TASTE THE STATE

Taste

the

State

South Carolina's
Signature Foods,
Recipes & Their Stories

Kevin Mitchell & David S. Shields

THE UNIVERSITY OF
SOUTH CAROLINA PRESS

Published by the University of South Carolina Press

Columbia, South Carolina 29208

WWW.USCPRESS.COM

Manufactured in China

30 29 28 27 26 25 24 23 22

10 9 8 7 6 5 4 3 2

Library of Congress Cataloging-in-Publication Data

can be found at http://catalog.loc.gov/.

ISBN: 978-1-64336-196-3 (hardcover)

ISBN: 978-1-64336-197-0 (ebook)

Frontis: Rhonda L. Wilson

Publication of this book is made possible

in part by the University South Carolina College

of Arts and Sciences Dean's Initiative Grant.

Designed and composed by

Nathan Moehlmann, Goosepen Studio & Press

CONTENTS

PREFACE

Taste the State is a guide for those who want to know South Carolina food more deeply. It treats the state's signature ingredients and dishes and their stories in more than eighty entries that supply descriptions, history, and sometimes classic recipes. While Lowcountry cooking has dominated media perception of Carolina cookery in the last three decades, we have ranged over the state looking for the prize fruits, grains, vegetables, and dishes. South Carolina is extraordinarily rich in heritage and distinct local foods. The legacies of Native agriculture appear here—corn, squash, and beans. As do foods, ingredients, and preparations of the African Diaspora. European garden vegetables and baked goods abound. Because Carolina cookery combines ingredients and cooking techniques of three divergent cultural traditions, there is more than a little novelty and variety in our food. It has inspired praise from visitors to the state since the 1720s. Because fakelore surrounds food that becomes important to places, we have taken care to supply the best documented information. You won't read here that pine bark stew contains pine bark or that collards came from Africa. Other foods that were once famous have passed into legend, no longer available. We remember several of these: groundnut cakes, rice birds, and tanya root.

When the University of South Carolina Press contacted us about writing a guide to South Carolina Food—something that would be informative to even the most schooled local cooks and historians, but also interesting to the visitor and the general reader—we knew that we didn't want to approach the book as a greatest southern hits collection. We wanted to focus more precisely on the state's food. So, chicken bog instead of fried chicken, no pimento cheese (more closely identified with Georgia, home of the "perfection pimento pepper," than South Carolina) or pimento burger, and no caramel cake, whoopee pies, cocoa cola, or pecan pie—all iconic southern foods that hail from elsewhere. With the exception of iced tea and punch, for reasons that will become apparent when you read those entries, we didn't much treat of beverages, since they are deserving of a study all their own. While some dishes received their own entries, others are included in more general entries about the primary ingredient, in which particular dishes are included. So, if you are interested in artichoke relish, you should look under Jerusalem Artichoke. Since there are a host of cookbooks that offer twenty-first-century takes on Carolina classics, in most cases we offered the most historical or traditional recipes that could be found—the ones that shaped the food that we now know. Older recipes look different than twentieth-century recipes. There is no ingredients list prefacing the cooking instructions. Instead, the recipe launches into the process of preparation taking up each ingredient in the dish when it matters in making it. There is sometimes a presumption that the reader knows what they are doing around the stove. So precise temperatures and length of time in the oven or on the fire are omitted. Most recipes here, but not all, post-date the widespread adoption of the cook stove, a kitchen appliance that permitted very exact temperature control. An experienced cook knew that sauces were made at low temperatures, fritters at high, and stews simmered at moderate heat on the back burner. We have left the old instructions as they first appeared in print, tweaking them only when something seems unintelligible or missing. Certain dishes developed multiple minor variations on a basic recipe template, so rather than select one specific recipe variant and suggest that it was more important than others, we have abstracted the base recipe from the multitude to include, usually in the narrative rather than as a stand-alone recipe. We invite the reader to make their own version using the base as a guide.

Our first collaboration was in 2015, when we worked together on Nat Fuller's Feast in Charleston, an event commemorating the 150th anniversary of the historic feast held by celebrated African American caterer Nat Fuller for Black and White guests to celebrate Emancipation and the end of the Civil War. Conceptualizing and writing this book was also a collaborative effort. Some entries were written individually, others together, and we both edited all of them. When one of us gets personal in our commentary, offering an experience or insight, a name (Kevin or David) will appear in parentheses to identify who's speaking. As with Nat Fuller's Feast and other shared projects, Mitchell's culinary expertise and training in historical research meld with Shields's extensive knowledge of agricultural history and culinary tradition. In addition to the historic and traditional recipes, others have been formulated by Mitchell to suggest to readers how South Carolina food traditions can be adapted to create one's own take on this deep and sumptuous cookery. We respect facts and historic recipes, so you will find a good deal of history in these stories and profiles; but this book was also meant to entertain and stimulate readers. Facts don't diminish fun—they make the stories richer and more real and give you a firm base upon which to build your own gardening or cookery.

Traditions are flexible things—that is what permits them to endure over time. By all means take advantage of that flexibility—seek out the ingredients, play with the recipes. We have white catfish stew and red catfish stew. Maybe you are the one to make peace between the warring camps with pink catfish stew.

— Kevin Mitchell and David S. Shields

Asparagus: The Palmetto

Manhattan millionaires of the Gilded Age made the asparagus the country's most cherished vegetable in 1880. Their insatiable demand for steamed asparagus with hollandaise sauce set the truck farmers of South Carolina to digging beds. The goal: to ship the spring's first spears to New York City and thus command the highest price.

During the era before California took over the produce industry, South Carolina ruled as a truck farming power. At various times it produced more cabbages, more strawberries, more radishes, and more asparagus than any state in the union. Asparagus was intensively farmed from the 1880s into the 1950s, first in the Lowcountry, then in the Piedmont in the region from Anderson to Union.

South Carolina's signature asparagus—the Palmetto—emerged in Mount Pleasant between 1882 and 1885. It was a luxuriously plump asparagus, the chubby kind favored by Americans prior to the rise of the skinny Mary Washington spears in the 1920s. The quality that ensured the adoption of the Palmetto as the standard crop asparagus in the South during the 1890s through the 1920s was its partial resistance to asparagus rust, *Puccinia asparagi,* a fungus that defoliates asparagus plants. Introduced to America in 1896 on a batch of European asparagus, rust spread everywhere because the popularity of asparagus had given rise to entire countrysides planted with the vegetable. Monocropping made the spread of rust rapid and lethal.

How did the Palmetto come into being? Almost by accident. The great New York seedsman Peter Henderson dispatched John Nix, his favorite vegetable man, to South Carolina in 1883 with instructions to plant extensively. "He always planted the Conover's Colossal until . . . he noticed his neighbor's Asparagus, under the same conditions, did considerably better than his own, being not only much earlier, yielding better, but more even and regular in growth. The difference, in fact, was so marked, that Mr. Nix deemed it advisable to purchase a supply of the roots of the new sort and since then he has been able to hold his own with any one on this crop" (1886). That neighbor, a French farmer named Alfred Jouannet, had planted the Argenteuil Asparagus in Mount Pleasant. But what Nix grew may have been a cross between the Conover's Colossal and the Argenteuil, a variety that had the size of the former, yet was more tender and prolific than the latter. Nix named it the Palmetto Asparagus and contracted with Henderson to make it a national variety. The tenderness mattered. Whereas most varieties of asparagus had sinewy stalks, the plump Palmetto was tender almost to the ground—no need to eat only the tips.

The Palmetto Asparagus monopolized Carolina fields in 1900. It would reign for a quarter century until two circumstances led to its eclipse. First, the Massachusetts Agricultural Experimental Station released the Washington series of rust-resistant asparagus plants, two of which, the Martha Washington and the Mary Washington, would win market traction. Second, physical culturists began insisting that thin asparagus would contribute to a thin torso, and fat asparagus would make one stout. With the slender flapper as the ideal body type for fashionable 1920s females, the Palmetto suffered from the rip tide of fashion. Farms began transitioning from

"Henderson's Palmetto Asparagus Roots," Peter Henderson & Co. 1900 Autumn Bulbs Catalogue, p. 58. Henry G. Gilbert Nursery and Seed Trade Catalog Collection, US Department of Agriculture, National Agricultural Library, via Biodiversity Heritage Library.

Palmetto to Mary Washington. In 1936, when ten thousand acres were under cultivation in South Carolina, Mary Washington exceeded Palmetto in terms of new plantings. Much of the Palmetto production went to canning plants in Fairfax and Gilbert, South Carolina. By the 1950s, Palmetto had been relegated to history. Farmers ultimately didn't mind because both Mary and Martha Washington varieties were more resistant to rust than the Palmetto.

South Carolina's reign as an asparagus power ended in the mid-twentieth century. Weather related crop disruptions from 1940 through 1943 led to a steady decline in harvests, particularly in the Lowcountry. California and New Jersey embraced the vegetable, and Carolina farmers turned away. By 1953 it ceased being a crop worth reporting. Solitary farms kept the vegetable in cultivation, but there were no longer consortia supplying canneries and packing houses. Today, Monetta Asparagus Farm, Watsonia Farms, and Asparagusto Farm in Conway supply locally grown hybrid strains of the pencil-thin asparagus varieties to South Carolina's diners.

As for the Palmetto Asparagus . . . it became virtually extinct. But Dr. James Kibler of Whitmire may have rediscovered a planting. Andrew Fallaw of the Monetta Asparagus Farm is growing it out alongside patches of Conover's Colossal and Argenteuil to determine whether it is, indeed, our state's famous fat asparagus. We may be on the verge of a renaissance for one of the most famous and cherished of South Carolina's vegetables.

[2]

Barbecue

In four polls conducted since 2000, South Carolinians named barbecue as their favorite "local food." By barbecue, the pollsters meant pulled pork. And it must be said that the average Carolinian in 2020 automatically thinks pig and then considers sauce—whether vinegar pepper, mustard, tomato based, or dry rub. Yet there was a time when barbecue described a broader world of choices.

In the early 1800s, when barbecue was a method of roasting low and slow, rather than the meat being cooked, the pit masters cooked goat, cow, chicken, rabbit, and even fish along with whole hogs. In the colonial era, the West Indian practice of cooking meats in the open air at controlled temperatures suspended over coals was altered somewhat; instead of cooking foods elevated above grade on grills supported by poles, Carolinians excavated pits in which fires were banked, and grills or spits were placed over the pits. What Carolinians retained from the West Indian practice was the social nature of the event, the open-air preparation of the meat, and enslaved cooks doing the preparation. The public event that introduced barbecue to the masses was the election. Candidates for office began offering free whiskey and pork flesh as enticements to vote. The religious conservatives objected to the practice as bribery for votes: In 1802, a commentator in the *Charleston City Gazette* wrote, "Till the election be over, be even Jews—I would not touch a piece of election-pork, particularly roast pork, vulgarly called barbecue."

Activating the Old Testament dietary restrictions against pork flesh was an effort doomed to failure. In South Carolina, like most parts of the South, the hog supplanted the cow as the chief livestock on the farm. Until the Civil War, the barbecues and open-air political meetings were inevitable pairings and pork always stood prominent among the offered meats.

Sporting events (the summer Georgetown boat races begun in the 1820s, the Charleston Race Week in winter) joined elections as large-scale events at which barbecue regularly appeared. Finally, the July 4th celebrations of clubs, associations, and military companies started featuring barbecue in the late 1820s. The scale of these events swelled in the 1830s and '40s, with a thousand or more attendees present for the food, the drink, the toasts, and the speechifying. The crowds demanded a diversity of foods and beverages. So, the big public barbecues were never restricted to pork. An attendee of the July 4, 1845, barbecue in Camden described the scene and the offerings: "Away for the dinner—the Barbecue under spreading trees, with the long pine tables and the chunks of roasted beef, after republican style. Bring on the smoking old hams—the mutton and the lamb, 'bacon greens and corn bread' if you please—bring them on, for the fatigues of the day have given us a vigorous appetite and we shall relish these barbecued meats under the fanning trees."

When ten thousand attendees crowded the October 3, 1856, barbecue honoring Congressman Preston S. Brooks in Abbeville (half a year after his infamous caning of Senator Charles S. Sumner on the floor of the U.S. Senate), they feasted on "ten thousand pounds of beef, pork, and mutton slaughtered and barbecued." Those who partook at the pine tables were White and free. Those who serviced the tables and plied the grills and rotisseries were Black and for the most part enslaved. There were also church barbecues where food preparation was done by corps of White women.

The defeat of the Confederacy and the liberation of enslaved Africans in 1865 led to consequential changes in barbecue culture. No longer were Black cooks compelled to perform their craft at the pits on command of planters. No longer could places at the grounds be denied them. When Hunter and Birge held a barbecue at Newberry in August 1866, a commentator noted: "As a consequence of freedom a large number of ladies and gentlemen of color filled up the outside setting, forming an artistic ebony frame work to the picture." Mixed public barbecues were a standard element in public

political life until the 1880s. Freedmen began holding their own barbecues as money raisers for their own purposes as early as 1867, such as one that supported M. T. J. Clary's School in Laurensburg. A thousand people attended. Black barbecue master Hampton Fletcher managed and catered the event.

After 1866, three sorts of people cooked barbecue: Black event cooks, White caterers, and women's groups. Often there were events managers in addition to cooks—persons responsible for publicizing the event, erecting tables, booking speakers, and ordering provisions (a task when the attendance exceeded eight hundred). By 1870, a handful of entrepreneurial manager-cooks who staged barbecues for profit emerged. H. H. Dent, a White cook from the midlands, was the

Whole Hog Barbecued prior to chopping and serving, James Helms barbecuist at Oldfields Plantation, Hopkins, SC, November 2016. David S. Shields.

major practitioner of the late 1860s and early 1870s. Solomon P. Kinard, county assessor of Newberry, earned the title, "the King of Hash," and held many feasts throughout the 1870s. Pat Lindler of Lexington was successor to H. H. Dent in the 1880s. There were several African American barbecue cooks deemed masters of the meats. Maybin Griffin of Edgefield, who ran the Black barbershop in that town, was a renowned barbecue cook from 1872 into the 1890s. Romeo Govan in Bamberg was a virtuoso at both barbecue and catfish stew. All of these masters operated as manager-cooks at the club or association level with eighty to one hundred guests present. Kinard and Govan had grounds around their own homes that served as outdoor eating and cooking areas. Serving a smaller group meant that one did not need to offer a diverse array of meats. It was in the private barbecue camps of the great cuists of the 1890s to the 1910s that the focus of barbecue narrowed to whole hog.

Barbecue came indoors just before the turn of the twentieth century. It began to be served at Jansen's New Restaurant in Augusta in December 1898, prepared by Gus Ferguson, the most famous cuist of the upper Savannah River valley. This African American innovator instituted Saturday barbecue at the restaurant. Augusta would be the first center of menu barbecue. After the turn of the century, James Selkirk's (a Ferguson protégé) Alcazar restaurant featured it in his late summer and early autumn bill of fare: "Roast chicken, barbecue pork, barbecued hash, steamed rice, stewed tomatoes, smothered cabbage, with picnic hams; cream potatoes, green apple roll." One sees already in the first decade of the twentieth century the fixation on pork.

One element of the barbecue that repeatedly appeared in accounts dating back to the first descriptions is hash. Barbecue hash differs from the chopped meat fries called hash that came into North American from Europe during the colonial era. It is boiled into its final shape rather than fried. Because the word hash originally referred to cutting up meat into small tidbits, and because this is the first step in making barbecue hash as well as fried hash, one can understand how the thickly textured gravy came to bear the name. There is no one hash recipe. Whatever meat was featured in a barbecue, whether goat, mutton, cow, or pig, went into the hash pot—and the offal (brains, livers, hearts, and lights [lungs]) were chopped and incorporated as well. It might include the hog's head, if that were not being reserved for head cheese. These were boiled in water along with vegetables (potatoes, peppers, onions, maybe tomatoes) and seasonings. Each cook had a proprietary formula, but common seasoning elements were salt, pepper, Worcestershire sauce, tomato catsup, mustard, brown sugar, apple cider vinegar, and hot pepper. The ingredients were cooked until the mixture lost its wateriness and became a thick, meaty agglomeration. Invariably hash was served on top of something—rice, grits, bread, or biscuits. The coloring ranges from pale orange yellow to rich reddish brown. The rice is always white (no red rice with hash).

If hash became a vehicle for asserting a cook's creative vision and sense of local ingredients, barbecue sauce proved much more conventional. The first barbecue sauce was an adaptation of the European vinegar and pepper sauce for meats, substituting red pepper (cayenne, bird pepper, or tabasco). This was the standard sauce in the West Indies and in colonial Virginia and is of course the base of the sauce found in the north and northeast of South Carolina. Sugar became cheap in 1825, and tomatoes only became standard ingredients in southern cookery in the 1830s. The 1840s saw an explosion of tomato catsup recipes that would be incorporated into barbecue, particularly in the western half of the state. The German preference for mustard as a condiment for meats no doubt stood behind the development of the mustard-based sauce identified with Orangeburg, Cayce, the Dutch Fork, and, to some extent, Charleston. The development of three Carolina styles of saucing reached maturation during the "homestead" period of barbecue cooking from 1900 to 1920. In this period, many freelance barbecue cooks would advertise barbecues held on their own properties. Solomon Kinard and Romeo Govan modeled this business path, and in the first decades of the twentieth century, the number of barbecues became so great that newspapers ran special columns of barbecue ads. In this competitive commercial environment, the sauces became signatures of schools of barbecue. For instance, the mustard sauce became associated with a network of cooks trained by Solomon Kinard: Levi Kibler, Jonathan Graham, H. M. Wicker, Ben Suber, O. A. Felker, John Nichols living around Newberry, and further afield, Jacob Sheely and A. C. Sleigh.

In the 1920s, the construction of state roads and the popularization of motoring gave rise to the roadside barbecue stand. The O. K. Barbecue stand on the corner of Queen and Meeting Streets in Charleston became a city fixture by 1927. Bootie's Barbecue in West Ashley supplemented meats with seafood, including barbecued shark. Another Lowcountry barbecue stand that served seafood was the "Old Rice Mill" in Ridgeland. Stands then began to proliferate in the midlands and western part of the state. The rise of the road house meant the end of the open-air fire pit; instead, cinder block fire beds and later metal rigs became standard. The stands operated at modest scale and had to supply beverages—sweet tea, water, lemonade, and (after 1935) beer—and "sides"—hash, red rice, coleslaw, pork and beans, potato salad, yams, green beans, hush puppies (red horse bread), and white bread. The final expression of motorized barbecuing was the crafting of large portable barbecue rigs, often propane fired, but permitting wood smoking. These enabled crews to continue the old work of onsite event cookery, obviating the digging of pits.

Today, barbecue culture in South Carolina is healthy and varied. Rodney Scott, a proponent of the vinegar-pepper sauce of Hemenway, has won the James Beard award for best chef Southeast. Whole hog barbecue still has practitioners, both commercial and private, many of whom were profiled in Rien Fertel's 2017 book, *The One True Barbecue*. A diversity of sauces (mustard, tomato, vinegar & pepper, and more) is available at nearly every commercial barbecue stand. Perhaps the greatest challenge to authentic local cookery that has arisen in connection with barbecue has been the reliance of barbecue stands on pre-prepared sides by major food processors.

Innovation has been encouraged by a contest culture that emerged toward the end of the twentieth century in which rival crews contend for honors at cook offs. The South Carolina Barbecue Association has organized among professionals to adjudicate important questions in the world of slow cooked meats. Amateur home barbecuists thrive and many an expert home cook has joined the rank of the professionals.

No ingredient epitomized the return of classic flavor to southern cooking in the 2010s more than the revival of benne. Benne biscuits appeared in a multitude of restaurant bread baskets. Benne oil once again lubricated southern greens thanks to Oliver Farm Artisan Oils. Benne and oyster stew sprang from the pages of antique cookbooks to the center of Lowcountry cookery. Gullah-Geechee cooks reclaimed parched benne seed as a condiment for rice and for cooked greens. And the traditional benne wafer, a cocktail party fixture in Charleston throughout the twentieth century, was joined by traditional confections such as benne brittle, benne sticks, and benne cakes. I suppose the dirty little secret of the benne revival was that some were using modern crop sesame (cheap and abundant at your local groceries) rather than the original heirloom benne.

Benne is a Mende word for sesame (*Sesamum indicum*). But the sesame that crossed the Atlantic as part of the African diaspora in the seventeenth century differs from that grown by modern farmers for market and oil processing. Benne is a landrace, tan hulled sesame with an oil content of approximately 45%. Its seed pods ripen at variable times from the bottom to the top of the plant and the pods shatter when ripe, broadcasting the seed. Modern sesame produces seeds with an oil content nearing 60% that is derived from non-shattering pods with a more regulated ripening to enable industrial harvesting.

African peoples of the Gold Coast and Slave Coast used benne seed in myriad ways: as a source for culinary oil; parched and mashed as a condiment; in stews as a flavoring; and milled into flour as a thickening agent and an element of flat breads. Enslaved Africans brought benne seed with them during the crossing and began cultivating it in huck patches for food and medicine (steeping the green leaves in cold water forms a mucilage that soothed gastric upset, particularly in children). Its use as a source of culinary oil immediately attracted the attention of European settlers. Lard, because it entailed the raising of hogs, was expensive. Experiments in olive planting in the American Southeast—and South Carolina particularly—failed because periodic cold snaps killed off olive trees. The need for an inexpensive salad oil and frying medium was great.

Sesame oil, with its long shelf life and high smoke point, became the focus of experiments, and in the 1810s, the basis of oil production that endured until David Wesson refined the stink out of cotton seed oil in the 1880s and created odorless, tasteless Wesson Oil. For sixty years, from 1830 to 1890, cold pressed sesame oil was a Carolina kitchen staple. Now if one asks for

Benne seeds in a calabash. Industrial modern sesame is hulled. Heirloom benne is usually cooked or processed with the hulls on, as in this image, giving it a darker tan grey hue. David S. Shields, taken in kitchen of Leonis O. Robert, Trinidad.

[7]

sesame oil, one is directed to the Asian food aisle in the grocery and shown dark brown, parched sesame seed oil with a pungent flavor—not at all like the sweet, mellow nuttiness of benne oil. The sole commercial, cold pressed benne oil producer in the United States is Oliver Farms of Pitts, Georgia, which uses landrace benne supplied by Anson Mills of South Carolina.

In 1820, John S. Skinner, editor of the United States' most important agricultural journal, *The American Farmer,* observed that "The Bene vine or bush, has been produced for some time, in small quantities, in the southern states, from seed imported directly from Africa . . . Many of the blacks of the Mississippi,

Mature benne plant in bloom with seed pods visible. Garden of Mills House, Historic Columbia Foundation, September 2019. David S. Shields.

have continued the propagation of the seed of the Bene, and make soup of it after parching. The seed may be procured from them and from the blacks in the Carolinas and Georgia."

The sole surviving recipe for benne soup appeared as a variation of groundnut soup in Sarah Rutledge's 1847 *The Carolina Housewife.* Though attentive to local vernacular cookery, Rutledge's collection was intended for a White readership with meat and seafood at its disposal. Oysters are added to benne and flour to make a dish that survives in Lowcountry cuisine as "Brown Oyster and Benne Stew."

Ground Nut Soup

Sarah Rutledge,
The Carolina Housewife (1947)

To half a pint of shelled ground nuts, well beaten up, add two spoonsful of flour, and mix well. Put to them a pint of oysters, and a pint and a half of water. While boiling, throw a red pepper or two, if small (45).

Bennie Soup

Sarah Rutledge,
The Carolina Housewife (1947)

This is made exactly in the same manner except that instead of a half a pint of ground-nuts, a pint and a gill of bennie is mixed with the flour and the oysters (46).

While soup was central to Gullah-Geechee cookery, other dishes held equal importance. Indeed, a complex constellation of dishes made use of benne, much like the rich benne cookery of West Africa: "The Negroes in Georgia boil a handful of the seeds with their allowance of Indian Corn" (1824). Three years earlier, a North Carolinian noted, "Mixed in due proportion with their hominy, it heightens its relish, and adds to its nutriment." Whole seed, because of its different cooking time than cornmeal, does not amalgamate well in hominy and can stick in one's teeth. The handful of benne cast into the hominy pot most likely was parched and pounded.

Thomas Jefferson wrote in the 1770s that sesame "was brought to S. Carolina from Africa by the negroes. . . . They bake it in their bread, boil it with greens, enrich their broth" with it. His observation that they boiled benne with greens accords with long-standing practice among a number of West African peoples. While casting a handful of whole seed into a cooking pot of collards (the premier cold weather green), turnip greens, beet greens, or mustard was convenient, it did not release all of the fat from the seed, so did not render the dish as luscious as if seeds were mashed. In the 1810s, when oil mills appeared in Columbia, Camden, and on a number of plantations, the mash cake left after pressing the sesame became a cooking condiment. The employment of benne mash as an oleo in boiling greens and root vegetables resembled North African practices of using tahini (sesame paste) as a condiment in vegetable cookery as well as the West African practice of adding mashed benne to one-pot preparations. It remained a feature of plantation cookery through the antebellum period.

One element of benne cookery developed entirely in the Western Hemisphere—confections. The molasses of the West Indies was combined with the West African sesame by the workers of the cane plantations. Benne candy evolved out of the simple mix of toasted seeds with cheap molasses, and over the course of the 1800s evolved into benne wafers, benne brittle, or the *pralines des bennés*. Each of these sweets incorporates whole benne into a honey, cane syrup, or molasses matrix. Francis Porcher's brief 1849 survey of the uses of benne among South Carolina's African Americans contains the first mention of benne confectionary as an established feature of Gullah cuisine: "In South Carolina the seeds are largely used by the negroes in making broths. They are also eaten parched, and are often candied with sugar or molasses." Benne candy was sold by the groundnut cake ladies on the city streets of Charleston in the 1870s, and the twisted benne sticks are visible in a famous stereograph portrait of a groundnut woman from the that decade. The sticks, benne cakes, and benne brittle were commercialized by Onslow's Confectionery store in the mid-1880s and were purchasable until the 1960s. Onslow's closing left the benne wafer the sole surviving form of benne confection.

Old landraces of benne survived in the Carolina landscape long after commercial sesame supplanted the market for baked goods and confectionery. It provided excellent feed for birds on shooting plantations. At least two old strains came down to the twenty-first century, and a third survives in Trinidad among the Merikans. These were revived beginning in 2011 and have since been reestablished as a feature of Carolina baking, cooking, and candy-making.

Biscuits

The star of breakfast, the partner of gravy, ham, and butter, the carrier of marmalade and fruit preserves, the biscuit has long been beloved throughout the South, and especially in South Carolina. Since the 1870s biscuits have been a quick bread made using flour made from soft white winter wheat, fat of some kind, one egg or two eggs, baking soda or powder, and buttermilk or some other liquid incorporating an acid. Baking biscuits was considered one of the basic kitchen skills. Despite its elementary standing in terms of baking technique, and despite its place within the ability range of beginning bakers, food companies began working to perfect premade refrigerated biscuit dough early in the twentieth century. They reckoned that convenience would be welcomed. Pillsbury introduced the instant biscuit—its "Grands"—to take the place of the homemade scratch biscuit. But the superlative flavor and texture of a traditional biscuit led to a revival of southern biscuit making both at home and in restaurants during the twenty-first century.

The biscuit as we know it was a product of a chemical revolution in baking. The protracted rise of breads enlivened by yeasts made old time baking time-consuming. Enlightenment chemists began looking for a chemical means to cause breads to rise rapidly. The idea was to inject chemicals into dough that upon activation by heat would release gas, causing the bread to inflate. Sodium bicarbonate, or baking powder, releases carbon dioxide gas when combined with an acid—vinegar, buttermilk, yogurt, cream of tartar, citrus juice, or acidic doughs such as sour dough. Baking powder is a dry chemical mix that combines sodium bicarbonate with one of the acids. Sodium bicarbonate was available in the South under the name salaeratus from the 1830s. It was not extensively used until the 1860s. In that decade commercial baking powder also became generally available.

Prior to the popularization of the soda biscuit in the 1860s and 1870s, the beaten biscuit was the standard bake. It survives as a traditional foodway in Maryland and Kentucky. The repeated manipulation of the dough, either by kneading or pounding with an ax handle or rolling pin caused the biscuit to puff and flake. In South Carolina, Elizabeth Sinkler Dubose (1829–1846) of Berkley County was a famous baker. Her surviving recipes, in Thomas Walter Peyre's plantation journal, reveal an interesting dichotomy. She used soda when making Poochee Corn Bread, but with soft wheat biscuits, hewed to the old beaten biscuit method:

Biscuits

Elizabeth Sinkler Dubose,
Thomas Walter Peyre Plantation Journal

2½ Tumblers of water—2 Salt-spoonsful of salt—1 Spoonful of lard & butter (half of each)—& as much flour as a strong person can knead in—will make 90 biscuits of ordinary size. Baked in 40 minutes—Miss S. Dubose

Since this recipe presumes much kitchen knowledge, it is useful to examine a later, more elaborate protocol for creating the classic beaten biscuit:

Beaten Biscuit

"Southern Biscuit. How to Make Them"
(September 30, 1889)

To a quart of good flour add a teaspoonful of salt and a heaping spoonful of lard (a piece about the size of a duck's egg). Rub the lard well into the flour until it is all thoroughly incorporated; then mix into a stiff dough with cold or warm water as you choose. I always use warm water in cold weather for comfort's sake. It requires very little water, for the dough must be as stiff as it well can be to be thoroughly mixed. Then transfer it from the mixing tray to a clean kneading board or table, and knead with all your heart, holding first one end of the dough and then the other until it is flexible and perfectly satin-smooth to touch, and will peel in flakes like tissue paper. Really well-kneaded dough will 'pop, pop' under the pressure of the hands like miniature champagne corks. It is very tiresome to knead, though it is good exercise for the muscles of the breast, shoulders and arms. . . . Many cooks who object to kneading beat the dough with the end of a rolling pin, but it is not so nice as kneading with the hands.

I always make twenty-four biscuit[s] out of a quart. Mold them into shapely balls, roll them out about as thick as your finger, say half and inch, or as much less as you choose, stick them through several times with a fork (a three-tined fork is de rigeur down South) and put them, just not touching, in the pan and set in a well-heated oven. They will require from twenty minutes to half an hour to bake according to the heat of the stove.

One great difference between the beaten biscuit and the quick bread biscuits was the degree to which the dough was worked. Extensively in the case of the former, barely in the case of the latter.

Buttermilk Biscuit

Abbeville Press and Banner
(November 7, 1888)

Sift together a quart of flour and a teaspoon of soda. Work into it a teaspoon of salt, and tablespoon of lard or butter (not melted). Add a pint of buttermilk, a little at a time until all is used. Do not work the dough longer than to collect it smoothly. Roll out one-half inch thick and cut with a biscuit cutter. Bake immediately in hot oven for about ten minutes.

An interesting choice facing biscuit bakers is the fat to be used in the mix. Lard stood foremost in early biscuit making and ruled for much of the nineteenth century. Butter stands currently as the preferred fat. During the twentieth century, Crisco (hydrogenated cottonseed oil, later, canola oil) and margarine had their moments. The trick with all of these ingredients was not to have them warm enough to melt when mixing. Using cold water or ice water in mixing the flour into dough has become standard practice.

When the soda biscuit established itself as the dominant southern quick-rise breakfast bread in the 1880s it became a matrix for the incorporation of other ingredients. Benne flour and/or benne seed, cooked onion, cheese, and cooked mashed sweet potato gave rise to families of flavored biscuits. The sweet potato biscuit became particularly popular. A parallel path of development was the sweet biscuit, with honey, sugar, or sorghum syrup pushing the baked product in the direction of confection. The incorporation of berries and small fruits was a hallmark of early twentieth-century sweet biscuit making. But in recent decades scones and muffins have become the more favored vehicles for presenting blueberries and blackberries.

The one dimension of effective biscuit making that remains from the long history of baking practice is the use of soft white winter wheat as the material for making dough. You can't have a superlative biscuit if you do not use soft wheat flour.

Blackberry

Skirting fields, roads, ditches, and banks the wild blackberry, with its thorny canes and sharp-tasting fruit, are the favorite wild berry crop of South Carolinians. Getting pricked by blackberry thorns is the initiation rite of a wild food forager. David S. Shields, Pelion, SC.

In the second week of June, 'Blackberry Time' begins across South Carolina. For four glorious weeks in every county in the state, the wild bushes, thickly laden with berries, turn from sour red to sweeter black. "We are living in better times than was that of the days when manna rained. Along the fence rows, the ditch banks, the old field—everywhere throughout this good land of ours—the blackberries are ripening" ("Blackberry Time" 1915). Children risked the thorns for the fruit, and home cooks processed buckets of berries into a host of dishes. Of native small fruits it vied with huckleberries as the finest—less insipid than mulberries, more flavorful than wild straw-

berries. Indeed, it rivaled cultivated fruits in popularity. Consider this comment by an Edgefield connoisseur in 1894: "The blackberry is a plebeian berry not to be named some say, in the same breath the plutocratic raspberry and strawberry, yet this same blackberry is the best all round berry in these United States. With cream and sugar they are delicious, in pies they are equally nice, and jam, wine, vinegar, cordial, etc., made of this abundant fruit are both wholesome and tempting to the palate."

Thriving on the margins of fields and forests, this member of the rose family possesses the prickles of its botanical ancestor. Growing in brambles or long canes, the wild blackberry

Cultivated blackberries found universally in groceries in South Carolina derive from the dozen varieties, all bearing the name of an Indian tribe, bred in the last forty years by Dr. James Moore of the University of Arkansas. David S. Shields.

bore small, sweet, often seedy fruit—hence the "plebian" reputation it had in some circles. Fruit breeders knew how to improve the blackberry—remove the thorns from the canes, diminish the seediness from the fruit and increase its lusciousness, and repress the astringency. Breeders wished to impose order on the genetics of the plant and farmers wanted to impose the regularity of rows in the fields. In the 1890s people began the large-scale planting of blackberry bushes. For a century and a half, small fruit breeders labored promoting varieties, but all too often, the flight from the sourness of wild blackberry led breeders to create inoffensive, even innocuous fruit. Wild berries had more impact and so remained the focus of much foraging, until Dr. James

Moore of the University of Arkansas created his twelve classic blackberries varieties named after Native American peoples and designed for cultivation in the South. If you buy a carton of plump blackberries in your grocery, it is one of Dr. Moore's varieties, grown by a Carolina or southern farmer: Arapaho, Navaho, Ouachita, Natchez, Apache.

Dr. Moore no doubt wished to honor the Native Americans who cherished the blackberries as food and medicine. Certain of the Native preparations became established in the folk medicine of the settler population. A decoction of the root counteracted diarrhea. Tea made from the leaves was an anti-inflammatory, particularly effective against sore throat. Settlers made their own medicinal adaptations.

[14]

Blackberry syrup and blackberry wine and blackberry cordial were reckoned tonics and restoratives. In 1858, when Dr. Teague of Edgefield began manufacturing Blackberry Brandy, the editor of the *Edgefield Advertiser* wrote, "It is a healthful, almost a medicinal berry. The cordial and jams made of it are thought worthy of a place among the various preparations of the medical dispensary; and we do not see why blackberry brandy should not also become a most useful as well as very genial drink."

Because of the blackberry's medicinal reputation, the enemies of Prohibition produced and defended blackberry wine, brandy, cordial, and spiked syrup (see recipe below) as "remedies" to circumvent the Volstead Act. Because of the ubiquity of the plant in the state, it became the favorite wild fruit for the home fermentation of wine after 1919, rivaled only by mulberry among the Gullah. The favorite commercial manufacturer of blackberry wine before Prohibition was the Sol Bear Company of Wilmington, NC. In 1920, the Bureau of Internal Revenue identified Blackberry cordial (a form of the syrup recipe noted below) to be an intoxicant and in violation of Prohibition. In 1923, in the midst of Prohibition, a reporter observed the following during the York County Blackberry festival: "Time was when blackberry juice was made into that most delicious and refreshing of all beverages—blackberry wine. But that was in the happy days of the past, before Volsteadian regulations rendered such practice a misdemeanor. There are those who hint—sh-sh—don't speak it loud—that in rural York the wine is still made, surreptitiously of course, but if this be true, it is strictly for home consumption and is seldom or never handed guests, as was the custom in days of yore." In 1928, farmers in Gaffney were fined for producing blackberry wine in one of the last cases prosecuted before the repeal of Prohibition.

When looking upon the classic recipes for blackberry beverages and foods, keep in mind that wild blackberries and pre-1970 cultivars contained more acid than the current strains bred by Dr. Moore. So, you might consider diminishing the sugar quotient in the recipes below. The repertoire of blackberry cookery was broad: "Blackberry pies, the blackberry roll, blackberry tarts and that ravishing triumph of culinary art, the blackberry dumpling" ("Blackberry Time" 1915). Jellies, jams, preserves, and pickled blackberries were standard pantry stock. Blackberry pies were so common that every home cook knew a version of the formula: one quart blackberries, three cups sugar, two tablespoons of flour, mix them together, spoon it into a crust, add a pat of butter if you want to cut the tartness, add a top crust, cut vents, bake until done. Other preparations required instruction:

Blackberry Syrup

Southern Patriot (August 12, 1847)

"an excellent remedy for summer complaint, with children"

To two quarts of blackberry juice, add half an ounce of powdered nutmeg, cinnamon and allspice, and a quarter of an ounce of powdered cloves. Boil these together, to get the strength of the spices, and to preserve the berry juice.—While hot, add a pint of fourth proof French brandy, and sweeten with loaf sugar.

Blackberry Jam

The State (June 28, 1908)

Pick over the berries carefully. Put in the preserving kettle over the fire, and after they have begun to cook stir frequently. Boil for 20 minutes. Rub through a fine sieve (if the sieve allows the seeds to pass through use a cheese-cloth bag) and measure. To every quart of juice allow three cupfuls of granulated sugar. Heat slowly, stirring often, and simmer for three-quarters of an hour.

Wild Blackberry Dumplings

Baltimore American (July 20, 1911)

Take a pint of freshly picked or preserved blackberries, add one teacup granulated sugar and one teacup water; simmer, slowly in enamel saucepan about five minutes. Then take one-half pound flour and one large teaspoon of baking powder sifted together, add two tablespoons of melted butter and one-fourth teaspoonful salt; beat well. Then heat one egg in a cup very light, fill the cup with sweet milk, add to the batter, beat well; add more milk, if necessary. Drop one tablespoonful of batter at a time in the berries until all is in; then put on a tight cover and cook slowly for about fifteen minutes. Serve with whipped cream.

Southern Blackberry Cobbler

The State (June 28, 1908)

Line a deep earthen pudding dish with pastry rolled out one-quarter of an inch thick, fill with fresh blackberries. Sprinkle with one half cupful of sugar, cover with a top crust and press down the edges. Bake slowly for three-quarters of an hour and serve hot with cream and sugar (18).

Blackfish

SEA BASS, *CENTROPRISTIS STRIATATROPRISTIS*

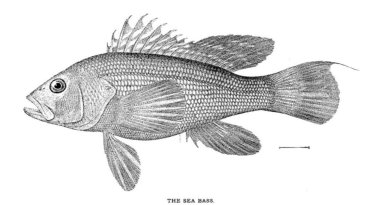

THE SEA BASS.

Blackfish, the Sea Bass, is historically the chief oceanic fish harvested commercially in South Carolina waters. H. L. Todd, engraving in George Brown Goode, The Fishes and Fishery Industries of the United States *(Washington, DC: GPO, 1887).*

Between four and five miles off shore at Pawley's Island, South Carolina, lay the blackfish banks, a worm-encrusted limestone reef projecting several feet off the bottom where the water stands one hundred feet or so deep. During the summer months, this outcrop teams with blackfish. An almond-shaped, large-eyed, and large-scaled resident of the coastal shallows, the blackfish is chubby yet agile, feeding on small crustaceans and fish. Capable of growing in excess of eighteen inches long, the standard size of an adult is a foot with a weight ranging from five to six pounds. Since the colonial period it has been the most abundant food fish available in Carolina markets and made up nine-tenths of the fish harvested by the commercial smacks that plied the coastal waters in the nineteenth and early twentieth centuries.

Before the Civil War, fifteen commercial fishing vessels, most northern owned, harvested the banks, sending the bulk of the catch northward for sale at the city markets in New York, Philadelphia, and Boston. After the Civil War, locally owned commercial fishing vessels vied with sport fishing smacks hired by local gentlemen (usually fifteen per boat) for access to the fish. The commercial fishing companies—Charles C. Leslie, the Terry Company, Thomas W. Carroll—brokered the harvest, and made sure an ample supply was available in the city markets and South Carolina's inland towns. Yet the great source of revenue remained the northern markets whose demand for the fish verged on being boundless. It can be said without reservation that the blackfish population has been overfished since the 1840s, yet the present population has remained stable since the 1980s, with an annual cap placed on harvest in waters under federal jurisdiction. Recreational fishermen could catch blackfish around the jetties of coastal settlements in South Carolina, but hurricane Hugo in 1989 caused the inshore population to vanish. Only recently have they been coming back. For the past three decades the old blackfish banks have been the commercial source for the fish.

Ichthyologist George Brown Goode observed, "The Sea Bass is considered one of our most available food-fishes, being especially excellent for use in chowders; in this respect a rival of the haddock, its flesh being very sweet, flaky, and firm. By reason of the hardness of its flesh it is especially adapted to packing and shipment in ice, and in summer is probably one of the most desirable fishes to be obtained in the city markets." The popularity of the blackfish is attested by the frequency with which one encounters it in the great cookbooks of the American Gilded Age. Felix Déliée's *Franco-American Cookery* (1884) features "Black-Fish à l'Americaine," "Broiled Black-Fish, Chili Sauce," and "Stewed Blackfish a la Newport." Charles Ranhofer's magisterial *The Epicurean* (1889) supplied instructions for "Blackfish a la Orly." But in South Carolina blackfish were baked and grilled, but the preparation that mattered most was that which Goode cited—chowder.

Thick fish and shellfish stews bring to mind more northern climes—New England's clam chowder, the fish chowders of Massachusetts, Maine's codfish chowder, Rhode Island's corn chowders, or Manhattan's tomato-laced clam chowder. For the most part the Lowcountry borrowed the formulae for these famous seafood stews. Beginning in the last quarter of the nineteenth century, the seafood houses on Sullivan's Island offered blackfish and oysters as regular fare, and Blackfish Chowder was the signature dish of the Jetty House. Like New England fish chowders there was fatback or bacon, onions, potatoes, milk, butter, fish stock, and the cubed flesh of the blackfish in the Jetty House version. Oscar Vick, the entrepreneurial cook and writer of the late twentieth century, updated the formula with sliced local okra in his self-published *Gullah Cooking: Fish Cooking* (1991). But an odd shift in taste occurred during the 1980s when baked blackfish and grilled fillets eclipsed chowder as the favorite way to prepare the dish. Baked blackfish was often stuffed. The version favored around Murrell's Inlet was published in Wilma D. Martin's 1990 cookbook, *Captain Murrell's Savory Seafood Recipes* with a classic bread crumb stuffing. It was coated in seasoned flour and had diced tomatoes strewn over the fish before being popped into the oven.

[18]

TASTE THE STATE

Boiled peanuts are available throughout the South, from Virginia to Florida, north into Ohio, and to the west in Louisiana. There are two main preparations for boiled peanuts, either boiled in their shell in plain salt water (brine) or with seasoning, such as Zatarain's Cajun Seasoning or Old Bay, added to the brine.

Originally called goober peas, pindars, or ground nuts in South Carolina, the original peanuts were the small, sweet Carolina African Runners. Boiling peanuts was a West African mode of preparation borrowed from the way people prepared the bambara, the native groundnut of Africa. The first printed recipe appears in Mrs. Washington's *The Unrivaled Cook Book* of 1886. The first ad for commercial boiled peanuts appeared in Spartanburg in 1925.

When preparing boiled peanuts, you only use raw or green nuts in the pods. Green are fresh picked and are not dehydrated; raw peanuts have been dried but not cooked. They must be rehydrated prior to boiling. Once cooked they can be frozen and eaten out of a can when peanuts are not in season. But the favorite way of eating them is fresh cooked, purchased at one of the roadside stands scattered across the state. The vendors usually serve them in a brown paper sack or a Styrofoam cup.

When it came to selling boiled peanuts, we must not forget "Tony the Peanut Man" Anthony Wright (1953–2016). The Peanut Man was a mainstay in Charleston, the most conspicuous purveyor of boiled peanuts in the city. He sold fresh fried and roasted peanuts for over twenty years. He offered three flavors: salt and vinegar, ranch fried, and garlic fried. The Peanut Man sang his jingle "Peanut Tyme"

Boiled peanuts are a preparation with African origins and the peanuts originally used were those that slave ships transported across the Atlantic as food for their human cargo—a small sweet peanut called the "Carolina African runner peanut." Long lost, this variety was revived and reestablished by Dr. Brian Ward of Clemson University in 2015. These are pods from his first crop. David S. Shields.

with his straw hat and red bow tie at every home Charleston RiverDogs game.

In the past decade the boiled peanut became a favorite for people living outside of the South. Having grown up in Charleston, the brothers Matt and Ted Lee so missed their beloved boiled peanuts that they started making boiled peanuts for themselves in New York and in 1994 started to sell them. They started the

Lee Bros. Boiled Peanuts Catalogue that includes other southern staples that they sorely missed.

Lee Bros. Boiled Peanuts

Adapted from *The Lee Bros.*
Charleston Kitchen (2013)

(Makes 4 pounds)
1½ cups kosher salt, plus more to taste
4 gallons water
2 pounds shell-on raw peanuts or
　　3 pounds green peanuts

In a large (10- to 12-quart) stockpot, stir ½ cup salt into 2 gallons of water until the salt dissolves, then add the peanuts. Use a large dinner plate or two to help submerge the floating peanuts. Allow to soak for eight hours or overnight. (This step saves a little time boiling, but you can skip if needed. If you're using green peanuts—which are freshly picked—you may also skip this step.)

Drain the soaking water and add 2 gallons of fresh water and the remaining 1 cup of salt to the pot of peanuts. Note the level of the water on the side of the pot. Bring to a boil. Lower the heat and simmer, covered, for 6 to 8 hours (2 to 3 for green peanuts), keeping the water in the pot within an inch or so of its original level with regular additions of water, until the peanuts are about as soft as a roasted chestnut.

Once the peanuts have boiled for 3 hours (1 hour for green peanuts), sample them to check their texture and salinity. Remove a peanut, and when it is cool enough to handle, crack open its shell and taste the kernel, slurping some brine with it. If the peanut crunches, it should be cooked further. If the brine lacks enough salt, add more to taste; if it is too salty, remove a portion of the water and replace with the same volume of fresh water. Allow the pot to boil for another hour before testing again. Sample every hour until they are pleasantly yielding and as salty as a good pickle.

When the peanuts are cooked to your satisfaction, turn off the heat and allow them to cool in the pot for an hour (30 minutes for green peanuts). When cool enough to handle, drain the water and eat immediately. If not eating, store the shell-on peanuts in a sealed container in the refrigerator or freezer. Boiled peanuts will keep for about 7 to 10 days in the refrigerator and up to 6 months in the freezer.

The South Carolina State Legislature designated boiled peanuts the official state snack food in 2006.

Butterbeans and Sieva Beans

Butterbeans and Sieva beans are one and the same thing—a native, modestly sized lima bean that flourished in the South and became a favorite garden vegetable, whether freshly shelled or dried and reconstituted. First known by settlers as a Sieva (pronounced "sivvy") bean, after the Sewee Indians of eastern South Carolina, or as the "Carolina bean," some southerners began calling it the butterbean in the 1860s because its cooked consistency was so creamy. There were two popular forms of the bean: a whitish green one and a reddish speckled one, both native.

The Sewee People were Siouan, related to the Santee, and lived north of the Cooper River, particularly around Bull's Bay. Known as traders, they probably conveyed the bean to the residents of Charles Towne in a barter transaction in the 1680s or 90s. While the Sewee

Butterbeans (Sieva beans) are pole beans and they grow up tall. The willow leaf butter bean is a rare variety with a skinny rather than broad bean leaf. David S. Shields, photograph of Dr. James Kibler's plant, Whitmire, SC.

made bean meal and bean bread from their beans, settler cookery viewed it as a standalone vegetable or a component of soups and stews. Cooks put Sieva beans in many classic dishes: Brunswick Stew, Succotash, and Sunday Beans in Cream. The mid-twentieth century saw butterbeans used to make bean dip for tail gate picnics.

Sievas were always understood as the diminutive alternative to the large lima beans that spread out of South America during the colonial period. While the large lima bean grew well in the North and the Midwest, it proved only marginally productive south of Maryland. So, the Sieva bean reigned supreme, which was fine with many: large lima beans were often chalky or mealy in consistency, but the Sieva beans had better texture and taste. The superlative flavor of the Sieva bean is best appreciated in simple preparations. The early recipes stress this. Theresa C. Brown of Anderson, SC, offered brief and clear instructions in her 1871 book, *Modern Domestic Cookery:*

To Boil Sewee Beans

Theresa C. Brown,
Modern Domestic Cookery (1871)

Gather them when tender; cover with water; boil until tender, and water pretty well evaporated; salt, and season with a little finely ground pepper. Serve them in a hot vegetable dish, with a piece of butter. When dried, soak them over-night in water.

Much of what passes for white butter-beans found in stores today are forms of the Fordhook bush limas. Classic Sieva beans are pole beans and are more heat tolerant, more productive, and longer producing than the bush limas, a creation of the Henderson Seed Company in the late nineteenth century. Encountering a dwarf lima on the produce stand, you probably couldn't tell on first view whether it was a white Sieva or a white bush lima. Only the red speckled butterbean can be recognized at first glance, and even that bears some resemblance to the Jackson Wonder bush lima. Those who seek out the famous old South Carolina bean, now primarily hunt the speckled Sieva. Its following is loyal to the point of fanaticism, and its growers vocal about its virtues.

How you see butter beans in a produce market's cold chest— fresh shelled in plastic freezer bags with initials inked on the front. Clockwise from top left: brown crowder field pea (BC), white butter bean, October bean (OCT), speckled butter bean (SP). David S. Shields, Cayce Farmer's Market, Cayce, SC.

South Carolina has its own distinctive cabbage, the Charleston Wakefield. In 1891, two things happened that tipped the minds of big farmers in the Lowcountry away from cotton and potatoes to cabbages: the Charleston and Savannah Railroad built a spur line from Ravenel Station to Yonge's Island and seedsmen Peter Henderson and Francis Brill sent the first batches of Wakefield Cabbage seed to Carolina growers. The growers who developed Yonge's Island intended from the first to grow a commodity crop, covering the landscape with cabbages, all to be shipped to northern markets. The proximity to Charleston enabled vast amounts of stable manure to fertilize the soil.

William C. Geraty and F. W. Towles, potato and tomato growers on Yonge's Island, South Carolina, saw that more money was to be made from spring harvest cabbages than from new potatoes. In the late 1880s they began planting various cabbage types experimentally, to supplement the potato crop. Systematic tests took place between 1888 and 1891 of every variety of cabbage for which bulk seed was available. No cabbage rivaled the quality and ease of cultivation of the Wakefield. Henderson realized the seed revenue that would arise if the Lowcountry growers succeeded, just as they had in most every other truck crop from 1870 onward. He developed a strain of Wakefield suited to the Lowcountry soil and clime. He named it the Charleston Wakefield Cabbage.

The heyday of the Charleston cabbage boom took place from 1903 to 1920. In 1905,

HENDERSON'S EARLY JERSEY WAKEFIELD CABBAGE.

Charleston Wakefield Cabbage, the cabbage that made South Carolina a national truck farming super power at the beginning of the twentieth century, is identified by its blunt conical shape and superlative taste. Peter Henderson & Co. 1900 Autumn Bulbs Catalogue, p. 59. Henry G. Gilbert Nursery and Seed Trade Catalog Collection, US Department of Agriculture, National Agricultural Library, via Biodiversity Heritage Library.

Norman Blitch, a Geraty partner, shipped 35 million cabbages. The scale of his enterprise can be judged from this report of 1908:

> It is possible to drive for miles through the truck belt about Charleston without being able to change the scene of growing cabbages which greet the eyes. . . . The section is traversed with many miles of railroad tracks, running through cabbage and potato fields, and at every mile, and in some instances at a less distance, are station platforms filled with barrels, crates and baskets of vegetables for shipment. Cars are being constantly moved and the places are scenes of much activity and business. Daily shipments go out of Meggett's amounting to several hundred cars, and fast freights of 25 or 30 cars solid of cabbages or potatoes are of daily occurrence during the shipping season, and this, in addition to the express business, which is of large proportions.

In 1920, California, using migrant labor, began underselling South Carolina and gradually wrested the cabbage business away. Now the USDA Vegetable Laboratory south of Charleston sits on Norman Blitch's old cabbage fields.

Though cabbage had long been a favorite winter vegetable in South Carolina, in the twentieth century it was cheap and ubiquitous. A local cabbage cookery made good use of the Charleston Wakefield cone heads.

Smothered Cabbage

A signature dish of the Dutch Fork and Orangeburg, smothered cabbage became one of the home preparations by which you could gauge the adventurousness of a household's taste. In homes where plain cooking prevailed, the dish was simply fine sliced cabbage steamed or boiled in water until soft, lubricated by a pat of butter or margarine with salt and pepper added. In more adventurous households the cabbage once steamed had a white sauce (flour and water and salt cooked as a white gravy) napped over it. The classic Dutch Fork version added vinegar to the white sauce. The Gullah version added a dash of cayenne to the gravy, with vinegar optional. There is also a Gullah version using tomato gravy instead of white gravy.

In the early twentieth century, the Plaza Café on Main Street in Columbia became famous for its smothered cabbage with ham, inspiring a period between the two World Wars when it became a fixture on the menus of small-town eateries. Since the 1950s it has reverted to being a home cooking dish.

Smothered cabbage with rice was a Gullah-Geechee cold weather dish, though it did not take on the symbolic significance that the dish had in Louisiana's Cajun country, where it became a New Year's Day good luck staple. Louisiana smothered cabbage frequently incorporates sausages into the cook pot. South Carolina smothered cabbage eschews sausage.

Calabash Fried Fish and Shrimp

In the 1940s a fish camp style of deep frying fish coated in cornmeal or wet batter in hot lard became popular in North Carolina's outer banks. In the small fishing port of Calabash on the northern side of the border between North and South Carolina, Lucy High Coleman popularized platters of fried fish, shrimp, and oysters, opening a restaurant (now called "The Seafood Hut") in 1940. Her sister Ruth followed suit, opening Beck's Restaurant, shortly thereafter named after her husband Vester Beck, and her brother, noting the success of his siblings, opened Ella's of Calabash, which in 2020 remains the finest of the three High family eateries that established the style. They are joined by fourteen more restaurants that now line the waterfront and Route 17 around "The Seafood Capital of the World." In the 1980s there were as many as thirty.

While the town's grandiose motto announces the ambition of its fishing fleet and cooks, Calabash's true influence extends less broadly. Calabash style cooking is recognized and copied in the outer banks of North Carolina and along the Grand Strand down to Charleston. While crusty, deep-fried seafood is popular throughout the Lowcountry down to Florida, the style is called fish camp fry south of Charleston. Today Myrtle Beach is the place that celebrates the style with the greatest zest besides Calabash itself. Captain Benjamin's Calabash Seafood on the King's Highway, Bennett's Calabash (three locations), Sea Captain's House, and Crabby Mike's at Surfside Beach are leading practitioners of the style.

While Calabash style frying eschews heavy breading for a more moderate coating, it does favor a robust brown exterior on the hush puppies that are the one inevitable side on the fish platters. While the original items in a Calabash fry were fish, shrimp, and oysters, the 1950s brought scallops into the fry basket, and the 1970s brought calamari.

Carolina Gold Rice

The most famous culinary ingredient ever produced in South Carolina, Carolina Gold Rice, provided the base for many classic dishes: Hoppin' John, Chicken Bog, Pilau/Perloo, Rice Bread, Rice Pudding, Rice Waffles, and Puffs. A non-aromatic subtropical japonica rice, it won fame for its pearly translucence, its wholesome mouth feel, and its versatility as a matrix upon which to mix flavors. It has existed in several forms over the centuries. The standard grain was the shortest of all of the varieties reckoned long grain in the United States at 5/16ths of an inch. Long Gold, a variant discovered in the mid-1840s at Brookgreen Plantation, was truly a long grained rice; it won gold medals at expositions in Paris and London in the 1850s and commanded the highest price of any variety on the world rice market in Paris. Carolina White was an out-mutation of Carolina Gold with a straw colored rather than golden hull; polished it did not differ in taste or quality. Charleston Gold was an aromatic and short-stature agronomic off-spring of Carolina Gold bred by Gurdev Kush and Merle Shepard early in the twenty-first century. Carolina Gold grew in commercial quantities in South Carolina from 1786 until the eve of the First World War. It was revived by Dr. Richard Schulze of Turnbridge Plantation in the 1980s. Its commercial restoration dates from the first decade of this century when Merle Shepard of Clemson University and Glenn Roberts of Anson Mills formed the Carolina Gold Rice Foundation and had Dr. Anna McClung of the USDA breed Carolina Gold Select, the seed now planted in several southern states for culinary use.

Genetically, Carolina Gold originates in South Asia, perhaps Indonesia. But rice varieties have traveled widely over the centuries. Bankorum, a close genetic relative, is found in West Africa, and numbers of related rices girdle the globe. History is silent on whence it came to South Carolina. What we know for certain is that it first appeared on the landscape in the growing seasons after the American Revolution—in 1785 and 1786—grown by Hezekiah Mayham of Pineville Plantation in Berkeley County. We also know that in within six years it had been embraced by the majority of planters north of the Ashley River and by 1800 it had become universally grown. The American Revolution had disrupted seed production for Madagascar White Rice, the variety grown since the 1680s, and Mayham's generosity supplying Gold Seed to planters insured its rapid domination of Carolina fields. It would remain in cultivation until its high cost to grow and the destruction wrought by hurricanes in the 1910s caused wide scale planting to cease.

England did not greatly influence the distinctive rice cookery that grew up in South Carolina. Much of the rice that England imported from its American colonies was resold and transshipped to Europe. Aside from rice pudding, the majority of the rice consumed in eighteenth-century England went to feeding invalids. The one pot dishes using rice as a grain base largely derive from West African models, albeit with different ingredients admixed. Rice fritters, too, had an African genesis. The rice breads emerged at the end of the eighteenth century in France and the New World, first as an effort to economize when wheat prices became exalted, by admixing boiled rice into

A stand of ripe Carolina Gold Rice in the field. The staple grain of South Carolina, it was restored to Carolina early in the twenty-first century. Named after the golden hulls that adorn the ripe panicles of rice, Carolina Gold has reasserted its culinary quality in southern cookery. Glenn Roberts, Anson Mills.

dough in mixture of roughly one part rice to four parts wheat flour.

A distinctive method for steaming the rice so that each grain was thoroughly cooked yet separate developed in the early nineteenth century. A Charlestonian published an instruction in the *Courier* in summer of 1829, a letter that newspapers across the country reprinted:

How to Boil Rice

Providence Patriot & Columbian Phoenix
(September 2, 1829)

Put you [*sic*] rice in an open pot, covering it with water then put it on the fire to boil. When it is boiled so as to become soft, (which is easily ascertained by means of a wood ladle, which we call a hominy stick) take it off the fire, drain off the water, and cover the pot so as to retain the heat; then put it on coals or hot ashes for about 15 or 20 minutes, so as to throw off the steam, or as it is usually called, to soak. Your rice is then ready for the table.

This basic instruction would be elaborated for two centuries, with additional comments on rinsing rice, choice of water, "graveling rice," the proper method of stirring, and a host of other fastidious instructions.

The most important category of rice dishes in which the grain was prepared by boiling in liquid is pilau. Originally called Pilaf, pilaus have collected a number of names. One of the most popular is perloo. Pilau flavors the rice by (a) employing a stock as the cooking medium, or (b) cooking the rice with meat or fowl or shellfish or a vegetable that flavors the grain. A separate entry detailing the varieties of pilau appears later in this book.

The commercial restoration of Carolina Gold Rice in the first decade of the twenty-first century was the tipping point of the Southern Culinary Revival, the first and most consequential of many ingredient restorations.

Modern chefs took up the classic rice and employed all of their technique and creativity to renovating its place in southern cookery. Rice bread is being baked in the Lowcountry and pilaus grace many a restaurant menu. Historically, some of the finest culinary uses of the rice took up the extinct long gold form of the grain. Dr. McClung's rebreeding of long gold as "Santee Gold" should be available in 2021.

"A catfish got cat whiskers." So, a range of fresh and salt water fish that have barbels under the chin are called catfish. This large family of fishes includes the Yellow Bullhead, the Red Horse, the Flathead Cat, the Channel Catfish, and the White Catfish. Most are caught from May to October in South Carolina's rivers and creeks. In the 1970s and 1980s they were farmed in state. For much of its history, catfish, because of its muddy habits and omnivorous tastes, had the reputation as being common food. Yet the clean, relatively fat-free flesh, has a sweetness and modesty of flavor that favored its discovery by restaurateurs over the last thirty years.

Because it was so common, catfish became one of the staple freshwater fishes employed in outdoor event cooking, along with bream and trout. When cooked outdoors, catfish was either stewed or fried.

Fried Catfish

At home one might fry catfish in bacon drippings, but at a fish fry, iron cauldrons of boiling lard stood at the ready while cooks either chunked or fileted the fish, dipped them in raw egg and coated them with salted cornmeal, cracker crumbs, or seasoned flour, and then dropped them into the bubbling fat. Catfish is cooked quickly and the sign of a rookie cook is overcooked fillets. It is ready when the fish start to look flakey.

In June of 1954, Shimmy's on Lady Street in Columbia became the first restaurant in the state to advertise fried catfish as its star attraction. With three sides it retailed for $1.25 and could be had at any time from 6:00 a.m. to 1:00 in the morning on Thursday, Friday, or Saturday. In the following decade a network of catfish-centered eateries sprang up in the state: Panorama in Ninety-Six, the Space Burger Drive-In, and the Sportsman Restaurant in Columbia; the Wells Marina Steak House in Ballentine; the Dock Restaurant in Moncks Corner, Jack's Diner in Hilton Head; The Fisherman's Wharf in Goose Creek. The Catfish Galley on Yeamans Hall Road outside of Charleston was the first restaurant to announce the fish in its name—in 1970. By 1965, the Winn Dixie grocery chain was advertising "Taste o' Sea French Fried Catfish fillets."

The appearance of catfish on the menus of a substantial number of restaurants can be tied to the rise of catfish farming—first in Mississippi then in South Carolina in 1969. Mississippian Ed Cliburn of the South Carolina Soil Conservation Service piloted a model farm at the Wadboo Hatchery outside of Moncks Corner. From the first the aim was to produce fish on a scale that could supply fast food chains. By the early 1990s there were fifty-three growers working 1,800 acres of catfish ponds. At that juncture the unforeseen consequences of intensive farming set in: the oversupply of catfish from farms over the South drove the price down to 59 cents per pound in 1991, pushing farms into the red. A number of farms experienced die-offs as disease raced through close-packed populations (this is why the disease-resistant tilapia supplanted catfish in South Carolina ponds after 2000). So, South Carolina did not endure as a major

Catfish and Crab Stew by Kevin Mitchell. Rhonda L. Wilson.

producer but has remained a major consumer, and catfish remains on many menus. It has become a staple of southern dining in the past half century.

Catfish Stew

Catfish stew belonged to the repertoire of open-air event dishes, usually cooked in kettles or large Dutch ovens over flames. Along with Pine Bark Stew (a stew of mixed fresh fish that included catfish and bream with tomatoes), Chicken Bog, Brunswick Stew, and Bream Stew, catfish stew became, in the nineteenth century, a fixture at fish fries, barbecues, political rallies, hunt club meets, camp meetings, fund raisers, and club outings.

Every part of the South boasted catfish stew in some guise—some called it "catfish soup," the name used by Mary Randolph in her *The Virginia House-Wife* in 1824. Louisiana

Catfish and Crab Stew

KEVIN MITCHELL

When I created my own version of catfish stew for a live demonstration, I chose a healthier preparation, using olive oil instead of bacon or butter. My contemporary interpretation is a red, tomato-based version, but I use fresh tomatoes and add okra, corn (which is traditional in white catfish stew), and crab.

½ cup olive oil
1 cup diced onion
1 cup diced green pepper
1 tablespoon minced garlic
1 cup sliced fresh okra
1 cup fresh or frozen corn kernels
3 cups low-sodium chicken stock
3 cups peeled, seeded, and diced
    fresh tomato
2 cups tomato puree

½ teaspoon cayenne pepper
Kosher salt and freshly ground
    black pepper
2 pounds fresh catfish fillets,
    diced
1 pound lump crab meat, picked
    through to remove any shell
1 cup chopped green onion
½ cup chopped parsley

Heat ½ cup of the olive oil in a medium pot over medium heat. Add the onion and pepper and sauté them until the onion begins to get tender, 3 to 5 minutes. Add the garlic and continue to sauté the vegetables for an additional 2 minutes. Add the okra and sauté for approximately 35 minutes. Add corn and sauté for 3 minutes more.

Increase the heat to medium-high. Add the chicken stock, tomato, and tomato puree. Bring to a strong simmer. Reduce the heat to low. Add the cayenne pepper. Season to taste with salt and black pepper. Cook for 10 minutes. Add catfish and cook for an additional 10 minutes until fish is cooked. Add the crab meat. Reduce the heat to medium and cook the stew for an additional 5 minutes to ensure catfish is fully cooked and crab is warmed through. Add the green onion and cook for an additional 3 minutes. Add parsley. Adjust the seasoning with salt and pepper if needed. Serve over steamed rice or grits if desired.

has its creole version replete with red pepper. Cooks argue about the optimal thickness of the liquid, the size of the fish chunks, the presence of vegetables other than onions and potatoes, and whether black pepper or black and red are used. Even within states there can be great variance.

In South Carolina each cook has their distinctive formula for the concoction, yet every cook belongs to one of two factions: white stew or red stew. In 1931, Harry Hampton noted the factional divide in catfish stew making: "There are two great classes of stew. In one are embodied large quantitates of tomatoes, ketchup and other seasoning along with corn and different vegetables. On the left wing is the 'straight' stew school—embracing in some instances nothing but catfish and potatoes, with slight seasoning, in other catfish and onions, and no potatoes."

The white stew was the older of the two preparations. The Gullah cooks of Colleton county called it Cush Stew. Its hallmarks: butter instead of tried pork fat as the lipid in the mix; lack of tomatoes; salt and pepper as the sole seasonings. In 1909, the editor of The *Laurens Advertiser* supplied a recipe that the fishermen of the Reedy River favored. It has the bulk measurements typical of dishes prepared for crowds and is a form of the white stew: "Take a peck of onions, a peck of Irish potatoes, 3 lbs. of butter, one-half gallon of green corn, and one gallon of sweet milk. To this add some water and let the whole boil three hours. While it is boiling you can be fishing. Now add one peck of nicely prepared cat fish but boil twenty minutes longer. Add pepper and salt."

A mid-twentieth century "Columbia Catfish Stew" collected by Robert E. Babb in 1974 typifies the more elaborate versions of catfish stew influenced by pine bark stew. It is a red stew incorporating two cans of whole tomatoes, a large can of tomato paste, tabasco, Worcestershire sauce, and hard-boiled eggs. In red stew Worcestershire is standard, the tabasco is an innovation. The usual practice is to add red pepper pods or flakes.

There were qualities that distinguished a superior catfish stew whichever way it was prepared: absence of bones, an abundance of fish in the stew, and liberal seasoning. Its frequent accompaniments were "red horse bread" named after the red horse sucker fish (the name hush puppy never found much favor in South Carolina until late in the twentieth century), and hot strong coffee.

During the twentieth century, an honor roll of South Carolina male event cooks became famous for their catfish stew: Romeo Govan of Bamberg in the 1900s and 1910s, Clarence 'Catfish Catoe' of Chesterfield in the 1910s and 1920s, Monroe Ridgill of Manning in the 1920s and 1930s, Earl Furman of Allendale in the 1920s and 1930s, H. M. Robertson of Rock Hill in the 1930s and 1940s, Herbert Stewert of Ridgeway from the 1940s to the 1960s, D. S. Lever of Columbia in the 1950s and 1960s, Bob Gregory of Moncks Corner in the 1960s and 1970s, and Ross Boulware of Elgin in the 1960s and 1970s. Boulware deserves particular honor for founding Elgin's annual Catfish Stomp, a celebration of catfish in all its splendor. Bob Gregory made catfish stew standard restaurant fare at the Dock Restaurant in Moncks Corner in the 1960s.

Chestnuts

Prior to 1920 chestnuts flooded the markets in October and remained available until the New Year. Chestnut dressing filled the rice field turkeys on holiday tables. Chestnut soufflé and chestnut pudding were popular desserts. David S. Shields.

Before the Horlbeck family began planting pecan nuts shipped from Texas in the fields around Boone Hall Plantation in the 1830s, and before Carolinians began calling pindars (*Arachis hypogeia,* a legume) peanuts in the 1830s, one nut loomed foremost in people's imaginations as the "nut of the country." It was the chestnut. The American chestnut (*Castenea dentate*) dominated the eastern hardwood forest and covered the hills and mountains in the western counties of the state.

The American chestnut was a fast growing, tall straight hardwood, ideal for timber. Every second year it bore massive loads of nuts, nestled within green vegetal spikey hulls. The creatures of the eastern forest feasted on chestnuts, waiting for the hulls to dry and split and the nuts to spill on the forest floor. The Cherokee, Catawba, Sugaree, Waxhaw, and Eno Shakori peoples harvested, broiled, boiled, mashed, and even dried the nut meats for a range of preparations. The boiled and mashed chestnuts (spoon meat) they mixed with cornmeal, fat, and salt, made it into a paste, wrapped it in a corn husk, and boiled it to create eastern tamales.

After European colonization of the southeast, settlers of the backcountry adopted the nut and substituted the American chestnut for the familiar European chestnut in a host of traditional recipes: chestnut bread, chestnut griddle cakes, chestnut pudding, deviled chestnuts,

[33]

and pickled chestnuts. Nut fall began in the second week in October and wagons carted the harvest to the coastal cities where roasted chestnuts became autumn fixtures, a signature of the holiday season. A rich repertoire of chestnut dishes developed over the nineteenth century.

In South Carolina, problems with the chestnut trees began shortly after the Civil War. The trees growing in the midlands began dying in great numbers, felled by a soil-borne disease of the roots, Phytophthora. Yet chestnuts survived in numbers in the western mountains. Harvesters mobbed the trees in October, sending bags eastward to the cities. Every year after 1913 the crop declined, leaving a commentator shortly afterwards to observe, "the chestnut crop in this country is being reduced each year by the chestnut-blight disease which is in some sections is gradually killing out the tree" (1917).

Shortly after 1900, a fungus (*Chryphonectria parasitica*) in imported Asian chestnut trees spread to American chestnut trees in the northeastern hardwood forests. Nothing could counter its lethal corruption of the cambium beneath the tree's bark. It spread steadily, first in the northern chestnut forest from Maine to Maryland, then in the 1910s, down the Appalachian ridge, until the whole eastern range of the tree sickened and died. The dominant tree of the eastern uplands expired in an ecological disaster that still haunts the minds of those who police biosecurity in the United States. Human foodways of great antiquity disappeared. By 1922 all that remained after the blight was the Christmastide appearance of imported European or Asian "roasting chestnuts" and perhaps a few additional nuts for the turkey's dressing at Thanksgiving.

For much of the twentieth century, forest ecologists, geneticists, and sylvaculturists

American Chestnut was once the dominant hardwood in the eastern forest and a major source of food in South Carolina. The blight wiped the tree out in the 1910s and 1920s. These seed chestnuts, bred to be blight resistant by the American Chestnut Foundation, promise the restoration of the tree and its foodways in the near future. David S. Shields.

labored to create a blight-resistant hybrid of the American chestnut and restore it to its traditional range. Using a breeding scheme devised by Charles Burnham, blight-resistant Asian trees are crossed with American trees, and their offspring crossed again with an American chestnut tree. The resultant tree from these back crossings are predominantly (94%) American chestnuts. The American Chestnut Foundation has chosen these hybrids as the vehicle for the reforestation of the old eastern range. By 2024, we should know once again the sweet, creamy taste of South Carolina's native nut. Here are some preparations for the day when it happens.

Chestnut Dressing

Abbeville Press and Banner
(December 2, 1904)

The chestnut dressing for the turkey is prepared from a quart of chestnuts which have been blanched then cooked until tender, adding a cupful of fresh bread crumbs, two tablespoonfuls of butter, a teaspoonful of salt, chopped parsley, pepper and milk or stock to moisten.

Chestnut Custard

Bay City Times
(November 29, 1903)

Boil a quart of large chestnuts, peel, skin and mash to a smooth pulp; add the grated yellow rind of a lemon, a tablespoonful of lemon juice, a grating of nutmeg and a custard made as follows: Beat three eggs with a third of a cup of granulated sugar, a pinch of salt and a grating of nutmeg. Pour a pint of scalded milk over the mixture, blend and return to the boiler and stir and cook until it is a thick, smooth cream. Take from the fire and stir in the whites of the eggs beaten to a stiff froth. Turn the custard into stemmed glasses, set on ice and when cold and ready to serve heap whipped cream on top.

Chestnut Soufflé

Augusta Chronicle
(September 27, 1903)

Boil a pint of shelled nuts in salted water until tender. Drain, remove the brown skins and rub through a fine sieve. Cream together ½ cupful of sugar and 4 tablespoonfuls of butter. Add the nuts, together with the beaten yolks of 4 eggs, a cupful of milk,

½ cup of breadcrumbs, and lemon juice and grated rind to flavor. Lastly, fold in the stiffly beaten whites of the eggs, turn into a buttered mold, cover and cook very slowly for fifteen or twenty minutes. Serve with sugar and cream. A soufflé can be cooked to perfection in the chafing dish by using the hot water pan.

One dish that appeared on local menus yet never had a recipe printed by a South Carolina newspaper or press, was deviled chestnuts. Here's a recipe from out of state:

Deviled Chestnuts

Philadelphia Inquirer
(December 30, 1899)

Cut a slit in the shell of each chestnut, put them in a popcorn popper over an open fire and shake them frequently. When they burst open they are done. Remove the shells and skin and then toss them about in hot water in the chafing dish. Sprinkle with salt and paprika, and add sufficient Worcestershire sauce to moisten them. Stir them till all have received a portion of the pungent dressing, and serve them hot.

Chicken Bog

First mentioned in a South Carolina newspaper in 1910, Chicken Bog gets its name from the fact that it appears that the chicken is bogged down by the rice, a texture that also recalls the bogs of the Lowcountry. Chicken Bog in essence resembles chicken pilau with the difference that a pilau is much dryer than a bog.

Originally, bog was cooked and served in a wash kettle or iron cauldron outdoors to accommodate large crowds. It became, like pine bark stew, one of the central dishes of large-scale outdoor and event cooking. (A pilau, by contrast, is meant to be cooked in the home.) Its first home was the Pee Dee region on the eastern side of the state, bog became so popular in the town of Loris that during the last quarter of the twentieth century they began hosting annual "Chicken Bog-Offs."

The best bogs are those that resemble a porridge with visible shreds of chicken with broth-swollen rice grains maintaining their shape, not broken. You can compare it in some sense to the Asian congee. Most cooks say the trick to a great bog is understanding the importance of the of the amount of each ingredient that goes into it and knowing the right moment to add the rice to achieve the proper consistency. The first recipes published in mass circulation media adjusted the ingredient proportions downward to suit family meals.

My introduction to chicken bog happened in 2013. The Culinary Institute of Charleston hosted The Lowcountry Rice Culture forum where I (Kevin) was to perform a cooking demonstration on chicken bog. Being a northerner, I had never heard of the dish. This meant a bit of research was in order. As I soon learned, tackling chicken bog would be a huge undertaking. Below is the chicken bog recipe created by Anson Mills, which I worked through and served at the forum.

Chicken Bog
Anson Mills

1 whole chicken (3 to 3½ pounds), washed, liver and gizzard reserved for another use, and neck bone, if present, along for the ride

2 medium yellow onions, chopped fine

1 large or 2 small carrots, peeled and chopped into ½-inch lengths

1 celery rib, chopped into ½-inch lengths

3 garlic cloves, peeled

6 fresh thyme sprigs or 1½ teaspoons dried thyme

1 Turkish bay leaf

Handful of fresh flat-leaf parsley stems

4 cups rich homemade chicken stock

4 cups spring or filtered water

10 ounces smoked sausage (½ inch in diameter), preferably dry-cured, cut into ½-inch rounds

7 ounces (1 cup) Anson Mills Carolina Gold Rice

1½ teaspoons freshly ground black pepper

Fine sea salt

2 tablespoons unsalted butter

2 scallions

3 tablespoons chopped fresh flat-leaf
parsley leaves

Day one: Combine the chicken neck (if using), onions, carrot(s), celery, garlic, thyme, bay leaf, parsley stems, chicken stock, and water in a heavy, nonreactive 5- to 6-quart stockpot. Place the chicken breast side up in the pot and bring the liquid to a simmer over medium-high heat. Reduce the heat to low, cover the pot, and simmer gently until the chicken legs pull easily from the carcass, about 1 hour. Remove from the heat and let cool for 30 minutes.

Using tongs, transfer the chicken from the pot to a rimmed baking sheet. Let stand until cool enough to handle, and then remove the meat from the bones and pull it into small pieces. Discard the chicken skin. Cover the meat and refrigerate. (Note: 1 pound or 4 cups of chicken meat is all you need for the bog. If you have extra meat, save it for a sandwich.) Return the bones to the stockpot, bring the broth to a simmer over medium heat, and simmer until

it is rich, flavorful, and reduced to generous 6 cups, about 45 minutes. Strain the broth through a fine-holed footed colander or fine-mesh strainer into a large mixing bowl. Refrigerate overnight.

Day two: Using a spoon, lift the congealed fat from the surface of the broth and discard the fat. Return the stock to the pot, set the pot on the stove, stir in the reserved chicken meat and the sausage, and bring to a simmer, covered, over medium-high heat. Reduce the heat to low and stir in the rice, pepper, and salt to taste. Continue to simmer very gently, uncovered, stirring occasionally, until the rice is tender and the broth has thickened, about 25 minutes. The stew should be thick but not dry, and the grains of rice should be full but not exploded.

Remove the pot from the heat and stir in the butter. Mince the scallions. Ladle the stew into 6 shallow bowls. Sprinkle with scallions and parsley and serve immediately. Pickled jalapeños are a perfect condiment to serve with this dish.

Chinquapins

Once the glory of the upstate autumn, the chinquapin, the sweeter smaller relative of the American chestnut, was roasted or boiled as a favorite autumn snack food. Victim of the chestnut blight, it hasn't been sold in generations, but now that it is beginning to return, it has the potential to be the novelty snack of the 2020s. Shelled roasted chinquapins from Seneca, SC. David S. Shields.

When you drive up I-26 heading out of South Carolina into North Carolina, note the signs for Saluda. It was the home of the last important market for chinquapins in the United States. At the train station in Saluda through the 1910s, knots of young boys would sell strings of hulled, boiled chinquapins to passengers. Each boy carried dozens of strings on the crook of his arm or around his neck. These filbert-sized nuts, a diminutive cousin of the American chestnut, were once an autumn delight. Boys would harvest ripe nuts in September, stripping off the prickly hull of five hundred chinquapins in an afternoon, knicking the nuts with a knife, boiling them, and wearing double and triple stringed necklaces of nuts to sell for spending money. But by 1912 lovers of the nuts were mourning its demise. The twin diseases of Chestnut blight and Phytophthora (a root rot) had killed most of the stands of chinquapins that grew on the margins of the eastern forest. These days the Alleghany chinquapin survives wild in isolated patches of the Piedmont and Appalachians.

A youngster wearing a string of chinqua-pins has not been seen in South Carolina in over a century. In the late 1800s there were a number of towns famous for their chin-quapins—Statesburg, Landrum, Pickens, and Union. A shame—because they taste better than the American chestnut, a nut sweeter more piquant than any Asian or Italian chestnut you have sampled at Christmastime. Boiled or roasted, salted or candied, Chinquapin meats are and were an addictive snack food. Four years ago, Glenn Roberts and I (David) secured a supply, had them hulled (at insane expense), and sampled them—then sent some to chef Travis Milton for an experiment. He milled the roasted nuts into meal and added it as flavoring to biscuits.

Chinquapins deserve attention in 2020 because we will soon have them as a culinary resource again. Dr. Joe James of Seneca has been breeding blight-resistant/ Phytophthora - resistant chinquapins using native stock and admixtures of resistant Asian chestnut ge-netics. His breeding program has produced resilient trees that can survive in cultivation. Dr. James is going into partnership with Nat Bradford, who will cultivate the crop. The great challenge before them is hulling. The small prickly burrs are the devil to get off the nut. But once the nut meats are exposed, then I don't doubt the demand. They taste better than hazelnuts, have a pleasant but not cloy-ing sweetness, and when roasted and salted disappear in an instant.

The last time someone tried planting chinquapin trees in South Carolina was in the 1950s when Waynesboro Nurseries of Virginia advertised that the way to make chil-dren happy was to plant a chinquapin in your yard. These were partially resistant trees being sold. The ads appeared for a number of years before Carolinians realized that the trees they purchased withered after two seasons in the ground. Phytophthora did them in.

There was not an extensive repertoire of chinquapin preparations, because they were so beloved as a snacking nut, shelled, roasted or boiled, and salted. The boiled chinquapins could be mashed into a paste and used in con-fectionery. But honey-roasted they tasted as sublime as any pastry. Before they were rare some cooks experimented with chinquapin flour. Yet there were other things one did with the nuts that had nothing to do with the kitchen—playing the old gambling game hully gully: "Hull Gull, Hand full, guess how many?"

As Dr. James's strains are becoming in-creasingly viable, soon there will be small trees laden again with the scrumptious nuts. Then we will need a nut huller suited to the small size of the nuts to process them into snack form.

☙ Collards ☙

Blue Stem Collard was the first variety for which a commercial seed demand developed after the Civil War. One of the "old stand by" collards like the white and yellow cabbage collard known for flavor and reliability in the field. David S. Shields.

No discussion about southern or South Carolina ingredients would be complete without greens, particularly collard greens. The name collard is a southern alteration of the English word "colewort," a loose-leafed form of cabbage. Native to Europe, cabbages were early settler food, but southerners discovered that heading cabbages, when grown in the South, bore seed that sprouted cabbages that would not head. These were coleworts, or collards.

If you wanted a heading cabbage you had to get seed from the North, from Europe, or after the 1840s from the mountains of North Carolina. Since coleworts were as edible as any other form of cabbage, settlers made due, and began in the 1850s to sell collard seed to one another. When USDA plant breeder Mark Farnham collected old collard varieties throughout the South at the end of the twentieth century, he and his team discovered over one hundred. Because the collard plants could draw salt out of fields suffering from salt water contamination, they were sometimes planted in vast quantities on coastal rice and corn plantations. So, fields full of collards grew along the coast and it became a cheap and plentiful mainstay of daily dinners. Picked for their

TASTE THE STATE

thick leaves, you can find them growing all year round. Their flavor peaks in the colder months after the first frost. For the best texture it is they should be picked before their leaves grow to maximum size.

While grocery stores don't identify collards by variety, backyard gardeners should be on the lookout for seed for one of the following if they love good eating: cabbage collards (yellow or white), Stoney mountain collard (an old South Carolina white stemmed sort), Georgia blue stem collard, Bradford collard, and if your garden is troubled by insects, glazed collards.

Traditionally cultivated for the most part by women in kitchen gardens, collard greens added to one pot stews that recall West African cooking and appear at the table at winter meals. Like okra, collards do not suit many taste buds in the North. As John T. Edge of the Southern Foodways Alliance observed, "collards more than any other food, delineate the boundaries of the Mason Dixon line."

Collard greens were known for their thickening properties. Added to simmering liquid or stew they will give it body. Some old school cooks liked to cook it until the leaves broke down and the plants "swapped flavor" with other ingredients in the pot. Yet they need not be cooked to be enjoyed. They can be chopped and fermented in salt like cabbage to create collard slaw. They can be eaten raw in salads, if the greens belong to one of the tender varieties.

A favorite of many African Americans, you will find a pot of greens on tables across the South. If not on your table during the holidays, you will definitely find them being cooked on New Year's Day. A pot of greens is a way to wish for plenty of green money for the coming year, served alongside a pot of Hoppin' John to handle change. Though Edna Lewis was not from South Carolina, she is heralded as a grande dame of southern cuisine and does have a connection to Charleston. She was executive chef at Middleton Place, where she served her greens. Like Lewis, we suggest diners season their own greens with as much vinegar as they want.

Cooked Greens

Edna Lewis, *In Pursuit of Flavor* (1988)

1 pound cured smoked pork shoulder,
    bacon or streak-of-lean
3 quarts of water
3 pounds collard greens
Salt and freshly ground black pepper

Cook the pork and water in a 5-quart-pot for 1½ hours or more, until the meat is very tender. Remove the meat from the stock and discard. Add the greens. You will have to pack them in but they will cook down quickly. Cover over medium-high for about 20 to 30 minutes. Do not cover the pot or the greens may turn dark. Be careful not to undercook the greens, which is as bad for them as overcooking. I will always test them for doneness after 15 minutes although they sometimes need 20 minutes of cooking. During cooking, season them with salt and black pepper. Lift them from the pot, shake off excess liquid, and serve hot.

At the beginning of the twenty-first century, when chefs and farmers realized that most of the classic ingredients of southern cooking had been replaced by modern agronomic grains and vegetables that had not been bred for flavor, they found only three items had remained stable and available from the antebellum period to the end of the twentieth century: okra, Jerusalem artichokes, and collards.

Spicy Collards with Red Peppers

KEVIN MITCHELL

I developed this recipe when I was tasked to create two New Year's dishes for *Charleston Magazine*. I wanted to celebrate dishes African Americans traditionally eat for the New Year, Collard Greens and Hoppin' John (see recipe in that entry). For the greens I did not move too far away from traditional recipes, however, I added red pepper to brighten up the dish and omitted the vinegar that is used in some recipes.

1 tablespoon vegetable oil
4 ounces thick-cut Applewood
   smoked bacon, diced
3 cups chopped yellow onions
2 tablespoons minced shallot
4 ounces bourbon
1 cup diced red bell peppers

1 pound collard greens, stems
   removed, and leaves cut
   into 1-inch pieces
3 cups chicken or vegetable
   broth
2 pinches red pepper flakes
Kosher salt and black pepper

Heat the oil in a large pot over medium-high heat. Add the bacon and cook until crisp. Add the onions and cook, stirring frequently until tender, about 5 minutes. Add the shallots and cook until just fragrant, about 2 to 3 minutes. Add the bourbon and allow alcohol to cook out, about 2 minutes. Add the red bell pepper and cook for 1 minute. Stir in the collard greens and cook until they start to wilt. Add the stock and red pepper flakes. Reduce the heat to low, cover, and simmer for 20 minutes, or until greens are tender and most of the liquid has been absorbed. Season with salt and pepper to taste.

Conch

Conch is the Lowcountry seafood that residents keep under their hats. Every Gullah seafood cook knows a source, has a fritter recipe, a stew recipe, even a salad recipe. The old families South of Broad have an ancestral chowder recipe handed down for at least half a century. But nobody talks up conch. They know what happens when an ingredient gets fashionable. The waters of South Carolina could be picked clean of conch just as Florida waters were in the early 1980s.

"Conch" has a rather broad designation when used by inhabitants of the southeastern coast. In Carolina and Georgia it means a large specimen of knobbed whelk (*Busycon carica*), maybe a channel whelk; in Florida it means the queen conch, *Strombus gigas,* the signature shellfish of Key West. In all cases the shells are rather large and twisty. Inside dwells a sizeable meaty mollusk, the queen conch being larger, weighing up to five pounds.

Conch has been a food resource of the sea islands since well before European settlers and enslaved Africans inhabited the Lowcountry. Conch Soup/Stew was surely the creation of the Native peoples. Conch fritters in the South are Gullah-Geechee. Conch chowder is Euro-American. Because a conch supplies an ample amount of meat, and because "conch ain't got no bone" it has always been a food source, albeit one that only intermittently gets registered in American mass media.

Beginning in 1971, southern newspapers began celebrating the conch—although by some odd trick of touristic imagination, insisting that conch foodways were Bahamian, and that preparing conch dishes was an excursion offshore to an exotic culinary culture

Conch, or knobbed whelk, is found all along the coast and a mainstay of sea island cookery. Kiawah Island coast.

(President Richard Nixon visited the Bahamas in 1971 and sampled conch chowder at Walker's Cay). Conch chowder (milk or half-and-half, streaky bacon, onions, maybe potatoes) was considered the signature main course of Key West cookery. Truth be known every conch dish imagined to be from elsewhere had been made in Carolina and Georgia from the colonial period on.

Conch is harvested alive and stored in salt water to the point of preparation, because dead conchs spoil quickly. Horseshoe crab is a common bait for conch traps. In the early twentieth century it was a common enough sight on the coast to see someone with a bucket of submerged whelks and conchs that they haul up from the tidal shallows. The shells were cracked with the butt of an axe and the meat processed immediately, usually boiled, sometimes chopped fresh.

[43]

The knobbed whelk doesn't suffer the same scarcity as the Caribbean queen conch, perhaps because of the careful regulation of the off-shore whelk trawl fishery. Commencing in early spring, boats harvest whelks over 4.5 inches long. When thirteen thousand bushels have been taken by the fleet, the season is closed. Since 2000, the harvest has tended to be below ten thousand, with occasional flat years. The problem for Carolinians is getting access to the crop, since customers in Asia purchase it at top dollar. So, the most reliable sources for citizens is their own harvest in their own bucket in waters that are open for public use, or their own creek. Still, there is some question that the in-shore population is overfished by recreational harvesters.

About the recipes: The classic Gullah-Geechee fritter recipe had peppers (hot and sweet), onion, and, when available, Worcestershire sauce added to a seasoned batter with chopped or ground conch. This was gussied in the twentieth century by city cooks with tomato paste and chopped celery. In the nineteenth century it was cooked in a skillet in an inch of melted lard or benne oil. In the 1900s they used Wesson oil.

The fastidious Franz Meier of the Colony House Restaurant in the 1970s and 1980s reputedly got his recipe from a Gullah fisherman on James Island. They assume the shape of irregular balls rather than batter cakes.

Colony House Conch Fritters

South Carolina's Historic Restaurants and Their Recipes (1984)

¾ cup conch meat, ground or chopped
2 tablespoons diced onions
2 tablespoons diced bell peppers
1 teaspoon chopped jalapeno peppers
2 eggs
1 ½ teaspoons baking powder
¾ cup flour
½ teaspoon salt
Oil for deep frying

Combine all ingredients except oil in a bowl until well mixed. In a heavy skillet or deep fryer, heat oil to 325 or 350F. Drop tablespoonfuls of batter into the oil, varying the size to suit your purpose (small for appetizers, large for side dishes). Turn fritters as they rise to the surface, and fry until golden brown and cook through. Serve with your favorite sauce.

Traditional Conch Soup/Stew recipes are quite simple: conch chopped and first cooked in fat, then put in a vessel with corn (the Native version was dried and cracked), water, salt, and long cooked. After the 1850s, tomatoes and onions were added, and sometimes supplanted corn.

In the twentieth century, the stew added Worcestershire sauce and some hot peppers and morphed into what Charlestonians began calling Conch Chowder. But the classic conch chowder was pretty much like any classic chowder: bacon and onions, chopped conch, milk or half-and-half as the liquid, and potatoes optional.

Not only is the conch a culinary delight but also marine scientists increasingly have taken an interest in the knobbed whelk because its presence in the coastal shallows is seen as an indicator of a healthy marine ecosystem.

Cooter Soup

Southern turtle soups and stews once stood at the heart of fine dining. Terrapin à la Maryland appeared first at any banquet worth its name in parts north of South Carolina, until Prohibition made its finishing splash of Madeira illegal. In South Carolina the terrapin took second place to readily obtainable cooter—originally an African American general designation for fresh water basking and sliding turtles. Biologists now identify the term with *Pseudemys concinna,* the River Cooter and its related species the Florida Cooter and the Suwanee Cooter. But when it comes to cooter soup, the original broader designation comes into play, and the yellow belly slider (*Trachemys scripta scripta*) finds its way into the pot under the name cooter too. Female cooters were traditionally preferred over males for cooking and contribute to two classic dishes: cooter soup (red or white) and cooter pie.

Allendale, South Carolina, in 1973 felt that the ecological, cultural, and culinary importance of the cooter had been neglected, and remedied the inattention by inaugurating a Cooter Festival, with turtle races, cooking contests, and other diversions.

Cooters, being fresh water turtles, lack the tinge of salt that characterizes the terrapin. Hence the flesh invites a liberal hand with seasoning. Two schools of soup/stew arose, red and white, paralleling the two schools of catfish stew in the state. The red soup incorporates tomatoes, ketchup, or tomato paste. The white soup does not, and tends to be flavored with pepper, mace, or allspice. It is usually charged with a pour of sherry before serving.

Prepping the turtle is not for the squeamish. First you chop off the head and hang the body inverted to drain the blood. You then immerse the body in boiling water for 5 to 8 minutes, or until the skin dislodges easily. Next, de-hinge the upper shell from the lower plates with a knife and separate them. Then extract the edible parts: eggs, liver, the front and hindquarters and the strip of white meat adhering to the upper shell. Wash and put all the turtle meat into cold water until ready to use. The meat will be cooked for an additional length of time during the soup preparation.

The first recorded recipe for the white version of the soup appeared in *Mrs. Hill's New Cook Book* (1867), by Annabella Hill of Lagrange, Georgia. The recipes given below simplify her instructions and adapts it to twenty-first-century practice.

White Cooter Soup

Adapted from Annabella Hill

Having extracted the meat and eggs from a female cooter, set a large pot with a gallon of water on to boil. In it put the turtle meat and liver, yet reserving the eggs, 1 chopped onion, and a ¼ pound piece of fatback. Boil moderately until the meat begins to break apart (at least an hour and half). Strain the meat from the stock, reserving the stock in another pot. Chop the meat fine and remove any skin and residual bones. In another poet make a roux with flour and oil. Brown it to your taste—then add 1 chopped sweet onion, stirring until it sweats, then stirring in the meat, and

[45]

immediately after all the meat has been added, begin introducing the turtle stock little at a time, stirring to prevent lumping. Once you have achieved the thickness you desire add mace, allspice, a pinch of cayenne, salt and black pepper. An optional ingredient is diced boiled potatoes. These can be added at this juncture. Cook the soup 15 additional minutes stirring and adding stock. Add boiled eggs. Add a ¼ cup of Madeira into the tureen before bringing it to the table.

Red Cooter Soup

Adapted from Annabella Hill

Having extracted the meat and eggs from a female cooter, set a large pot with a gallon of water on to boil. In it put the turtle meat, and four strips of streaky bacon. Boil until the meat begins to break apart. Strain the meat from the stock, reserving the stock in a pot. Chop the meat fine and remove any skin and residual bones.

Return the prepped meat to the stock pot, add 4 onions rough chopped, two carrots chopped, 2 cups of ketchup, one can of tomato juice, ½ bottle of Worcestershire sauce, salt, lots of pepper, a tablespoon of red pepper. Bring to a boil, then after 5 minutes of rolling boil, turn it down to a just bubbling. Cook four hours. Then add 4 diced potatoes and cook an additional 45 minutes. Some add tabasco before serving, but this is optional. Serve with rice.

White Cooter Soup became a restaurant dish in the 1860s in South Carolina. Mrs. R. W. Torck's restaurant, Our House, on the corner of East Bay and Queen Streets, served it in Charleston for lunch from 1868 to 1880. Thereafter it has appeared on menus with some regularity throughout the Lowcountry and midlands. Red Cooter Soup tends to be an outdoor event dish, prepared in large quantities. The White Soup retained sufficient importance in the local repertoire to earn a place in Blanche Rhett's *200 Years of Charleston Cooking* (1930) and *Charleston Receipts* (1950).

Corn Bread and Corn Pone

"Give me corn bread when I'm hungry,
Corn whiskey when I'm dry."

At the dawn of the twentieth century, Carolina's home bakers made rice bread in the east, corn bread in the west. Wheat bread and rye could be had at the town bakeries and at hotels. After the collapse of rice culture in the 1910s, corn bread has reigned supreme as the chief creation emerging from home ovens. Whether made from scratch or prepped from a mix, it retains a welcome place in the Carolina bread basket, nestling there with biscuits and benne rolls. How did this come to be?

In much of the South, spring wheat proved difficult if not impossible to sustain as a crop—Hessian fly, rust, joint worm, and other diseases ravaged it, and the soft white winter wheats that escaped these pests and pathogens were suited to cake flour and biscuits rather than bread. So, there is little wonder that southerners made bread from the one grain that would grow throughout the summer without difficultly—maize. Native peoples in the southeast had a variety of preparations made from doughs and batters made of ground maize and water and some sort of fat: fried breads, round pones baked in ceramic pots using a second pot of coals, batter cakes poured on hot stones. A similar variety of preparations arose when colonists took the maize and the recipes, adjusting them to European tastes: corn pone, corn bread, corn dodgers, corn cakes, and fried cornmeal fritters.

In the 1790s, the British-American scientist Benjamin Thompson, or Count Rumford, became interested in the potential of baked Indian meal as a staple to feed the world's

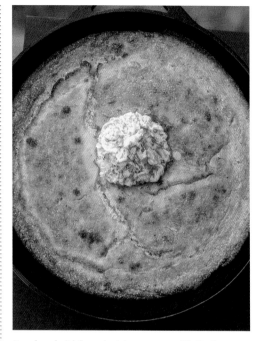

Corn bread with honey herb butter prepared by Kevin Mitchell. Rhonda L. Wilson

poor. He even developed chemical leaveners (among the first baking sodas) to enable cornmeal bread to rise when heated despite its lack of gluten. He theorized a diet entirely based on corn, little realizing that the practicalities of hardscrabble life in the southern upcountry would restrict settlers to just such a corn diet in decades to come. Surviving on corn bread, grits, and corn whiskey subjected settlers to a vitamin deficiency disease, pellagra, because maize does not supply niacin, unless it is ash-treated and made into hominy (see entry for Hominy Grits).

Classic corn bread is made with cornmeal, made from the dried kernels of field corn. Originally, it was a rather coarsely ground white flint corn, as opposed to the varicolored

[47]

flint corns known by millers as Indian Meal. After the southern white dent corns became available in the 1840s, some millers and cooks began to favor the more easily milled Cocke's Prolific, Carswell White, Boone County White, and Hickory King corns. In the 1880s, when industrial milling emerged in much of the United States, the mills offered corn flour processed from white and, after 1900, yellow dent. "The meal of . . . commerce, [is] kiln-dried, bolted and ground altogether too fine" to make traditional corn bread (1899). Indeed, there was a general decline in the production of corn bread early in the twentieth century, if newspaper complaints may be credited. In South Carolina, however, corn bread was too important an element of home cooking to be allowed to decline. The state supported an array of small-scale toll and water mills. By the 1920s, brands like Birdsey's Meal from Columbia advertised that they were "Old Fashion Stone Ground." Adluh Flour in Columbia advertised stone ground meal from 1918 to 2018.

If a textured meal is necessary for any corn bread worthy of the name, milk and eggs are optional. If you bake a cornmeal loaf without milk and eggs, and if the shape is round, it is called a pone. If it has it milk and eggs, it is corn bread. If it has many eggs and a lot of butter and milk, it is a batter bread, or spoonbread—a cornmeal soufflé (see separate entry).

The twentieth-century turn to yellow corn in corn bread must be viewed in light of the national transformation of corn agriculture, making Reid's Yellow Dent and its offspring the standard corn planted in the corn belt Midwest. Each decade of the twentieth century saw the plantings of yellow dents

increase and white decrease. What is available and cheap is what will be promoted by processors. During World War II, when an emphasis on quick preparation (battlefield speed) brought us minute rice and instant mashed potatoes, the first corn bread mixes appeared in the state, all using yellow corn: Miss Chambers and Clinch Corn Bread Mix. Convenience corn bread never left the grocery shelf thereafter with Jiffy, Martha White, Marie Callender's, Betty Crocker, and Krusteaz offering variants. What the mixes supplied were seasoning and leavening agents beside the meal. The ideal of these mixes was fluffy corn bread—with a high rise and a big crumb. One ingredient present in some mixes and not another provokes noisy arguments among devotees of corn bread nowadays: sugar. Jiffy has it. Martha White does not.

The very earliest corn breads using white flint cornmeal did not, since sugar was not cheap enough to be a common household commodity until 1825. But by the time Sarah Rutledge published *The Carolina Housewife* in 1847, sugar had entered into some recipes—her Chicora Corn Bread for instance. Some argue that sugar in corn bread is an African American foodway, while savory corn bread is Anglo-American. But the documentary evidence indicates that there has always been a range of corn bread preparations—some with admixtures of wheat flour, some with sugar, some mixing cooked grits with meal, some jettisoning leavening agents. The most famous recipe of the latter nineteenth century in South Carolina was chef Christian Mugel's corn bread served at Charleston's Pavilion Hotel. It contained sugar.

Pavilion Hotel
Corn Bread

Christian Mugel,
The Weekly Union Times (July 17, 1883)

First, half pound butter; second, half pound sugar; third, one dozen eggs; fourth two quarts of milk fifth, two pounds white Indian meal; sixth one-pound wheat flour, and two and a half ounces Royal Baking Powder. Mix the above ingredients one after the other as they are numbered and be sure and mix the baking powder in with the flour before putting it in the mixtures. Bake in small moulds or in square pan, in a hot oven.

Conforming more to the imaginings of no sugar purists was the rather austere savory version that circulated in print in the early 1920s, "Spider Corn Bread," named after the three-legged or more Dutch oven in which one baked corn bread before the advent of the cook stove (1840s to 1870s). Using sour milk or buttermilk in conjunction with baking soda was a standard way to activate the rising agent in skillet bread recipes.

Spider Corn Bread

Bessie R. Murphy,
Charleston Evening Post (July 31, 1923)

1½ cups corn meal
2 cups sour milk
1 teaspoon soda
1 teaspoon salt
2 eggs
2 tablespoons butter

Mix dry ingredients, add the eggs well beaten and the milk, place the butter in a frying pan, melt it and grease the pan well, heat the pan and turn in the mixture, and place the mixture in a hot oven and cook 20 minutes.

Matching the diversity of corn bread recipes are the ways corn bread is garnished—with butter, with apple butter, with cane syrup, with gravy, with pot likker. No one way is more authentic or proper than another, except the garnish should never eclipse the flavor of corn bread itself, for if you have meal from a good old corn variety, an effective rising agent, and a lipid with some point (bacon grease, butter, lard, pecan oil), you will be tasting a wonderful thing indeed.

Cracklin' Bread

In 1928, a connoisseur of traditional southern cookery remarked, "when cracklin' bread was recently served to members of a Columbia, South Carolina, luncheon club, some said it was the first they had tasted in years." It stood foremost in this man's estimation of the old dishes "fit for the gods" that used to grace the region's dining tables: "rice bread, hopping john, hoe cake, batter bread [spoonbread], turnip soup, pot-liquor, rice pilau, tomato and okra soup, sally lunn, corn-starch pudding, trifle, marble cake, stickies, hard ginger cake."

What exactly is cracklin' bread? A 1911 commentator said "no latter-day baker knows anything about cracklin' bread. It is a product of the soil, so to speak, and is found only in the rural districts where old-time cooking is still in vogue." It was a corn pone—baked at least three inches thick whose interior is "bedecked with little brown cracklin's which look for the world like raisins." And if you don't know what cracklin's are—they are the residue when hog fat is cut into small chunks to be rendered for lard—crispy and dark reddish brown.

While cracklin' bread may have been going out of favor a century ago, it survived and was indeed revived in the twenty-first century as an autumn-time black skillet favorite preparation in the Carolina countryside. Cracklin' bread was one of the staples of old southern Christmas cookery. Because hog killings took place during the cold on the verge of Christmas, there was always a multitude of cracklin's left from the lard kettle. It graced the breakfast table, consumed with "sausage or bird pie, or even roasted sweet potatoes and plenty of butter" (1938). The enduring popularity of cracklin' bread has given rise to meat processing companies offering packages of cracklin's for sale over the internet. One need no longer render your pig's leaf fat into lard to have cracklin's ready to hand. Manda Fine Meats of Baton Rouge, Louisiana, offers a high-quality product—an important consideration since some snack food companies sell deep fried pig skin chips (bbq spice rub optional) under the name cracklin's.

The simplest form of cracklin' bread was to add a cup of cracklin's to your standard corn bread recipe, leaving out any other shortening. Though it should be observed that this minimalist version always used baking soda instead of powder, and eschewed eggs or sugar in the mix. Some may find the old formula too dry, so add 3 tablespoons of drippings (rendered lard) as well. There were variations and elaborations of course.

Duck

For many a hunter duck reigned as the most versatile, flavorful, and plentiful game bird to be encountered in the autumn. Whether Redhead, Widgeon, Wood Duck, Scaup, or one of the breeds that visit and soon depart, the wild ducks excited the hunter, and challenged the cook. While the canvasback, a duck more proper to the Chesapeake, stood first in culinary repute among restaurateurs and hoteliers, the home cook in South Carolina cherished the Wood Duck and the Redhead. They were processed quickly—plucked and gutted—with some effort made to extract the shot. Then the duck was hung up in a cool protected place to age. The classic Carolina cookbooks had instructions on how to roast the duck. Here is one such recipe.

To Roast a Duck

A Southern Lady,
The Centennial Receipt Book (1876)

Let your duck hang always for a day, and longer if the weather is cold enough; stuff with sage and onion stuffing. Put it before a clear fire, turn and baste it frequently; let it roast about an hour. Just before it is done, draw it nearer the fire; dredge it with a little flour, baste it with a little butter to crisp the skin. Make some brown gravy in the dripping pan, and pour it in the dish around the bird.

While this method serves equally for domestic and wild ducks, another method was reserved almost exclusively for game birds: they were trussed and impaled on a spit that rotated before an open fire. Because of the mystique of game, wild duck was one of the few things prepared hearthside or before an outdoor fire long after the advent of the cook stove in the 1840s. If a wild duck was old and tough it would be rubbed in vinegar and pepper and then hung to age. The duck would then be parboiled before roasting. In the last half of the twentieth century the old vinegar rub was supplanted by a marinade—lemon juice and soy sauce being popular.

Carolinians had decided opinions on which ducks one could stuff without ruining their flavor. Good stuffed: Redhead, Canvasback, Mallard, Black Duck, Pintail, and Wood Duck. Do not stuff the Bufflehead, Bluebill, Baldpate, Mottled, Florida duck, or Shoveller. Stuffings included onions, celery, apples, sausage, and stale bread. In the Dutch Fork, duck might be stuffed with sauerkraut and roasted.

Another preparation thought to have originated among the Carolina Huguenots was duck with turnips (*canard aux navets*). Numbers of recipes survive, the chief difference being the treatment of the turnips—are they simply roasted in the duck fat, or are they butter roasted elsewhere, half of them mashed, half of them whole and the mashed turnips softened with cream? The following version hails from the "My Mother's Cook Book" column of the *Lancaster News:*

Wild Duck with Turnips

"My Mother's Cook Book,"
Lancaster News (October 24, 1919)

Cut the bird in neat piece for serving. Slice one large onion and one carrot; melt four tablespoonfuls of sweet fat in a saucepan, add the vegetables; cook until nicely browned. Strain off the fat, add a cupful of stock and one bay leaf, place in the oven and cook for one hour. Peel eight turnips, cut four of them into quarters and fry in hot butter until brown; put them with the duck to finish cooking. Boil the other turnips until tender in salted water; mash and rub through a sieve; put them in a saucepan with one tablespoonful of butter to season and salt and pepper to taste; add a quarter of a cup of cream and heat again. Take up the duck, dish in on the hot mashed turnips and arrange the fried quarters around it. Strain the sauce from the duck, thicken with flour, season and serve in a sauce boat.

In the twentieth century, Duck à l'orange became popular, first as a restaurant dish, then as a home preparation in the 1920s. The orange sauce was a litmus test of kitchen skill—if one used flour and the juice and pulp of an orange, the intensity of the fruit's color would diminish, even if one managed to keep the sauce lump-free. If you used arrowroot starch as the basis for the sauce, the color remained intensely vibrant.

Of other duck dishes that emerged during the twentieth century, wild duck bog, made like chicken bog, is probably the most endearing. Dallon Weathers, an event cook popular in the 1970s and 80s, became famous for this old-style duck pilau made of few ingredients: duck, fatback, onions, celery, rice, and butter.

Duke's Mayonnaise

"The Queen of Mayonnaise in the South." The South's favorite mayonnaise was created by Eugenia Thomas, born in Columbus, Georgia, in 1881. At the age of 19, she married Harry Duke and moved to the city of Greenville, South Carolina. After moving to Greenville, she started selling sandwiches with her home-made mayonnaise to soldiers at Fort Sevier. After years of selling her sandwiches she bottled her mayonnaise and sold it as well. Sales took off and she decided to step away from retailing sandwiches to sell her mayonnaise exclusively. In 1926, the demand grew so great that Duke moved from her kitchen into a processing plant.

Popularity sometimes gives rise to problems. Demand grew so great that she could not handle it and decided to sell the business to the C. F. Sauer Company on February 29, 1929. She stayed on as C. F. Sauer's chief salesperson. Sauer, though from Richmond, kept the Duke's operation in Greenville. Eventually Eugenia Duke moved to the West Coast to be closer to family and returned to selling sandwiches under another name. Eugenia Duke passed away in 1968.

Seventeen years later the company introduced a light form of mayonnaise and sales began a steady expansion. In 2006, the company created a chocolate cake recipe that stands as their most requested recipe to date. Though popular in the South, Duke's mayonnaise lags behind sales of two other brands nationally: Hellmann's and Kraft. Used to make many a southern favorite, from pimento cheese, deviled eggs, tomato sandwiches, coleslaw, and, of course, potato salad, Duke's flavor appeals to southerners more than any other brand.

James Beard Award–winning chefs such as Sean Brock and Dolester Miles use Duke's in their professional cooking and of course at home. As one of the few store-bought items in his restaurants, Brock says "if someone else is doing it better than you can make it, let them do it." Better because it contains more egg yolks than other mayonnaise products and no added sugar. Sugar's absence may be due to wartime rationing and makes Duke's the preference of dietitians for persons with diabetic tendencies or weight concerns. For the healthy consumer, Duke's unique flavor suits it for making for the best tasting tomato sandwiches and the most delicious baked goods.

Chocolate Mayonnaise Cake

ADAPTED BY ERIKA CLINE

3 cups cake flour
1½ cups sugar
6 tablespoons dark cocoa
    powder
1 tablespoon baking soda
¼ teaspoon salt
1½ cups Duke's Mayonnaise
1½ cups water
1½ teaspoons pure vanilla
    extract

CHOCOLATE CREAM CHEESE FROSTING

1 cup (2 sticks) butter, softened
4 ounces cream cheese, softened
1 cup dark cocoa powder
1 teaspoon pure vanilla extract
5 to 6 cups confectioners' sugar
6 or more tablespoons milk
Chocolate shavings for garnish

Preheat the oven to 350°F.

Evenly apply baker's pan spray to two 8-inch cake pans. Sift the cake flour, sugar, cocoa, baking soda, and salt into a medium bowl, mix well. Combine the mayonnaise, water, and vanilla in a bowl and mix until combined. Add the dry ingredients in thirds to prevent over mixing, mix until incorporated. Pour the batter into the prepared pans and bake for 30 minutes or until done. Cool on wire racks.

For the frosting, beat the butter, cream cheese, and cocoa in the bowl of an electric mixer with a paddle attachment until smooth. Add vanilla. Alternate adding confectioners' sugar and milk until icing is spreadable.

Frost the cake and garnish with chocolate shavings.

Dumplings

A dumpling is handful of dough, shaped in lump or strip form, often containing a filling, usually cooked in hot liquid, sometimes baked. Filled it can be a stand-alone food (the classic apple dumpling), unfilled it can supply a hearty adornment to a stew; a wholesome, hot spoonful of sumptuous carbohydrate. European in origin, the first dumplings had a set formula: suet, flour, yeast, water, and salt. In the American South where the hog supplanted the cow as the dominant animal on the farm, lard replaced suet in the classic formula, although suet remained an option. In the twentieth century, Crisco, or even butter, supplanted lard in some kitchens. Though modern dumplings are made with self-rising flour and expand by chemical reaction of the leaveners when cooked, the old suet dumpling was made with winter soft wheat (biscuit wheat) with yeast and water and formed into balls, and set in a warm place to rise. They were cooked by boiling, not frying. Fritters differed from dumplings.

Certain dishes had a near universal following in the early United States. Chicken and dumplings and apple dumplings appeared in a multitude of cookbooks and family recipe collections. Other preparations had more local followings. Tomato dumplings emerged in the 1840s in the South; rice dumplings served in stews became a feature of Lowcountry cooking at about the same time. Potato dumplings in beef stew found favor in Germanic enclaves, including Orangeburg and the Dutch Fork in South Carolina, and Salem in North Carolina. Liver dumplings were another Germanic boiled pastry—and enjoyed a vogue through the South in the late 1920s when national newspapers became interested in Pennsylvania Dutch food. They existed in southern sites of Germanic settlement prior to 1926, but never inspired the wider adoption of potato dumplings until the eve of the Great Depression. They were made with chopped poached calves' livers, eggs, bacon, and bread crumbs or flour.

It was perhaps inevitable that cornmeal would be substituted for wheat in those districts that did not grow winter wheat, and cornmeal dumplings came into being; they did not rise, so were not fluffy, and were made by scalding the meal with hot water, not wetting it with cold like classic wheat flour dumplings. Cornmeal dumplings simmered in a stew didn't have the flavor interest of that same water scalded cornmeal ball when pressed flat and fried in bacon fat. Called "hot water corn bread," it is one of the classic African American comfort foods of the Piedmont South. Cornmeal dumplings were generally eaten without many added ingredients; hot water corn bread often incorporated scallions, greens, herbs, and peppers.

The first regional cookbook to devote a chapter to dumplings was Annabella P. Hill's *Southern Practical Cookery and Receipt Book* (1872). This Georgia matron captured the repertoire of professional boarding house cooks in her collection. She was only interested in filled dumplings. Three recipes for apple dumplings appear, boiled, stewed, and baked, a filled rice ball that was boiled in cloth called a "snow ball," and several fritter recipes including two "Puffs" forms of that southern favorite, the fried pie.

Dumplings could be savory or sweet. Hill's sweet dumplings imparted dulcetness in their fillings. One chopped and cooked apples, rolled out the dough to a saucer shape, stuck the apples in the center, and crimped the pastry into a pouch or ball. One of the tricks of apple dumpling makers was to supplement the cooked apples in the center with pre-prepared apple jelly or marmalade. Sweet dumplings could be made another way—taking the regular dumpling dough and cooking it in syrup. The syrup could be flavored by fruit, could be maple syrup, or could be a plain simple syrup. These were dessert dumplings.

The first extended discussion of dumplings in South Carolina occurred in an 1824 newspaper article on indigestion in which we learn, "Plum-pudding, dumplings, and all boiled flour, are poison to dyspeptic people." In the hands of an unpracticed cook, dumpling could become weighty wads of undercooked dough. But with a properly risen dough made of purple straw wheat flour, they could be fluffy, sumptuous and aswim with the flavor of yellow chicken gravy.

≈ ℰ *Field Peas* ℰ ≈

South Carolina's favorite field peas. While sea island red peas—the traditional Lowcountry component of Hoppin' John—and white rice peas generate the bulk of the positive comment, old favorites such as pink eye purple hull, brown crowders, whippoor-will peas, iron and clay peas, white acre, and Dixie Lee all have devoted followings. David S. Shields.

The field pea (*Vigna unguiculata*) is also known as the cowpea and southern pea, because it was once used to feed cattle and became a mainstay on southern tables. Varieties of field peas can be split into several categories, such as field, crowder (so named because the seeds are so jammed in the pod they have flat ends), and lady (small white) pea.

Field peas originally came to the New World from Africa, shipped as part of the provision store on slave ships. Remnant food stocks provided the seed for the first plantings in the southern colonies. In the 1840s, farmers discovered the soil-building benefits of field peas. They fixed nitrogen, replenishing the soil's nutriment load after being taxed by staple crops such as cotton, corn, cane, and rice.

The field pea also proved to be drought resistant and saved labor for farmers. The most popular varieties during the nineteenth century were the iron, clay, black-eyed, sea island red pea, Tory pea, and whippoorwill (shinny) pea. In the twentieth century, the most desirable were the white lady pea, the black-eyed pea, sea Island red pea, brown crowder, black crowder, Mississippi Silver Hull, and pink eye purple hull. Dr. Richard Fery of the USDA's Vegetable Lab in Charleston introduced many of the field peas such as the Baby Cream, the Knuckle Hull, the Charleston black-eyed pea, and the whippersnapper that enjoy popularity among farmers in the twenty-first century for their disease resistance and productivity. The lab now has the importance for field pea research that Alabama's Tuskegee Institute had at the beginning of the twentieth century, when George Washington Carver directed efforts there.

The field pea was something that George Washington Carver "was equally devoted to as much as he was to the peanut and the sweet potato." Carver extensively wrote the best

[57]

ways to grow them as well as cook them in the *Tuskegee Agricultural Experimental Station Bulletin No. 5* in 1903. Carver's work was revitalized by a group including myself (Kevin) in a November 2015 field pea tasting hosted in Charleston. The tasting was held at the William C. Gatewood House, the same home in which caterer Nat Fuller lived as an enslaved laborer. There were twenty-two varieties cooked for a documentary on southern food. Some of the varieties included the lady, the pink-eyed purple hull, sea island red, the whippoorwill, the Mississippi silver hull, the brown crowder, the clay, the rice, the white acre, the Texas cream, as well as more localized specialties such as South Carolina's rice pea and Louisiana's black crowder. I remain partial to the black-eyed pea, which was one of the first things I learned to

cook in my grandmother Doris's kitchen. As for others in the category of the black-eyed pea, a favorite was the pinkeye purple hull. In the tasting, the brown crowder, cream pea, lady finger pea, petit rouge (due to its rich pot likker), and Tresimino White were favorites in their categories.

Many cookbooks contained recipes that treated the pea as king. Most famous were Mary Randolph's *The Virginia House-Wife* (1824), Lettice Bryan's *The Kentucky Housewife* (1838), and Sarah Rutledge's *The Carolina Housewife* (1847). The recipes run the gamut from soups, fritters, to plain boiled peas. The most famous would be Rutledge's pea soup made from the sea island red pea, king of the cowpeas in the Lowcountry.

Red Pea Soup

Sarah Rutledge,
The Carolina Housewife (1847)

One quart of peas, one-pound bacon (or ham-bone), two quarts of water, and some celery, chopped; boil the peas, and when half done, put in the bacon; when the peas are thoroughly boiled, take them out and rub them a cullander or course sieve; then put the pulp back into the pot with the bacon, and season with a little pepper and salt, if necessary. If the soup should not be thick enough, a little wheat flour may be stirred in. Green peas may be used instead of the red pea.

The famous sea island red pea, the sine qua non of Lowcountry Hoppin' John, the base of red pea gravy, and the treasure of Gullah-Geechee kitchen gardening. Here the late matriarch of Sapelo Island Cornelia Bailey shows her family's red peas. David S. Shields.

Black-Eyed Peas

This is one of my favorite recipes, as it holds a special place in my heart. My love for cooking was fostered in the kitchen of my Grandmother Doris. Growing up, peas (preferably black-eyed peas) and collards were mainstays in her kitchen. These ingredients were always cooked in separate pots. As an ode to her I wanted to bring them together into one pot. In place of collards I used Lacinato kale. My Grandmother Doris has not tried this rendition yet, but I am sure she would be proud.

- 1 pound dried black-eyed peas or sea island red peas, soaked overnight
- 2 sprigs thyme
- 4 cloves garlic, divided (2 whole and 2 finely chopped)
- 2 tablespoons coconut oil or olive oil
- 1 small onion, finely diced
- 1 teaspoon grated fresh ginger
- 1 teaspoon red pepper flakes
- 1 teaspoon curry powder
- ½ teaspoon ground turmeric
- 1 28-ounce can diced tomatoes, drained
- 1 cup vegetable stock
- 1 can coconut milk
- 2 bunches lacinato kale or greens of your choice, bottom stems removed
- salt and freshly ground pepper, to taste

Drain soaked peas, place in a large pot, and cover with plenty of cold water. Add thyme and 2 garlic cloves and bring to a boil over high heat. Reduce heat to medium-low and simmer, covered, about an hour. (After peas have been cooking 20 to 25 minutes, add a generous pinch of salt to the pot.) Once peas are tender, remove pot from heat, let stand 5 minutes, then drain. Reserve 2 cups of the cooking liquid and set aside.

In a wide, heavy-bottomed pot, heat oil over medium-low; add the onion and cook until tender, about 10 minutes, then add ginger, chopped garlic, red pepper flake, and salt and cook, stirring occasionally, until softened and just starting to brown, about 10 minutes. Add the curry powder and turmeric and cook, stirring, until fragrant, about 2 minutes. Add the tomatoes and cook, stirring occasionally, until softened, about 10 minutes. Add the stock, coconut milk, and reserved cooking liquid to pot, bring to a boil, then reduce heat and simmer, stirring occasionally, until the tomatoes break down and the sauce thickens a bit, about 20 minutes. Add the peas to the sauce and cook over medium-low heat, stirring, until the peas are lightly coated, about 10 minutes. Stack kale leaves on top of one another, roll tightly, and slice into thin ribbons. Fold greens into peas and remove pot from stove (greens will cook from the residual heat). Adjust seasonings and serve as is or over rice.

Certain field pea varieties (the rice pea, a lady type for instance) can be picked when the pod is green and prepared like green beans. But most are shelled and sold fresh for immediate cooking or dried down for storage in the pantry and later rehydration.

Field peas remain important for agriculture as well as human nutrition. They remain a rotation crop for corn planters, a green manure plowed into the soil to boost nitrogen, a forage crop for livestock, and an inexpensive source of food for humans. Because they grow in climates hotter than those that snap beans can endure, they provide the most reliable leguminous protein available in the deep South and Lowcountry. With USDA climate zones shifting northward, the dominion of the field pea is expanding as the twenty-first century advances.

Fig tree–bearing fruit. South Carolina abounds in yard trees that bear fruit from the end of May into October. David S. Shields, Cheraw, SC.

The fig tree grows vigorously and produces lavishly in most parts of South Carolina. The Spanish planted fig trees on Parris Island when they settled "Santa Elena" there in 1566. It is an open question whether Natives secured fig cuttings from the Spanish or from the English in Virginia, who began planting figs in 1621 around Jamestown. Whichever the source, Natives began planting the countryside of Carolina, so that Robert Sanford in 1666 encountered "some store of figge trees very large and very faire," on the banks of the Broad River in South Carolina. Two qualities of the fig recommended them to settlers and Natives: they could produce fruit without sexual fertilization, and they grew large quickly. The intentional importation of European varieties of figs to gauge which performed optimally in Carolina dates from the garden experiments of Eleanor Laurens in 1760s Charleston.

All of the figs imported into early Carolina were female trees of varieties originating around the Mediterranean. The earliest growers designated them by colors rather than by names. John Bachman in the 1840s noticed "black, blue, brown, lemon and white figs. One variety, the large white lemon an abundant early crop, whilst the large brown fig, when attended to, continues ripening its fruits til late in autumn. The black and blue figs seldom bear early, but usually [supply] a very abundant crop." During the later 1830s, Carolina fruit growers began receiving varieties from Louisiana that originally derived from the south of France. The Celestial fig was the most important of these importations, "small but delicious."

Traditionally, some figs were grown to be consumed or processed when fresh; others were grown to be dried. "The latter are left of the tree till they are dead ripe, which is known by a drop of sweet liquid hanging from the eye. As soon as they are gathered, they are placed on wicker hurdles in a dry, airy shed" (1848). In Georgia, where dried fig production was greatest in the South, a method of dipping the figs in strong boiling lye water twice for a brief duration before drying insured quality desiccation. The majority of figs in the South were eaten fresh, and they were particularly savored as a breakfast fruit. "When ripe the Fig is mild, rich and luscious, without being at all cloying; and can be eaten to almost any extent, even by those of most delicate constitution" (1858).

Three luscious varieties of fig, long grown in South Carolina: the silver leaf, the celeste, and the green Ischia. David S. Shields.

Through the early twentieth century, southern nurseries carried ten standard varieties: Angelique (very early, yellow, and fair quality), Black Ischia (blue-black, crimson pulp, good quality), the Brown Turkey (large, brown, and sweet), the Brunswick (large, violet, sweet), Celestial (small, violet, sweet), Green Ischia (medium, green skin with crimson heart, late season, best quality), Large Blue (large, bluish, and moderately sweet), Lemon (medium sized yellow, ribbed, white fleshed, sweet), Magnolia (Dalmatian-large, tender, greenish amber, good quality), White Marseilles (Genoa-medium, yellow skin, white flesh, good quality).

The repertoire of fig dishes was narrow: fig syrup (a favorite children's laxative), fig jam, fig preserves, fig pudding, fig cake, candied figs, spiced figs, and stewed figs. While fresh figs tended to be a summer and early autumn fruit, dried figs were employed year-round and became a fixture in holidays. There are many recipes for fig pudding, several for fig cake, but this recipe for fig candy gives us a glimpse of an old holiday season treat worthy of reviving.

Fig Candy

Charleston Women's Exchange Cook (1901)

Boil one cup of sugar and a third of a cup of water together without stirring them until the mixture is a pale amber color. Stir in a quarter of a teaspoonful of cream of tartar, add half a pound of figs chopped fine and turn into a buttered dish. When cool cut into squares.

Southern-fried . . . that's what a fritter is. Whether in boiling lard, in bubbling Crisco, in peanut oil, or even canola, the fritter transforms from a heaping spoonful of batter into a crispy golden handful of savory or sweet sumptuousness. It has myriad faces: the beignet, the hush puppy, the oyster fried in cracker meal. They are eaten hot, or at least warm. And since they are finger food, the finger tips will feel a lick of heat.

The fritter family is large, organized by the grains used for the flour or meal, and also by the main ingredient. In South Carolina, you had fritters made from rice flour, from cornmeal, and from wheat flour. You had salty or sugary fritters. Fruit fritters tended to sweet (orange, banana, and pineapple had particular favor) and vegetable fritters to savory (salsify, peanut, green corn, potato). Seafood and fish fritters also tended to savory. Grain fritters included: cornmeal fritters (hush puppies/red horse bread); rice fritters (rice flour puffs or boiled rice fritters); and wheat fritters (beignets, doughnut holes, etc.), and could be either sweet or savory depending on the whim of the preparer of the tastes of the audience.

There was one imprecision about the use of "fritter" in instructions—besides the deep-fried items discussed here, the term sometimes applied to batter-fried vegetables—for instance, eggplant fritters were slices of eggplant dipped in batter and fried. It was also used for deep-fried fish in a coating—what people in the Lowcountry refer to as "Calabash style" (see separate entry). A distinction should also be made with croquettes, an amalgam of minced matter dipped in egg yolk and coated in bread crumbs before deep frying; often there is not grain-based batter or meal per se in croquettes (deep fried balls of mashed potatoes in a crumb crust for instance).

Both Europeans and Africans fried dough laden with ingredients in bubbling fat, so the genesis of individual fritter dishes is sometimes difficult to trace. Most students of southern cookery have since the 1880s identified the bulk of the fritter repertoire with African American cooks. The fat employed has shifted over time: benne oil and lard after the 1810s; Wesson Oil (cotton seed oil) and Crisco after 1890; Peanut oil after 1920; and Canola oil nowadays. The cooking temperature should register 385°F. The average cooking time lasts six to seven minutes depending on the size of the fritter.

All fritters employed one of three kinds of batters. The following three formulae can be adjusted but supply a template for a multitude of varieties. Fritters that incorporated other ingredients usually maintained a one cup ingredient to one cup batter ratio.

Basic Fritter Batter
[Wheat Flour fritters]

1 cup flour
¼ cup sugar
½ teaspoon salt
1 teaspoon baking powder
1 egg
1 to 3 cups milk
2 teaspoons melted lard or Crisco

Sift flour, measure, and sift again with dry ingredients. Beat eggs, combine with milk, and add gradually to dry mixtures. Stir until batter is smooth. Add lard or Crisco.

Rice Fritter Batter
[Rice Puffs]
New York Commercial Advertiser
(March 17, 1830)

To a pint of the [rice] flour add a tea-spoonful of salt, a pint of boiling water—beat up four eggs—stir them well together—put from two to three spoonsful of fat in a pan—make it boiling hot, and drop a spoonful of the mixture into the fat as you do in making common fritters.

Cornmeal Batter
David S. Shields

Two cups white cornmeal, 1 cup flour, 1 teaspoon of baking powder, 1 teaspoon black pepper, 1 teaspoon salt, 1 cup buttermilk, 1 beaten egg, bacon drippings mixed together. Add cooked onions and bell pepper and you have the base for a good hush puppy/red horse bread with this formula.

VEGETABLE FRITTERS

Corn Fritters
[corn oysters]
Abbeville Press and Banner
(November 11, 1891)

Many housekeepers are not aware

that fritters or "oysters" of corn can be made almost as well with canned corn as with fresh. Pour into a clean chopping bowl a can of nice corn (it always pays to get a nice brand), chop quite fine and add three well-beaten eggs, a dessertspoonful of sugar, a teaspoonful of salt, tablespoonful of melted butter, two tablespoonfuls of cream, about a half a pint of flour, in which has been sifted a large table-spoonful of baking powder. Use some judgment about the flour, taking a little more or less, as seems necessary. Mix thoroughly, shape into thin fritters and fry quickly in hot fat.

Potato Fritters
Abbeville Messenger (December 14, 1887)

Boil eight or nine large potatoes, mash them through a colander, beat five eggs light, and mix with the potatoes, adding a tablespoonful of wheat flour, butter the size of a walnut, and a quarter of milk, with one teaspoonful of salt. Beat well, and drop in large tablespoonfuls into boiling lard deep enough to float them. They are done as soon as they rise to the top and are a light brown.

Rice Fritters
Edgefield Advertiser (July 5, 1911)

Beat two eggs until thoroughly broken, then add one pink of milk, on fourth teaspoon salt, one table-spoonful melted butter, two level teaspoonfuls of baking powder, one pint cooked rice, grated rind and juice of half a lemon, and flour enough to hold the mixture into a deep batter. Drop by dessert spoonfuls into smoking hot fat, and when the fritters float and are delicately browned removed to a brown plain paper; dust with pulverized sugar when ready to serve.

Salsify Fritters
Abbeville Press and Banner
(February 1, 1905)

Wash and scrape the salsify and drop into cold waters as fast as scraped, for this vegetable turns dark on exposure to the air. Cook in plenty of boiling salted water until nearly tender, but not soft. Grate, season with salt and pepper, a rounding tablespoon each of flour and butter and two beaten egg yolks to two cups of salsify. Drop in spoonfuls into hot deep fat and cook until brown.

Sweet Potato Fritters
Abbeville Press and Banner
(May 30, 1906)

A pint of hot mashed sweet potatoes, two eggs, a cupful of flour, into which has been sifted a teaspoonful of baking powder, salt, and enough milk to make a batter. Drop the batter, a tablespoonful at a time, in deep fat, smoking hot, and cook to a light brown. Tomato sauce may be served with the fritters.

Tomato Fritters
Weekly Union Times (August 25, 1893)

Boil, peel and pound to a pulp four tomatoes. Beat up with this the yolks of four and the whites of two eggs, two tablespoonfuls of cream, two tablespoonfuls of white wine, seasoned with a little grated nutmeg and dash of cinnamon. Beat until very light; then divide into small fritters and fry in a pan of heated butter; drain on paper and send to the table with a sauce made of an ounce of melted butter, the juice of two lemons and a tablespoonful of caster sugar.

FRUIT FRITTERS

The orange fritter often employed the Seville Sour Orange, a variety that had naturalized throughout the Lowcountry, in the seventeenth century. It took two forms—a simple deep fried marinated orange slice and a battered segment. The latter was considered the ideal complement of broiled ham in the early twentieth century.

Peach fritters were popular throughout the South and frequent entries on banquet menus, often at the end of the meal. In general, there was a preference for freestone peaches over cling for making fritters because they were easier to process. Macon, Georgia became an experimental center for peach fritter cookery. In South Carolina, the standard preparation was the recipe registered below.

Truck farming after the Civil War made strawberries a cash crop in South Carolina.

Okra Tomato Fritters by Kevin Mitchell. Rhonda L. Wilson.

Okra Tomato Fritters

KEVIN MITCHELL

This recipe came about through sheer experimentation. I had been gifted a bunch of beautiful okra and wanted to try something different from the norm of making fried okra. Fritters came to mind. I added some tomatoes, as I have always thought tomatoes and okra go well together. There you have okra and tomato fritters.

3 tablespoons vegetable oil, plus 3 to 4 cups oil for frying
4 cups fresh okra, chopped fine
1 cup onion, minced
1 egg, beaten
1 cup chopped tomato
1 teaspoon smoked paprika
1 teaspoon kosher salt
1 teaspoon fresh cracked black pepper
1 cup buttermilk
2 cup self-rising flour

In a large skillet heat the 3 tablespoons of oil over medium heat. When oil is hot, add chopped okra and onion and cooked until onion is translucent and okra has color, approximately 8 to 10 minutes. Remove from heat and let cool. In a stainless-steel bowl add all the ingredients except the buttermilk and flour. When the okra mixture is cool add to buttermilk and mix until thoroughly incorporated. Slowly fold in flour a little at a time until it is all mixed in. Add 3 to 4 cups of oil to a Dutch oven and heat to 325°F. When ready to fry, in batches drop a heaping spoonful in the hot oil and fry until golden brown, approximately 5 minutes. Place on paper towel to remove excess oil. Continue until the fritter batter is gone. You can sprinkle with additional salt or Cajun seasonings. Serve warm.

Two strawberries developed in Charleston—the Neunan's Prolific in the 1860s and the Hoffman's Seedling in the 1880s—became the chief strawberries grown in the South because their firmness permitted shipping and their heat tolerance permitted them to grow during spring heats. Both were sour-sweet strawberries, with an acid kiss and a sugar finish. No modern strawberry approximates this older taste ideal. What is consequential is that the old strawberries required a bit more sugar to counteract their bite than modern varieties. Strawberry fritters were popular in both North and South Carolina and were always served dusted with powdered confectioners' sugar.

Apple Fritters

Sarah Rutledge,
The Carolina Housewife (1847)

The yolks of three eggs, beat up with wheat flour to a batter; the whites beaten separately, and added to it. Pare your apples core and cut them into slices, lay them in a bowl, in brandy and sugar, about three hours before dressing them; dip each piece in the batter, and fry in lard. Sprinkle white sugar over them.

Fig Fritters

Edgefield Advertiser (May 2, 1917)

Sift together three-fourths of a cupful of flour, a teaspoonful of baking powder, a third of a teaspoonful of salt, add the yolk of an egg a teaspoonful of olive oil, a third of a cupful of milk; mix well and add six soaked figs, coarsely chopped and last of all fold in the beaten white of the egg. Drop by spoonfuls into smoking hot fat and cook a golden brown. Serve with any hot fruit sauce.

Orange Fritters

Anderson Intelligencer (May 22, 1901)

Peel and quarter the oranges, remove the seeds and all the extra outside skin; make a batter of two eggs, one tablespoonful of olive oil, one teaspoonful of sugar, one cupful of flour, half a cupful of cold water. Roll the oranges in sugar, dip them immediately into the batter and fry in hot fat.

Strawberry Fritters

Abbeville Press and Banner
(March 21, 1888)

Beat separately the whites and yolks of two eggs, then mix them and add one teacup of cream and a pinch of salt, stirring in sufficient flour to form a thick batter. Beat the mixture thoroughly until smooth and throw on a pint of strawberries. Fry the same as ordinary fritters, in a frying-pan filled with boiling fat. When the fritters have taken a rich brown color remove them from the fat, drain, and served on a napkin, strewing the tops with sifted sugar.

Frogmore Stew

Frogmore Stew prepared by Kevin Mitchell. Rhonda L. Wilson.

Beaufort Boil, Lowcountry Boil

Like chicken bog, Frogmore Stew is a communal dining dish. Named by Richard Gay of Gay Seafood for Frogmore, a community located in St. Helena, a stone's throw from Beaufort, the dish has existed in a number of variants under different names since the 1970s. It was not mentioned in Dee Hryharrow and Isabel Hoogenboom's 1965 *The Beaufort Cook Book.* There are at least three origin myths, none of which has a paper trail to verify it: it was created ad hoc at a National Guard meeting in the 1960s; it was created by Richard Gay; or it was created at a Gullah fish camp in the 1960s. Ben Moïse is perhaps the most authoritative commentator on the origins of the stew.

Its first citation in print dates from January 1977, and Frogmore Stew has been featured in just about every cookbook on Lowcountry cooking published in the last twenty years. Its simple components have been deconstructed, reconstructed and otherwise fiddled with in every imaginable mutation. Originally, however, it was a simple, rustic, one-pot delectation chiefly eaten with one's fingers.

The boil or stew mainly consists of sausage, usually kielbasa or smoked sausage, fresh corn, shrimp, and seafood seasoning. Some cooks, not content with the elemental goodness of the traditional receipt have periodically augmented the pot with crawdads, blue crabs, chicken strips, potatoes, onions, and even broccoli. Frogmore Stew is not soupy. It is more about the ingredients cooked in the liquid than the liquid. While most cook in water, others use beer with seafood seasoning. The stew was known to have been cooked over open fire in large trash cans. The cans were always brand new and never used for anything else but the stew or boiled peanuts. The earliest recipes specifically called for Old Bay as the seafood seasoning employed. In recent years, as seafood spice mixes have proliferated, the seasoning is the cook's choice.

Some serve the stew spread out on newspapers on a picnic table. The more delicate served pieces from the stew pot tonged onto individual plates or bowls. There is a great deal of variety about the accompaniments of the stew: some like mustard for the sausages, some like a mayo based dipping sauce for the shrimp, still others prefer to have some sort of hot pepper sauce to up the heat quotient of the cooked corn, seafood, and sausage.

Frogmore Stew
John Martin Taylor

1½ gallons water
3 tablespoons commercially prepared shrimp boil such as Old Bay Seasoning plus 3 tablespoons salt or 3 tablespoons homemade boil (see below)
2 pounds hot smoked link sausage, cut into 2-inch pieces
12 ears freshly shucked corn, broken into 3- to 4-inch pieces
4 pounds unpeeled shrimp

In a large stockpot, add the seasonings to the water and bring to a boil. Add the sausage and boil for 5 minutes.

Add the corn and count 5 minutes. Add the shrimp and count 3 minutes. Do not let the water return to a boil. Drain immediately and serve.

I usually serve Frogmore stew with coleslaw, corn bread, and red rice. Leftover Frogmore Stew helps make a delicious soup. Peel the shrimp, cut the corn from the cob, slice the sausage thinly, then add to simmering duck stock or tomato juice to warm through. Season with hot peppers.

Seafood Boil for Shrimp, Crab, & Crawfish

¼ cup mustard seed
2 tablespoons black peppercorns
2 tablespoons crushed red peppers (dried)
6 bay leaves
1 tablespoon celery seed
1 tablespoon coriander seed
1 tablespoon ground ginger (dried)
a few blades of mace
¼ cup kosher, sea, or pickling salt

Place all of the ingredients except the salt in a blender and blend until evenly ground. Add the salt and blend briefly to incorporate the salt into the seasonings. Store in well-sealed jars in a cool, dark, and dry place.

When the Carolina Expedition set out in 1670 to settle the South Carolina colony, its leader Captain Joseph West, received instructions on what to plant, both trade crops and provision crops. West stopped in Bermuda en route to pick up "Cotton seed, Indigo Seed, ginger roots which roots you are to carry planted in a tubb of earth" (1856)—none of these were provision crops, plants that could feed colonists—they were what the Lords Proprietors of the colonies envisioned as the materials that would support trade. While cotton and indigo would in the course of time prove valuable commodities, what of ginger? Why were such hopes being placed on that pungent Asian root?

Extraordinary medical virtues were ascribed to ginger in Medieval Europe, where it was believed that the "hot" and "dry" qualities contained in ginger counteracted a predominance of phlegm in one's system. The English understood themselves to be a phlegmatic, "watery" people in need of dry and hot substances to counter their constitutional defect. After black pepper, ginger was the Asian ingredient (both fresh root and dried powder) that had the greatest efficacy in restoring humoral balance in phlegmatic peoples. The Spanish had smuggled roots out of India and Southeast Asia, planting them in Hispaniola in the sixteenth century. When the English conquered Jamaica from the Spanish in the latter 1650s, they found ginger fields growing on the island. Not enough to serve the need of the English people, though, so the Lords of White Hall determined it should be grown in the next colony to be formed in America, South Carolina.

South Carolina's ginger cultivation experiment shut down quickly and thereafter it became one of the avid importers of Jamaican ginger. Its pharmacies stocked Holloway's Concentrated Essence of Jamaica Ginger, "efficacious in all cases of Chill from exposure to cold or dampness, colic, cholera morbus, Dysentery, Diarrhea, &c." (1868). As early as 1817, newspapers printed recipes for ginger beer using white Jamaican ginger.

To make Ginger Beer

Camden Gazette (April 24, 1817)

Take of acid of Tartar 1⅓ oz. of the juice of 2 Lemons, Ginger 2 oz. Lemon peel 2 oz. refined Sugar 2½ lbs. Water 3 galls. Boil the Ginger, Lemon peel and Sugar together for 15 minutes, then add the acid and strain; add 2 table-spoonfuls of Yeast, let them stand for 24 hours and bottle cork and wire them firmly, lay them in cellar and in three days they will be fit for use.

There was a problem with recipes of this sort, if someone bottled them prematurely and there was an excess of sugar, the effervescence generated by fermentation would cause the ginger beer to pop its corks, and many cases exploded in the cellar. This gradually led to to a preference among manufacturers and consumers in Carolina for ginger ale, which was manufactured by flavoring soda water with ginger extract or ginger syrup instead of attempting to induce fermentation. Controlled carbonation made ginger ale a more manageable beverage. J. Dalton on the corner of King and Church Streets in Charleston advertised the sale of ingredients for making "Aromatized soda water or near beer" in September of 1818. In the early nineteenth century there was a belief that carbonated waters could induce intoxication like alcohol because it was observed that when soda water and alcoholic spirits were mixed one got drunk quicker than when drinking straight alcohol. What was happening was that the gas from the carbonation forced the alcohol into the blood stream quickly when ingested together. It wasn't until the 1840s that temperance people realized that soda water did not intoxicate of itself. So ginger flavored soda water, or ginger ale, became preferred to ginger beer in which minor alcoholic fermentation could occur. Johnson & Maynard's Medicinal Fountain at 5 Broad Charleston was the first establishment to sell mineral waters, seltzer, and flavored soda waters in South Carolina in 1819.

Ginger ale was first sold with that name in 1817 in Baltimore by De Gruchy's "Soda Water and Ginger Ale Manufactory" at 26 Great York Street. When the temperance movement took off in the 1840s, it championed ginger ale rather than ginger beer. In South Carolina, E. F. Bedford's grocery began importing Irish Ginger Ale in 1871. The vending of imported rather than locally manufactured ginger ales (DeLatour, Vartray, Corry's, and Ross brands) persisted in South Carolina stores until the Harris Lithia Carbonated Water company of Harris Springs began offering ginger ale, first at the spa in Harris Springs, then bottled in South Carolina stores in 1896.

Harris Lithia hit upon the hot marketing idea of the 1890s by combining the old health associations of ginger with the old health associations surrounding natural mineral water. In 1903, G. D. Matheson decided that the tonic qualities of the mineral spring at Blenheim recommended its use as a base for ginger ale. The high iron content of the water gave it a sharp taste to match its boldness, which came from Matheson and Dr. Charles R. May using a very potent Jamaican ginger extract. The erection of a bottling plant enabled Blenheim Ginger Ale to establish regional distribution in 1915 when it began advertising seriously.

Because of its fiery flavor, Blenheim's never became a mass market brand. It survived the twentieth century as a novelty soda, and the business changed hands on several occasions. Bill Dennis bought it in a tax auction in 1974. At that time the bottling works paid the smallest crown tax in the United States. Eddie Dennis diversified the offerings, the original peppery formula being designated "Old #3" and a milder brew, Extra Pale, for cocktail mixing. It would be "Old #3" that would eventually win Blenheim's a national following. "Strong ain't the word for it," Bill McDonald memorably opined in 1982 in an article that won the ginger ale broader notice. At the time the antiquated brick plant was producing five hundred cases of ginger ale per week—very small scale. Alerted by McDonald's article, TV personality Charles Kuralt made a visit to the Blenheim Ginger Ale plant the headline story in an "On the Road" segment in summer 1983. By August of 1983 the plant was generating eight hundred cases per day.

Blenheim's Bottling had been raised from the death bed by the Dennis family. Yet they lacked the capital to rebuild the antiquated

Blenheim Ginger Ale bottle caps are color coded to indicate the fieriness of the brew. The red cap is the famously hot old formula that won Blenheim Ginger Ale a national following in the 1980s. Rhonda L. Wilson.

plant. In 1993, they sold to beer distributor and developer Alan Schafer. Schafer invested $5 million for the renovation of the plant. A second plant was erected in Dillon, outside of Schafer's South of the Border attraction. The boosted output enabled large-scale distribution. Schafer also expanded the line of offerings, premiering a diet ginger ale and a clear version. In 1994, advertisements for Blenheim's appeared in the New Yorker and it made its first impression on the mixologists who were setting in motion the cocktail renaissance. Now Blenheim's has the enviable situation of being the one brand of ginger ale that has both local identity and distinction of flavor. No other ginger ale on the market approximates its profiles. It has become a signature beverage of South Carolina.

Gravy

If Louisiana cooking is all about sauces, Carolina cooking has been all about the gravies, from the refined shrimp and oyster gravies of the Lowcountry to the pigfoot gravy of the midlands, to the red eye gravy of the backcountry. What exactly is a gravy? It is the most treacherous dish in the whole art of cookery, showing immediately the mastery or incompetence of the maker. A perfect roast can be spoiled by a lumpy spoonful of fat and flour. And what of the watery gruel spooned over a pristine mound of mashed potatoes? Gravy when perfect is poetry, recognized as good by everyone from the mindless feeder to the epicure.

In 1859, a French chef resident in New York asked, "What is an American's idea of gravy? Fat is one; and fat, flour and water is another; for poultry, a hash of the giblets and fat, so thick that the spoon can stand upright." The chef had it right. Gravy was a broad category encompassing the deglazed pan juices of roast meats to the gelatinized daubes and hashes favored by Creole kitchens. But for most Carolinians, the second of the commentator's three versions of gravy prevailed: a hot liquified fat, into which flour and water or stock was added to thicken it, and seasonings added to give it savor. It was always served hot. It tended to savory, not sweet (cooked emulsified fruits were sauces, not gravies). And it always accompanied another preparation.

Red eye gravy is the one great exception to the flour rule. It is pan drippings from fried ham or bacon deglazed with a cup of coffee. It was considered the ideal accompaniment to breakfast ham and biscuits. We have provided a classic recipe below but note that in about 1960

people began putting a tablespoon of brown sugar, flour, and water into this mixture to give it the look and texture of other gravies.

In South Carolina, the liquid added to the fat and flour determined whether something was a gravy or a sauce. If the liquid was pan juice, water, stock, or wine it was reckoned a gravy. If milk, cream, or eggs were added, it was a sauce. There was one indeterminate zone—seafood gravies were called sauces indiscriminately, though they were made like most other gravies.

Browning the flour to make a roux began to be a widespread kitchen practice after the Civil War. A dry browning process in the oven is described in Theresa C. Brown's *Modern Domestic Cookery,* published in Charleston in 1871. After it is toasted the flour is added to butter or rendered fat. Roux-based gravies fall under the old category of brown gravies. White gravies—veloutés—did not brown the flour and often used water or veal stock to maintain the lightness of color.

Every respectable southern cookbook since the 1820s contained instructions on how to make it, for it was one of the kitchen mysteries that required tutelage, as much as any pudding or cake recipe. Furthermore, every region of the South had one or more local versions that lent a distinctive accent to the dish. South Carolina was rich in gravies—red pea gravy, shrimp gravy, pigfoot gravy, oyster gravy, and red eye gravy and classic brown gravy. Brown gravies were flavored by the fat and juices of the roasted meat from which they were made. Turkey brown gravy was considered the best thing to serve over rice. Pork brown gravy vied with butter as the ideal complement to mashed turnips. Beef gravy was the best for mashed potatoes. Chicken brown gravy was ideal for biscuits.

CLASSIC GRAVIES

BROWN GRAVY: Made from a brown roux in which pan drippings from roasted meats or fouls has been added to the fat. The liquid added tends to be water or stock.

WHITE GRAVY: Made from wheat flour, melted fat, and water or sometimes milk. This is a matrix into which many ingredients can be incorporated.

OYSTER GRAVY: Is a white gravy or brown using bacon fat into which a quart of shucked oysters and a modest amount of oyster liquor is added. Sometimes spiced with mace and braced with Madeira.

PIGFOOT GRAVY: There are two styles. In the Lowcountry tomatoes are the base—you cooked down tomatoes and an onion into tomato sauce that you added 2 pig feet into and simmered it low until the red sauce became smooth. In the Dutch Fork, it is a flour-based gravy with pig foot stock and gelatinous bits, with lots of pepper and some mace or nutmeg. You cook the pig feet in salted water and a little vinegar on steady simmer overnight. The gravy has got to be glossy and slide off the spoon. Most use bacon fat rendered up to put the flour in. Then you slowly add the pig foot stock, letting chunks of the meat and gristle to join the gravy.

RED EYE GRAVY: Bacon fat or the drippings of fried ham into which a cup of brewed coffee is stirred and simmered.

RED PEA GRAVY: Made with sea island red peas that have been soaked, long simmered in chicken stock onion and seasonings until the peas break down.

SHRIMP GRAVY/SHRIMP SAUCE: Using a stock made by boiling fried shrimp shells that is cooked until reduced, butter, and minced shrimp meat in a white gravy.

Groundnut Cakes

For 150 years, from 1800 to 1950, Charleston had a signature candy, the groundnut cake. It was a beloved dish of the city, sold by African American women on city street corners. Just as shrimp and grits, she-crab soup, and Frogmore Stew were iconic foods of the Lowcountry in 2000, groundnut cakes belonged to the list of local delicacies in 1900: "Charleston submits groundnut cakes, palmetto pickle, waffles, shrimp pie, Bull's Bay oysters, and ricefield turkey, among other strictly local dishes for the delectation of her guests" (1915). When Carolina expatriates dreamed of returning to Charleston, the candy came first to mind.

Similar to a praline in configuration, the groundnut cake combined peanuts (the small Carolina African runner peanut grown in the Lowcountry since the colonial era), some form of sugar (molasses, cane syrup, brown sugar, loaf sugar), and a flavoring. The street form of the cakes used lemon as the flavoring. The upscale version found in cookery books used vanilla.

For close the fifty years the price of a groundnut cake remained the same—a penny. As was perhaps inevitable, a gentrified, White-folks' version of the candy emerged and found its way into later editions of Sarah Rutledge's landmark *The Carolina Housewife:*

Groundnut Cakes

Sarah Rutledge,
The Carolina Housewife (1847)

Blanch one pound of peanuts; grind very fine in a marble mortar, adding a little brandy while pounding to prevent oiling. Add ten eggs, one pound of sugar, and one pound of butter. Beat the whole well together; make a puff paste, lay it on your tins, and fill them with the mixture; grate lump sugar over them, and bake in a slow oven.

These fancy peanut tartlets were too costly for street consumption at a one cent price point. Besides, they minimized the peanut flavor by blanching instead of parching the nuts. Astute observers of street food noted "in Charleston . . . a fine molasses is used for it instead of sugar" (1909). An 1895 reporter elaborated this point: "It has been asserted that these vendors of sweets go down on the wharves, where the molasses hogsheads and casks are being unloaded, and scrape up such of the molasses as chanced to leak out or overrun, straining it for use in their confections. Be that as it may, the groundnut cakes are delightful,

Stereograph photograph of a Charleston groundnut cake seller by George N. Bernard, 1874. She holds a fly whisk and her platter displays benne twists, monkey meat (a molasses coconut candy), and groundnut cakes. Located at many busy street corners, the hucksters were legislated out of business by the fly ordinance of 1914. Schomburg Center for Research in Black Culture, Photographs and Prints Division, The New York Public Library. "Margaretta Van Wagenen" New York Public Library Digital Collections.

crisp and wholesome, the syrup boiled to just the right consistency, the nuts selected with care." The final product was small and round and regarded by many visitors as "Charleston's greatest charm" (1899). Besides molasses and peanuts, an egg white would be added to clarify the syrup. Furthermore, they were "highly flavored with lemon peel" (1902). One does not doubt either that the molasses was pulled repeatedly to make it glossy and silver as a matrix for the nuts.

From 1909 to 1919, municipal sanitation officials waged a war with the vendors, driving the candy off the streets. In 1909 Charleston enacted a regulation popularly known as the "Fly Ordinance" that required all food items sold in the open air to be covered to prevent possible contamination from house flies. Traditionally the groundnut ladies displayed their wares on open trays—groundnut cakes, monkey meat (molasses and coconut candy), benne twists, and gungers (ginger cakes). Officials ruled that the fly whisks used by the vendors could not prevent the candies' contamination. Popular support for the groundnut ladies made the enforcement of the "fly ordinance" a problem until World War I when proclamations from Washington, DC that unsanitary food threatened troops stationed in the city made the enforcement absolute.

From 1919 to 1926, a single seller, "Mauma Chloe," sold the homemade cakes during the intermission of theatrical performances and public celebrations occurring in enclosed spaces. Her final recorded sale took place at a December 1, 1926 concert of the Plantation Melody Singers at Charleston High School. The city's most famous African American–made street food ceased to be available from its creators.

In 1938, Miriam B. Wilson, an Ohio-born entrepreneur, collector of African American

material culture, and commercial cook, purchased the Charleston Slave Market and turned it into an attraction. She had been running a Williamsburg type colonial kitchen and had popularized peach leather in the city. At the Slave Market Museum, she revived the classic street candies. Her "Slave Recipes Company" presented itself as an appreciation of old African American foodways, though now seems a rather bald act of cultural appropriation. In 1940 she published a recipe pamphlet from the Old Slave Mart, including her versions of groundnut cakes using parched peanuts, butter, brown sugar and molasses. The 1876 *Centennial Receipt Book* of Charleston includes the following recipes. Neither makes mention of the secret flavorings, noted by astute tasters: vanilla for the cake, lemon juice for the candy.

Groundnut Cake

A Southern Lady,
The Centennial Receipt Book (1876)

A pint of parched and pounded ground nuts, one pint of sugar, whites of five eggs. Froth the eggs, stir in alternate the sugar and nuts. Bake in patties.

Groundnut Candy

A Southern Lady,
The Centennial Receipt Book (1876)

To one quart of molasses, add a half pint of brown sugar, and a quarter lb. of butter. Boil for half hour, then add one quart of ground nuts parched, and boil quarter of an hour.

Guinea Squash

EGGPLANT

With its plush curves, lustrous smooth skin, rich color, and ample size, the eggplant vies with the tomato as the most sensuous plant on one's kitchen counter. It became a summer mainstay in South Carolina and Virginia before any other of the United States. At first, we knew it by another name. South Carolinians called eggplants guinea squash for a century and a half before national wholesale produce suppliers forced grocers to change their nomenclature. Certain foods that crossed the Atlantic with enslaved Africans had their African genesis recognized by prefixing the common English name of the generic item with "Guinea," the West African territory in which the Mandingo and Fula peoples lived: Guinea corn (*Sorghum vulgaris*), Guinea fowl (*Numida meleagris*), Guinea pea (*Abrus precatorius*), and Guinea Squash (the eggplant; *Solatium melongena* and *Solanum aethiopicum*). The name eggplant arose shortly after it was introduced into England as a horticultural novelty at the end of the sixteenth century. A small white fruited variety shaped like a goose egg became a garden specimen plant. The long purple fruited variety did not gain a foothold in European cuisine until the 1840s. In the American colonies, however, it became a fixture in those regions where enslaved Africans labored: the West Indies, the mainland South, Central America, and Brazil.

Two kinds of guinea squash crossed the Atlantic: the familiar long purple that would become the ancestor of the Black Beauty and the Florida Highbush varieties that dominate southern produce stands, and a red tomato shaped variety (*Solanum aethiopicum*) that was

Red Guinea Squash (Solanum aethiopicum), *the rarer of the two varieties of eggplant brought from Africa to South Carolina in the colonial era. The red eggplant became functionally extinct eleven years ago when seed for the last known strain in the South was destroyed in an arson fire. This plant was grown from seed procured from Brazil where it also took hold. Now the long purple black eggplant rules the market uncontested. Lawrence Melton's garden, Columbia, SC. David S. Shields.*

more bitter and almost exclusively maintained in African American families (the last known strain of seed was burnt in an arson fire in a Louisiana seed house a decade ago). Though it has not survived in the South, the red gilo eggplant remains a favorite street food of Brazil, sliced and batter fried as finger food or sauteed with onions as a bar treat.

In the United States, there was a regional division over the merits of the vegetable. Some northern writers found the purple tasteless or lacking in wholesomeness. Northern commentators sympathetic to the eggplant noted its lack of a following there. From 1839, "This is considered a delicious vegetable; but little attention has, however, been paid to its cultivation, and it is seldom seen in our markets; but in the southern States great quantities are cultivated, and sold in their markets."

The hucksters who sold goods in antebellum southern markets were predominantly African American, so the eggplant joined okra, benne, and the cowpea as foods that spread from the slave garden to general sale and consumption. In the earliest printed descriptions from White southerners of how guinea squash should be prepared for the table, we encounter the African mode of preparation—frying. William N. White, the south's most eloquent horticulturist on the eve of the Civil War, preserved a version of the traditional preparation: "Cut the egg-plant in slices a quarter of an inch thick. To remove the acrid taste, pile the slices on a plate with alternate layers of salt; raise one side of the plate, that the juice may run off. In half an hour wash them well in fresh water, and fry them quite brown in batter." White observed that eggplant was an acquired taste; "they are not commonly liked at first, but after a few trials become very agreeable to most tastes, and are esteemed a delicacy."

The nineteenth century supplied several classic treatments found below. The twentieth century saw the nationalization of the food press in syndicated newspaper columns and Carolinians had the odd sensation of seeing a familiar and favorite vegetable treated as an exotic, and subject to all sorts of experimentation.

Fried Egg Plant

Mary Randolph,
The Virginia House-Wife (1838)

Purple ones are best. Take young fresh ones, put out the stem, parboil them to take out the bitter taste, cut them in slices an inch thick without peeling them, dip them in the yolk of an egg, and cover them with grated bread, and a little salt and pepper; when one side has dried, cover the other in the same way, then fry them a nice brown. They are very delicious, tasting much like soft crabs.

Broiled Egg Plant

Pierre Blot, *What to Eat* (1863)

Split the egg plant in two, peel it, and take the see out, put it in a crockery dish, sprinkle on chopped parsley, salt, and pepper; cover the dish, and leave thus about forty minutes; then take it off, put it on a greased and warmed gridiron, and on a good fire; baste with a little sweet oil, and seasoning from the crockery dish, and serve with the drippings when properly broiled. It is a delicious dish.

To Bake Guinea Squash, or Egg-Plant

Sarah Rutledge,
The Carolina Housewife (1847)

Parboil the squashes until they are tender, changing the water two of three times, to extract the bitterness. Then cut them lengthwise in two, and scoop out the inside, being careful not to break the skin.—Season the pulp of the squashes with pepper, salt, crumbs of bread, butter, and a slice of onion, chopped fine (this last ingredient, if not liked, may be omitted). Mix all well together and fill the skins of the squashes with the mixture lay them on a plate, and bake in a Dutch oven. They do not take long to boil, but require two or three hours to be baked brown.

Egg-Plant Pudding

Mrs. R. L. O. Marion Cabell Tyree,
Housekeeping in Old Virginia (1879)

Quarter the egg-plant and lay it in salt and water the overnight, to extract the bitterness. The next day, parboil, peel and chop fine, and add bread crumbs (one teacup to a pint of egg-plant), eggs (two to a pint of egg-plant), salt, pepper, and butter to taste; enough milk to make a good batter. Bake in an earthen dish twenty minutes.

We need to understand a few terms: big hominy, small hominy, and hominy grits—or grits. Grits are so Carolina that they were called "Carolina Grits" or "Charleston Grits" in other parts of the South in the antebellum era. The ad below appeared in the December 28, 1853, issue of the *Alexandria Gazette:*

CHARLESTOWN GRITS, OR, SMALL HOMINY, just received, in store, and for sale by [dec 23] JOHN A. DIXON

Grits scrambles the spelling of "grist," "what you get when a grain that has gone through a coarse grind in a mill." The advertisement gives a second name: small hominy. Small hominy differed from big hominy, or plain hominy— what is now called posole.

Eliza Leslie, America's foremost cookbook author of the antebellum period, supplied a definition of plain hominy in her *Lady's New Receipt Book*: "Hominy is white Indian corn, shelled from the cob, divested of the outer skin by scalding in hot lye, and then winnowed and dried. It is perfectly white. Having washed it through two or three waters, pour-boiling water on it, cover it, and let it soak all night, or for several hours. Then put it into a pot or saucepan, allow two quarts of water to each quart of hominy, and boil it till perfectly soft."

The lye treatment of the corn kernels— nixtamalization—is the Native process to make maize more nutritious. It breaks the chemical bonds that prevent niacin in corn from being taken up by the body (niacin deficit gives rise to the disease pellagra), and the freed niacin can be ingested. The nutritional benefits of nixtamalization were not understood medically until the twentieth century—many early southerners thought the lye bath made slipping the hulls off corn kernels easier.

Eliza Leslie also supplied an introduction to "small hominy" or hominy grits: "The small-grained hominy must be washed and boiled in the same manner as the large, only allow rather less water for boiling. For instance, put a pint and a half of water to a quart of small hominy. Drain it well, send it to table in a deep dish *without a cover,* and eat it with butter and sugar, or molasses. If covered after boiling, the vapour will condense within the lid, and make the hominy thin and watery."

Leslie also spoke of samp, a more finely ground form of cornmeal, that was usually eaten with milk and some sweetening. The name derives from the Narragansett language—*nasaump*, meaning "softened by water." The finer grind of corn gave rise, when cooked in water, to mush, a cornmeal porridge whose smoothness recommended it as infant food as well as adult breakfast fare. Samp was the name of the meal, mush the name of the dish, though some also referred to the cooked version as samp.

Two important facts were conveyed by Eliza Leslie: that hominy, big or small, was made from white corn; that the white corn, great or small, underwent lye treatment before processing and cooking. These are important because over the course of time, grits would be made from yellow corn and without the lye processing. In South Carolina the conviction that hominy grits must employ white corn remained firm throughout the nineteenth century. Indeed, white flint corn (sea island white flint) was specified. In other parts of the

South "hominy corn" or "rare-ripe corn" was understood to be white flint corn.

By the 1850s the use of lye in the processing of corn for grits had become optional. The *Camden Journal* of February 20, 1852, provides a new method for processing the grist: "After shelling your corn, winnow and clean it of all dirt and trash . . . then soak your grain for five minutes or longer in clear boiling water, let it drain, then grind in a steel mill, and spread immediately upon a clean cloth and upon a table, in the sun; after drying, winnow it thoroughly of the bran, which slips from the grist in grinding." There is no mention of lye washing.

This did not mean that lye treatment or ash treatment of corn vanished entirely from the processing of hominy big or small. Theresa S. Brown supplied an upcountry method of nixtamalizing corn practice through the Reconstruction era in the state. This is a recipe for big hominy:

Lye Hominy

Theresa S. Brown,
Modern Domestic Cookery (1871)

Take a gallon corn—flint is preferable; put it into a vessel. Have a lye ready made of wood-ashes, hickory is best; put one quart of lye and two gallons of water into the vessel with the corn; let it boil until the husks crack; then wash and rub until all the husks come off and the corn is white—boil it tender in clear water. If the weather is cool, it will keep several days. Mash and season with pepper, salt, and ham-gravy or butter, when wanted for table.

People will make porridge from whatever meal grows most conveniently; but reports of grits made from yellow dent corn prompted Carolina commentators to assert their preference for white flint grits. William Gilmore Simms, the South's most famous novelist in the nineteenth century, offered this opinion in 1853:

Now, your yellow corn won't do for hominy—the color and the flavor are alike against it. It must be the genuine semitransparent flint, ground at a water-mill, white as snow, and swelling out in two huge platters at convenient places upon the table. A moderate portion of each plate is provided with this vegetable, boiled to a due consistency: neither too soft, like mush, nor too stiff, hard, and dry for easy adjustment with a spoon. It requires long experience on the part of the cook to prepared this dish for the just appreciation of an adept. There must be no rising lump in the mass; there must be no dark speck upon the surface. The spoon should lie upon it without sinking below the rims. . . . The Carolina breakfast-table would be a blank without hominy.

Because dent corns are easier to mill, the state's millers promoted the use of white dent corns as a "best substitute" for white flint and priced the meal so that it was the more affordable of the two kinds of grits. But it wasn't until 1880 that a rival emerged for sea island white flint in South Carolina, when Hickory King Corn, a large-kernelled skinny cobbed white dent, was introduced to the southern market by A. O. Lee of Hickory, Virginia. When lye was processed for big hominy, the hulls rubbed off more easily than white flint. Ground, its consistency when boiled proved agreeable, and the plant was more prolific. Indeed, the explosive popularity of Hickory King led to the eclipse of white flint corn early in the twentieth century.

It is too easy to view the twentieth century as the era that saw the decline of grits from a sumptuous staple of the Carolina table to a quick cook abomination with the flavor and consistency of library paste. This dire picture obscures that emergence of a number of local grist mills (Allen Brothers, Anderson's Mill, Blizzard Branch, Boykin Mills, Calhoun Mill, Cotton Hills Mill, Gilreath Mill, Golden Creek Mill, Keisler's Mill, Hagood Mill, Hogbear Hollow, Issawueena Mill, Palmetto Farms, Swansea Mill, Suber's Mill, Timms Mill) featuring local heirloom corns over the last half of the century. Then too, chef Bill Neal's championing of "Shrimp and Grits" at Crook's Corner in Chapel Hill, North Carolina, drew attention to grits and posed the question of quality once again. One of the curiosities of the small mill revival in South Carolina was that the corn varieties many featured were yellow dent corns, not a traditional grits category. The national organization of the corn industry around yellow dent corns at the end of the nineteenth century influenced local planting and milling, and even resulted in yellow grits being milled in state.

There is of course no rule the dictates that grits can only be made of one variety of corn. Even the centuries of Native knowledge that made white flint hominy grits the preference for nutrition and flavor, operates only as a recommendation. Truth be told, when the grits revival that Anson Mills and Marsh Hen Mill (formerly Geechie Boy Mill) spearheaded in the South took place, sea island white flint corn was a functionally extinct variety. It had to be reconstituted from seed saved by Ted Chewning and others. In its place the most historically minded millers looked to other available heirlooms—pencil cob corn, white gourd seed corn, Jimmy Red corn, and perhaps most spectacularly, orange Guinea Flint corn, the other major flint corn of the southeast. So, in 2020 we have the peculiar advantage of once again having the classic white flint, a yellow flint, and a range of historic white, red, and yellow dent corns with which to experiment.

Should you put sugar in the grits? Molasses? Cheese? Hot peppers? Should you dowse them with gravy? Cream? Syrup? Those, my friends, are more your concerns than ours. The first mention of the preparation, by Mark Catesby who visited the Carolina colony in the 1720s, observed that the African American cooks liked to prepare grits by boiling them in cider! We are content if the grits are made from heirloom corn.

Hoppin' John

Hoppin' John is collard greens' counterpart as a lucky food. When asking how the famous rice and field pea pilau Hoppin' John got its name, you may get one of the following stories. A man named John would peddle the dish his wife made through the streets with a noticeable limp. Or, a couple celebrating the New Year allowed an unexpected guest to join in on the celebration, calling it a "hop in John." Lastly, it is said to come from a French dish called "Poi Pigeon" that was introduced to the Lowcountry by slaves from the Caribbean. *Poi* is pea in French and is the basis of this dish traditionally eaten on New Year's Eve and said to bring luck and prosperity. In the case of the pea, we look to the black-eyed pea, one of many field peas domesticated some five thousand years ago in West Africa. They crossed the Atlantic with enslaved Africans and were planted in their food gardens. They soon became a field crop in the Carolinas and were exported to the Caribbean before the Revolutionary War.

When you discuss the history of a beloved dish or ingredient, there is always some debate. Many people associate the dish with black-eyed peas, however I (Kevin) soon found out that in certain areas of the south that black-eyed peas should never be used. This I learned while teaching my students how to make Hoppin' John. A student told me with conviction that she was not going to make the dish because we were to use black-eyed peas in the recipe and that is not how her grandmother taught her how to make it.

The first recipe appears in Sarah Rutledge's *The Carolina Housewife* in 1847. It describes the standard Lowcountry practice of using sea island red peas with Carolina Gold Rice. The instructions are classic and simple and it is clearly present as a legume pilau; we should consider it a cousin to the Gulf Coast's red beans and rice.

Hopping John
Sarah Rutledge,
The Carolina Housewife (1847)

One pound of bacon, one pint of red peas, one pint of rice. First put on the peas, and when half boiled, add the bacon. Then the peas are well boiled, throw in the rice, which must be first washed and graveled. When the rice has been boiling half an hour, take the pot off the fire and put it on the coals to steam, as in boiling rice alone. Put a quart of water on the peas at first, and if it boils away too much, add a little more hot water. Season with salt and pepper, and, if liked a spring of green mint. In serving up, put the rice and peas first in the dish, and bacon on the top.

It is not uncommon these days for the rice to be cooked separately and be intermixed with peas cooked with bacon, onions and seasoning just before serving.

Hoppin' John prepared by Kevin Mitchell using Sea Island Red Peas and Carolina Gold Rice from Anson Mills. Rhonda L. Wilson.

Hoppin' John Fritters

KEVIN MITCHELL

I developed this recipe alongside the Spicy Collards earlier in the book for *Charleston Magazine*. Wanting to update the traditional recipe, I thought frying would be an interesting way to eat Hoppin' John. I used arborio rice, as one would for arancini, due to its high starch content, which helps it hold its shape when formed into a ball. You can also use Carolina Gold rice but it must be cooked slightly longer to develop enough starch. You can make these fritters as big or as small as you want; just adjust the cooking time to get a golden-brown exterior.

- 1 tablespoon vegetable oil plus more for frying
- 4 ounces bacon (about 5 slices), chopped
- 1½ cups minced onion
- 1 cup peeled and minced celery (about three ribs)
- 1 cup Arborio rice
- 3 cups chicken or vegetable stock
- 1½ cups cooked black-eyed peas
- 1 tablespoon chopped thyme
- 1 tablespoon chopped flat-leaf parsley
- 2 dashes Tabasco sauce
- 2 tablespoons Kosher salt plus more for seasoning
- 1 tablespoon black pepper plus more for seasoning
- 2 cups all-purpose flour
- 5 eggs, beaten
- 3 tablespoons water
- 3 cups panko bread crumbs
- ½ cup benne seeds, optional

Heat the tablespoon of oil in a large saucepan over medium heat. Add the bacon and cook until the fat has rendered and the bacon has browned, about 5 minutes. Add the onion and cook, stirring frequently, until softened, about 5 minutes. Add the celery and cook, stirring frequently, for an additional 3 minutes. Stir in the rice and cook until the grains turn translucent, about 2 minutes. Add the stock ½ cup at a time and cook, stirring frequently, until all of the liquid is absorbed and rice is just al dente, 15 to 20 minutes. Stir in the peas and cook for 5 minutes. Season with salt and pepper. Spread the mixture out onto a rimmed baking sheet and refrigerate until completely chilled. Once completely chilled, stir in the thyme, parsley, and Tabasco. Divide the mixture into 10 balls and pat into cakes. Place on a rimmed baking sheet lined with parchment paper and refrigerate for 10 minutes.

Place the flour, eggs, and panko in three separate shallow dishes. Add 2 tablespoons of salt and 1 tablespoon of black pepper to the flour. Whisk the water into the eggs. Add the benne seeds to the panko and mix well.

Dredge the fritters in the flour. Tap off any excess and then dredge them in the egg wash. Shake off any excess and roll in the panko mixture. Place them on the parchment paper lined baking sheet and freeze for 20 minutes. Preheat an oven to 200°F. Line a rimmed baking sheet with paper towels.

Put approximately 3 inches of vegetable oil in a large pot. (You want enough oil to cover the fritters as they fry.) Heat it to 350°F over medium heat. Working in two batches, fry the fritters for 5 to 8 minutes, until hot on the inside and golden brown on the outside. Place them on the prepared baking sheet and keep warm in the oven until ready to serve. Serve with collard greens. Fritters can be made ahead of time and kept in the freezer until ready to cook.

Sweet tea deserves something more than a baggy collection of facts about its early manifestations. It merits a myth of origin at the very least. So here is one—Trajan Brisket invented iced tea, though he didn't realize it, in 1832. He grew up a flash bachelor in Charleston. He was a punch drinker. He particularly loved those punches that included as many drugs in one bowl as possible: alcohol, sugar, caffeine, spice. Artillery Punch, St. Cecilia's Punch: the ones with a lot of green tea in them, a lot of rum, and a modest splash of brandy. Sad to say he imbibed the bowls too frequently and too deeply. One evening he found himself lying miserably in a Charleston gutter, asking, "what have I done with myself?" The Washingtonians (the hard-edged temperance evangelists) got to him and turned him into a teetotaler. The punch bowl, however, had marked his soul deeply. He couldn't give it up entirely. So, he compromised. He left out the booze, and drank the sugared lemony tea with the stray cinnamon stick left in the mix. The vessel still contained enough drugs to send a charge through his bloodstream. He didn't call it sweet tea. He called it sobriety punch.

Now the mundane truth: we don't know who created sweet tea, or where. The print record indicates just a few things: iced tea, so called, was popular in the North before it was in the South; that 1868 was the year in which iced tea impinged on southern consciousness; that the original iced tea was made from green tea, not the black tea now preferred; that 1874 was the break out year for iced tea in the South; and 1874 was the year when a southerner theorized that sipping iced tea from a straw was morally, physiologically, and gastronomically more satisfying than drinking it from a glass.

The New York Tribune reported in midsummer of 1868 that "Ice tea is becoming very popular. It is a beverage easily prepared, costs little, does not intoxicate and can be taken at any house. Sweeten the hot tea to suit your taste; then pour it, spoonful by spoonful, into a tumbler filled with ice." While a number of advertisements suggest that iced tea was a regular consumable in the years 1868 to 1872, the first published description of someone in the South drinking it comes from a letter written for the New Orleans *Times Picayune* describing a trip to the Virginia Springs: "Last of all comes a jostling stage ride to the springs; then we find ourselves beneath a hospitable roof, regaled with ice tea, real gunpowder flavor, and snowy rolls" (1871). How unexpected! They are drinking iced tea made from green gunpowder tea!

In 1874, the *Times Picayune* reported that iced tea had become the most popular drink in Cincinnati. Indeed, 1874 might be said to be *the year of iced tea* when virtually every metropolitan paper in the South hailed the onset of "Iced Tea Season" in June and pointed readers to emporia that sold the best varieties for use. It was in August 1874 that the *Dallas Daily Herald* first advanced the theory that drinking iced tea through a straw amplified the chill while intensifying flavor in an essay entitled "Tube Drinking": "During these warm days, the temptation always is to drink more liquid that is best for us. A good way to obviate this, and at the same time to slake the thirst fully, is to take water, lemonade, or iced tea, through a small tube—the smaller the better. By this method the liquor seems to reach the palate more directly, and certainly quenches the thirst with half the quantity taken after the ordinary manner."

Two developments spurred the explosive growth of iced tea beginning in the 1890s—the increasing substitution of fermented black tea for green tea in its preparation (the higher caffeine content of black tea seemed to call for an additional charge of sugar) and the growing controversy about the health effects of drinking iced tea. Drinking iced drinks in summer seemed a dire risk to some guardians of public health. But those things that the archons of morals and hygiene condemned took on a greater mystique in the eyes of consumers seeking summer refreshment.

The phrase "sweet tea" invariably meant hot tea that had been sweetened with sugar or honey throughout the nineteenth century. When iced tea first began to be consumed it was sugared tea that was chilled. Unsweetened tea existed only to assuage that portion of the population on a diet or heedful of the newspaper monitors of excessive consumption. The phrase "sweet tea" meaning iced sweet tea enters into common usage in the 1930s in Georgia and Louisiana. It doesn't supplant the original usage meaning sweetened hot tea until the mid-1970s, the beginning of the second "great age" of iced tea popularity. Television advertising and magazine articles touted iced tea. In 1988, Christine Arpe Gang, a reporter for the Scripps Howard news agency, observed: "Ten years ago half the tea consumed in this country was hot and half iced. Now 75 percent is iced." In 2018, the statistics would be further complicated by the explosive growth of herbal tisanes (herbal teas) diminishing the consumption of actual hot tea. Iced herbal teas in no way compete with iced black teas in terms of popularity.

Something should be said of the rise of commercial sweet teas since the 1970s. In one regard, they mark a return to the idea of a beverage that combined caffeine with sucrose and fructose. The Snapple Company, founded in the 1970s, was a fruit juice company that hit upon tea as a carrier for their product. Though based in Long Island, they found their strongest following in the South. Lemon, Peach, Mango, and Apple were the original fruit flavors. The company is now owned by Keurig Dr. Pepper of Plano, Texas.

Jerusalem Artichoke

Often pickled, sometimes boiled with gravy or a cream sauce, the Jerusalem artichoke is a late autumn root crop with a fine taste and a confusing name. The name "Jerusalem" is an English mangling of the word *gerisole*. This is Latin for "turning toward the sun," something all members of the sunflower family do. Yes, it is the root of a member of the sunflower family, not an artichoke, and its taste has no resemblance to that of artichoke. Because the name is such a botch, some marketers have taken to calling it sunchoke (coined in the 1960s and copyrighted by Frieda's Finest-Produce Specialties Inc. of Los Angeles), or sunroot.

The Jerusalem artichoke is a wonderfully refined vegetable. Horticulturist N. L. Willet of Augusta, Georgia, when asked about the finest winter vegetables, without hesitation would reply that the Jerusalem artichoke was "the most edible tasty vegetable. . . . It melts like butter in the mouth and the taste to me is delicious." He preferred it the way hotels prepared it, "cooked like carrots in cream" (1912). There is something ethereal, precisely delicate and yet satisfying about well-prepared creamed Jerusalem artichoke. Yet South Carolina chefs in the twenty first century favor the crispness of the raw sunroot and prefer to serve it pickled.

The dietary fiber of the tuber is high in inulin, a substance that has been deemed highly beneficial in human nutrition. Though these nutritive benefits have led to breeding numbers of varieties and clone lines for cultivation, there is little variety recognition among farmers. There are long copper-colored roots, and clumped straw-skinned varieties. People usually plant whatever local landrace they can procure, because most will flourish. Native to North America, they do well in a variety of American soils, thriving without much maintenance, and multiplying until they take over a field in a relatively short span of seasons. Then hogs are loosed upon them for feeding, and

Jerusalem Artichokes appear in the autumn at South Carolina's produce markets. Here Wendy Eleazer of Eleazer Farms, Elgin, SC, offers the last of her 2016 harvest to home makers of artichoke relish. *David S. Shields.*

[88]

TASTE THE STATE

they savor the tubers so much that they will uproot every last one. Some Georgia farmers logged three hundred bushels per acre yields on sandy loam soils.

Artichoke relish has been the cherished dish fashioned from Jerusalem artichokes since the 1920s when it supplanted whole pickled chokes. Sarah Rutledge described Jerusalem Artichoke Pickle in *The Carolina Housewife* (1847): "peeled whole tubers immersed in boiling vinegar and salt with no other ingredients." Mrs. Annabella Hill, in her post–Civil War cookery manual immersed the chokes in sugared and spiced vinegar, a mixture that prevailed until the 1940s. Artichoke relish, in contrast, was and is a composite sweet pickle including chopped chokes, onions, bell peppers, mustard seed, turmeric, sugar, and vinegar. Recipes for this chopped choke preparation begin to appear about the time of the First World War. Mrs. Nelson D. Sassard of Charleston made artichoke relish the anchor of her line of local pickles in 1917 and suggested that gifting a jar of relish would be the ultimate local food treat for Christmas. In 1921, the South Carolina Home Producers' Association, a USDA-sponsored group promoting canning, made Sassard's chopped style of relish a special project in its training sessions for home canners. The Association brokered the sale of home-produced relish. Almost immediately, versions containing items besides Jerusalem Artichokes began to be sold. The Barrett's Food Company of Augusta, Georgia, began retailing an artichoke relish in 1923 and enjoyed marked success until the Great Depression (its recipe appears below).

The most controversial additive in mixed artichoke relish was cabbage—an ingredient that pushed the relish too much in the direction of Chow Chow for purists. Less controversial as additives were slices of hot pepper, or chopped celery, allspice, and mace. Braswell's offered its version of relish in a jar in 1953, which galvanized artisans to take up canning local versions. Harold's Cabin, during its twentieth century heyday, advertised these among the signature Charleston dishes, though the relish is loved from Texas to Virginia.

Barrett's Artichoke Relish

Barrett Food Company,
Augusta, GA (1929)

(adjusted for home preparation in terms of measures)

2 quarts of Artichokes, peeled & chopped

1 dozen white onions, chopped

1 dozen green bell peppers, chopped fine

1 half dozen red bell peppers, chopped fine

2 cayenne peppers sliced

2 cups brown sugar

1-ounce turmeric

½ lb. white mustard seed

1½ pints apple cider vinegar

Salt

Celery Seed

Spices

Lady Baltimore Cake

If there is a mystery about any southern dessert, this is it: How did this elusive and beautiful southern sweet, the Lady Baltimore cake, originate? Who created it and when? We know that the cake makes its first appearance in print in Owen Wister's 1906 novel *Lady Baltimore.* In that fiction a man soon to be married gets cold feet about his impending wedding and goes into a bakery to purchase the Lady Baltimore cake. He becomes smitten with the young lady who sells him the cake and winds up marrying her. The recipe for this love-inspiring cake is printed in the novel.

The cake was named for Lady Baltimore, Joan Calvert, prior to Wister's visit to Charleston and the writing of the book. Under a different name, Silver Cake, a similar but less elaborate confection appeared in the August 1889 issue of *Lady's Home Journal.* The recipe was for a plain white cake containing English walnuts.

So, what is mysterious about the origin? Well, there are two claimants to the title of maker—the socially connected Alicia Rhett Mayberry who served the cake to Wister during his research trip to Charleston, and Florence Ottolengui, who claimed to have been given the sole right to make the cake by the board of the Charleston Women's Exchange in 1889. She sent Wister cakes after he left Charleston. Ottolengui's claim to sole possession of the secret recipe was disputed in Camilla Pinckney's letter to the *Evening Post* of July 23, 1906, indicating that Ottolengui was *not* the sole authorized and capable maker of the cake. What is not in dispute is that the Women's Exchange was the "home" of the cake, and an organization to which both Mayberry and Ottolengui belonged. Oddly Lady Baltimore cake doesn't appear in *The Women's Exchange Cookbook* published circa 1913, despite the cake section being the amplest of any in the pamphlet. Did everyone already have the recipe?

The recipe below is adapted from *American Cake,* written by Anne Bryn in 2016 and from the *Two Hundred Years of Charleston Cooking* by Blanche Rhett, a relative of Alicia Rhett Mayberry.

Lady Baltimore Cake

Erika Cline, adapted from Anne Byrn's *American Cake* (2016)
and Blanche Rhett's *200 Years of Charleston Cooking* (1930)

½ cup yellow raisins

¼ cup chopped dried apricots

¼ cup chopped dried figs

⅔ cup Grand Marnier

½ cup chopped walnuts

2 cups cake flour

2 teaspoons baking powder

¼ teaspoon salt

½ cup (1 stick) unsalted butter,
   at room temperature

1¼ cups granulated sugar

¾ cup whole milk, at room
   temperature

½ teaspoon almond extract

3 large egg whites, at room
   temperature

Citrus Simple Syrup

½ cup granulated sugar

¼ cup water

½ teaspoon vanilla extract

¼ teaspoon almond extract

1 tablespoon fresh lemon juice

½ teaspoon grated lemon zest

Seven Minute Frosting

1½ cups sugar

⅓ cup cold water

2 large egg whites

2 teaspoons light corn syrup

¼ teaspoon cream of tartar

Pinch of salt

1 teaspoon vanilla extract

Candied Lemon Slices
   (optional, make ahead)

1 to 2 lemons

1 cup sugar

1 cup water

Place the raisins, and the apricots and figs in two separate containers and add ⅓ cup of the Grand Marnier to each to soak for 3 to 4 hours. Cover with plastic wrap till needed.

To make the cake, place a rack in the center of the oven, and preheat the oven to 375°F. Spray three 8-inch pans evenly with baking spray and set aside until needed. Toast the walnuts in a small oven-safe pan in the preheating oven until lightly browned, 3 to 4 minutes.

Sift the flour, baking powder, and salt twice into a large bowl.

Cream the butter and sugar in a large mixing bowl with an electric mixer on medium speed, about 2 minutes. Alternate adding a quarter of the flour and ¼ cup of milk, mixing on low speed after each addition until just combined. Finish with the last of the flour. Add the almond extract and mix to combine.

Beat the egg whites in a large mixing bowl with the electric mixer on high speed until stiff peaks form, 3 to 4 minutes. Fold the egg whites into the batter in four parts until all is incorporated and smooth. Divide the batter between the prepared pans. Bake the layers until golden brown, approximately 16 to 18 minutes. Cool on a wire rack with a sheet pan under the rack for 10 minutes. Gently shake the cakes from the sides and remove the cakes and place on the wire rack.

To make the sugar syrup filling, add the sugar and water to a medium saucepan and cook over medium-high heat, stirring, until the sugar dissolves and the mixture bubbles. Continue stirring until it thickens slightly, about 1 minute. Remove the pan from the heat and stir in the remaining ingredients. Let cool for 5 minutes. Poke holes in the cake with a skewer and drizzle the sugar syrup over the layers so it soaks down into the holes.

Prepare the frosting immediately before you plan to use it. Bring water to a simmer in the bottom of a double boiler; the water should not rise high enough to touch the top of the double boiler. Add all of the ingredients except for the vanilla to the top of a double boiler, away from the heat. Beat with an electric mixer at low speed for 30 seconds, then move over the simmering water. Increase the mixer speed to high and beat for 7 minutes, until the frosting is stiff and glossy. Remove from the heat, add the vanilla, and beat for 1 to 2 minutes.

To assemble, place the first layer of the cake on a platter. Spread about 1 cup of frosting on the cake. Top with half of the Grand Marnier–soaked raisins, apricots and figs, and walnuts. Place the second layer on top, spread with 1 cup of icing, and top with the remaining fruit and nuts. Place the third layer on top. Frost the top and sides of the cake with the remaining frosting. Garnish with candied lemon.

CANDIED LEMON SLICES
Slice the lemons as thin as possible. Add the sugar and water to a wide-bottomed pot and heat until the sugar is dissolves. Add the lemon slices and cook until translucent. Be patient, this can take 25 to 45 minutes depending on how thin you sliced them. Lay the slices out on a silicone- or parchment-lined baking sheet. Let them dry overnight or bake the chips at 200°F, turning them over occasionally, for about 1 hour or until they start to stiffen. Let the lemons cool before using.

Liver Pudding

Originally a seasonal food appearing in butcher stalls in December, liver pudding had two styles in South Carolina: one incorporating cornmeal as its grain binder, the other rice. Made from hog liver and lights (lungs), stomach and lips, and sometimes the head, cooked long and chopped fine, it made use of one of the two most popular grains in the region cooked to a porridge when mixed with the meat, then seasoned. The mixture was either put into casings for sausages or poured into molds to cool into bricks. Both forms appeared on the winter breakfast table prior to the Second World War. Nowadays it can appear at any meal—even with fried slices appearing as the focus of sandwiches at lunch.

Traditionally liver pudding was homemade as the culmination of the cold weather slaughter of hogs. As a do-it-yourself preparation, makers introduced a fair amount of variation in the formula. Liver pudding composed of offal but no liver—double charges of sage and black pepper—garlic.

From the Civil War onwards, complaints arose when another's pudding tasted different from one's own. Against the DIY chaos, certain butchers defined a norm of flavor and texture. Butcher Brill in stall eight at the Columbia market shaped the public sense of what the cornmeal version of liver pudding should be immediately after the Civil War. Mrs. Stoudemeyer of Newberry and J. A. Darwin of Yorkville specialized in the German seasoning of liver pudding (pan parching the cornmeal brown before adding sage, thyme, black pepper, mace, and salt). Darwin moved to Charleston, secured the services of butcher Charles Boppe, and at a stall in the market sold liver pudding using a German seasoning and a rice binder. This would become the standard formula for Lowcountry liver pudding. He announced "Liver pudding is one of the delicacies that the people of Charleston have been missing for a long time, for the reason that it has been a long time since there has been a man in Charleston who could properly prepare the ingredients and give it a proper flavor. My Mr. Boppe thoroughly understands the preparation of the ingredients and the seasoning for Liver Pudding and is producing an article that is delicious."

Boppe's style of liver pudding employed rice as a binder, as well as sage, thyme, pepper, and onions. It was housed in sausage casings and was equally savory cooked hot or cooked and sliced cold. But it was not unusual for liver pudding to be sold in rectangular loaves like scrapple. Palmetto Farm Brand Liver Pudding, a mainstay of the third quarter of the twentieth century, sold it in this form, double branding it as liver mush/liver pudding. Liver mush is the preferred name for liver pudding in western North Carolina. No hog hearts were used in their formula. Most of the commercial brands available hereabouts deviate from the classic recipe. Neese's from North Carolina adds wheat flour to the cornmeal. Four Oaks farm from Lexington has the classic rice, onions, and pig parts, but no liver.

First known to Americans as the Japanese Medlar, the loquat (*Eriobotrya japonica*) became a garden fixture in Charleston the 1850s and early 1860s when pomologist A. Pudgion sold hundreds of trees from his nursery on King Street Road. Then it was viewed as the Asian equivalent of the American persimmon—a yellow-orange stone fruit that was "ripe when it was rotten." It attracted Carolinians because it set fruit over winter and ripened in March and April, making it the first ripe fruit in the year cycle.

An evergreen, long-leaved tree, the loquat flourished in urban yards and grew to a respectable height (30 feet), providing shade in gardens. A gardener in the 1880s observed that it "is a fine table fruit, and very desirable for jellies and preserves" (1888). It rarely, however, found its way onto breakfast tables, for the town boys pillaged every tree that was unprotected by walls. Wildlife, too, took its share.

The loquat was introduced into Great Britain from Japan in 1787. Thence individual specimens made their way across the Atlantic to the United States. It did not, however, capture the popular imagination until the early 1830s, when it began to be exhibited in state horticultural society shows. The foliage in particular impressed in the 1832 display at the Pennsylvania Horticultural Society at Masonic Hall in Philadelphia. In the North it was a solarium tree; in the South it adorned the yard and the walled garden. The fruit was never sufficiently sumptuous to inspire orchard plantings for market. It was an ideal specimen tree to show one's fruit loving friends and neighbors. The first tree for which a record exists in the

Deborah G. Passmore USDA watercolor portrait of the Olivier variety of Loquat, 1905. U.S. Department of Agriculture Pomological Watercolor Collection. Rare and Special Collections, National Agricultural Library, Beltsville, MD 20705.

South was one planted by Miss M. Smith on Broad Street in Charleston, South Carolina in 1838. "It is an evergreen and bears flowers of a delicate almond-like fragrance, twice a year, but bears fruit but once a year." It remained sufficiently rare during the antebellum period that its appearance in a horticultural exhibition insured print until the early 1850s.

Nurseries took the tree up in the period after the Civil War, often selling it under the name "Japanese Plum," and it became a fixture throughout South Carolina, much of the lowland South, and in California, loved particularly for its handsome foliage and its generally uniform habit of growth. Several varieties of the loquat were bred in the final decades of the nineteenth century. Breeders became concerned with improving the flavor of the fruit (a cross between apricots and mealy peaches) and reducing its sometimes-granular mouthfeel and its blandness by giving it a more subacid taste. Several varieties came into being. The Blush improved the disease resistance of the plant. The Premier gave a large salmon-colored alternative to the normally yellow-orange fruit. The Advance was, for many nurseries, the standard market breed, noted for its large clusters of fruit. The Pineapple came closest to offering a fruit with more vibrancy of taste. It produced a yellow-skinned, white-fleshed fruit that tended toward roundness rather than oval or pear-shaped configuration. In 1900, the Commercial perfected a pear-shaped version of the loquat.

In the kitchen it had various applications: "It makes a remarkably fine jelly; stewed with sugar it is far superior to 'apple sauce'; it forms an incomparable 'filling' for that much maligned American institution called 'pie'" (1910). Loquat jelly became an article of commerce in the southern reaches of the Lowcountry, in Jacksonville, Florida. When prepared from half-ripe fruit, the heightened tartness of the pulp gave the jelly a striking flavor.

Loquat Jelly
Daily Herald (May 22, 1910)

Thoroughly wash loquats and put in a kettle whole; nearly cover with water and boil until done. Strain through a cloth. Do not squeeze it or it will be cloudy. Measure the juice and add equal portions of cane sugar. A small quantity will cook in twenty minutes. Drop a little in a cup and if it will jelly when cold it is done. In making any kind of jelly use fruit which is just ripe—no more. Cut the blossom end from the loquats; wash or wipe with cloth and cut in half, using skin and seeds. Cover with cold water about two inches above the fruit, and boil slowly until soft. Put in coarse flannel bag and drain overnight. In the morning strain juice through muslin bag. Measure juice and put on to boil, not more than six cupfuls at a time. When it has boiled up once, add equal measure of sugar and boil rapidly until when dropped from a spoon into a little cold water it will not run, but drop heavily. Have glasses previously rinsed in cold water standing on thick cloth wrung out of cold water. Pour jelly into glasses, hot but not foaming. Stand glasses, uncovered, out of draught until cold. Keep in cool, dry, dark place.

The durum wheat now used in pasta is not grown in South Carolina. Nor have the few artisan cheese makers in the state directed their efforts to manufacturing the "yellow cheese" favored in make that dish that many consider quintessentially ours—mac & cheese. Not from here . . . yet well and deeply installed in every tailgate, church buffet, and family picnic.

Food historian Adrian Miller has traced in *Soul Food* the history of how northern blacks and New Orleans Creoles of Color came to embrace macaroni and cheese in the twentieth century. His story of Italian influence and the industrial manufacture of macaroni until it permeated the southern countryside ends in the African American embrace of the dish on a national scale. But South Carolina has a more local history. Its spread from an urban upscale dish to one with a broad black and white following took place in the nineteenth, not the twentieth century, and occurred because of its embrace by the African American caterers such as Eliza Seymour Lee, Nat Fuller, Tom Tully, Velma Middleton, and William Barron, who made it a fixture on menus and taught it to the multitude of Black chefs they mentored from the 1840s to 1900. Black caterers served both White and African American clienteles, and the dish captivated all who ate it. The cooks spread it across the state, so Gullah Fish Camp chefs such as Matt Brooks and Romeo Govan made it a feature of open-air fish fries. Where did the professional Black caterers learn the dish? The Italian–African American exchange that Miller noted took place in South Carolina, too, perhaps as early as the 1830s.

Angelo Santi, a native of Bologna, Italy, came to Charleston in 1794 and set up a confectioner's shop under Charleston's City Tavern at 86 Church Street. He was South Carolina's first pasta maker. During the winter season of 1795 to 1796, he interrupted his production of chocolate bonbons and cordials to manufacture both vermicelli and macaroni. He used Timilia durum wheat—a classic Sicilian pasta wheat that had been grown in parts of the Lowcountry since the Salzburgers of Ebenezer, Georgia, introduced it in the 1750s. Because South Carolina did not produce cheese on any scale in the 1700s, importing it from New York or Europe, we can be fairly certain that Santi, like Thomas Jefferson, another devotee of macaroni, probably used Parmesan cheese in his saucing of the macaroni.

The shape of macaroni sold on the Edmonston wharf in Charleston 1821 differed from the short elbows familiar to today's mac & cheese lovers. It was a pasta corta—short straight tubes of pasta—not bent. It did have the yellow coloration, derived from saffron added to the pasta flour before its extrusion through a metal die. In the most important sense—that it was hard and dry and made of hard wheat, that it was a pasta secca—the pasta was fundamentally the same.

The baked mac & cheese that we in the twenty-first century cherish first became widely popular in the dozen or so years after the Civil War. Here is the recipe in a recognizable form, albeit with an odd name:

Stewed Macaroni

The Port Royal Standard and Commercial
(July 13, 1876)

Break the macaroni into small pieces, wash it, put into salted hot water, and cook about twenty minutes; drain and put in a vegetable dish a layer of macaroni, sprinkle on it grated cheese, bits of butter, pepper and salt; proceed in this manner until the dish is full omit the cheese at the last); set the dish in the over for a few minutes, and let it get thoroughly hot. For baked macaroni pour a few spoonfuls of milk over the top, and bake half an hour.

Two things worth mentioning about this recipe. Grocers sometimes sold macaroni in the form of long pasta tubes that the customer broke up to bite size after purchase. This was apparently the case here. The second is that the variety of cheese to be grated and baked with the boiled macaroni is not specified. This was the case in most places where Italian expatriates were not preparing the dish in the United States. Cheese selection, therefore, became the area that showed the cook's particular taste, level of refinement, and wealth.

In around 1875, both vermicelli and macaroni (the elbow variety) were available in the groceries in middling towns from Port Royal to Landrum. By 1890 the grocery that did not carry dry pasta was an anomaly. It had a long shelf life, was relatively cheap, and was portable. In South Carolina until World War II, the challenge was in obtaining a cheese worth eating.

In 1937, while the Great Depression still stalked the United States, Kraft Foods introduced its boxed macaroni and cheese at nineteen cents per box. Cheap and convenient, it could serve four people. From that point on, students, poor people, single people with minimal kitchen skill, and the elderly had a grocery staple that would provide a familiar form of pleasure. So, mac & cheese was as much the comfort of the solitary diner as it was the social dish of the picnic, tailgate, and party.

Mullet and Mullet Roe

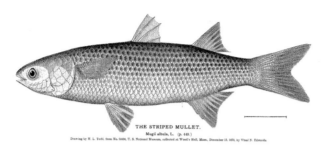

THE STRIPED MULLET.
Mugil albula, L. (p. 449.)

Drawing by H. L. Todd, from No. 74456, U. S. National Museum, collected at Wood's Holl, Mass., December 15, 1879, by Vinal N. Edwards.

The striped mullet, H. L. Todd engraving from vol. 2 [illustrations] of George Brown Goode, The Fishes and Fishery Industries of the United States *(Washington, DC: GPO, 1887).*

All along the south Atlantic coast, the striped mullet (*Mugil cephalis*)—the jumping fish, or popeye mullet—abounds; for sport fisherman it is bait fish. But for lovers of Lowcountry cookery, it has deep charms. Smoked, it was a favorite breakfast when the weather turned cooler. Cooked down with tomatoes it was one of the favorite Gullah fish stews. Yet the most cherished of preparations was cured mullet roe, traditionally called pickled mullet roe—which arrived in November and was a signature of the season.

The favored name for the dish suggests some acidic fermentation, and perhaps a bath in vinegar or citrus juice. Yet this was not the mode of preparation. The roes—compact cylinders of eggs four to eight inches long sheathed in membrane—were extracted from gravid mullet when they came to spawn in the salt creeks and rivers beginning in mid-September. The fresh roes were laid out in layers in wooden kegs with a liberal casting of salt on each layer (dried mullet roes were lightly salted and air dried; but they were always a decided second in preference to the pickled roes). By November the curing had become complete and the kegs found their way into groceries and restaurants.

Other parts of the world had equivalent dishes. The salt and dried mullet roe in Japan is known as Karasumi. Sardinian bottarga uses the gray mullet in preparation. In the Lowcountry the pickled mullet roe became a centerpiece of breakfast from Thanksgiving to New Year. Gullah fisherman would catch them on nocturnal expeditions with a burlap sheet, lanterns, and an old oyster scow, scaring schools of mullet into the burlap barrier. Their song was sung for decades along Jeremy Creek:

> Oh de mullet roe is sweet,
> And de meat is good to eat,
>   So Sally, hot de pot for cook 'um
>   You can cook them in a pot for stew
>   And they fries up pretty too
>   So Sally, hot de pot for cook 'um

The three preparations celebrated in the song—mullet roe, mullet stew, and fried mullet—have remained the standard dishes of mullet cookery in the Lowcountry. The roe was cured by fisherman the same way for two centuries.

Two schools of thought arose concerning how to stew mullet. The Grand Strand approach layered thinly sliced sweet potatoes and onions with split mullets and interlarded the layers with butter, salt, and pepper. (See Joe Blake's "Mullet Stew" in *McClellanville, S. C. Favorite Recipes,* 1956). The Sea Island approach is found in a number of stew recipes from Edisto and St. Helena. There was some variability to the recipe—tomatoes, sometimes okra, red pepper, and bacon or butt meat (a strip hog jowl). A Gullah fisherman from Edisto observed in 1944, "Mullet stew with red pepper and a chunk of butts meat make you bite your mouth." Edisto Islanders did have one dish that stood mid-way between these two preparations, "Pop Eye Mullet and Sweet Yellow Yam." This was a poached mullet accompanied by baked yellow sweet potato: "For more than a century it has often been the piece de resistance at Edisto dinners. Island cooks usually prepare it this way: To a cup of water add a tablespoon of vinegar, a bay leaf, pepper, salt; put in a whole mullet and cover. Cook gently for 15 minutes and serve with baked yellow yams" (1953).

In the twenty-first century, interest has turned from the fish to the roe. This is the latest in several shifts in taste. During the post–Civil War period, the pickled roe was manufactured in large scale from North Carolina to Georgia, shipped in kegs to Charleston, and then shipped to the West Indies. Most of it did not reach consumers along the coast. Around 1910 grocers began stocking it as a featured item, and in the period between the two world wars there was a pickled mullet roe rage.

In the 1940s the mullet population came under stress, leading to a decline in the catch. The roe industry shrank. One seafood store in Charleston, Carroll's on East Bay & Market,

made cured roes available in season through the 1960s. In 1973 the mullet population burgeoned in the coastal waters of South Carolina. But writer Jack Leland in the 1970s pointed out the problem facing the revival of a mullet fishery in the state. Freezing fish had supplanted corning as the convenient method of preserving the harvests. "Today the mullet one gets is usually of the frozen kind, flabby from time and strong of taste" (1974). The fish had gained the reputation as a "stinker" and the roe, well it wasn't real caviar was it? The last decades of the twentieth century marginalized the fish completely. It wasn't until the international bottarga boom of the twenty-first century that Florida producers sprung into existence. When you charge $57 for a pair of cured roe sets weighing 5 ounces, the level of return is sufficiently high to reboot an artisan curing industry in the Lowcountry.

Charleston Gullah plate of fried mullet, braised Charleston Wakefield cabbage, cabbage collards, and crab rice (crab pilau) prepared by B. J. Dennis, 2019. David S. Shields.

The old folk wisdom of the countryside insisted that winter eating led to a deficit of iron in one's body, and that the table in April and May had to feature spring vegetables to recoup the loss: "We get it [iron] from eating radishes. English peas, onions, and especially from eating a nice mess of greens—mustard greens, spinach, turnip greens, dandelion greens, lettuce, cabbage and salad generally" (1922). Two things stand out about the list: the absence of collards (it was a winter, not a spring vegetable in general estimation) and the primacy of mustard (*Brassica juncea*) in the list of tonic greens. More than spinach, more than turnip greens, mustard seemed the star of the greens pot. In truth, there was pointed debate about which greens were superior in terms of flavor and nutrition, mustard or turnip. "Turnip greens contain more manganese than do mustard greens. The trouble with turnip greens is that most people never get the greens washed clean. Sand is always in them. You have to wash them and wash them and wash them" (1936). In terms of convenience, there was no argument—mustard greens ruled.

Several varieties have enjoyed enduring favor over the decades: the Florida broadleaf mustard, a plant that grows to gigantic proportions in good tilth; the southern curly mustard (also called Creole mustard on the Gulf Coast); and the fancy Ostrich Plume mustard grown in Georgia. Nearly every twentieth-century South Carolina vegetable seed broker offered southern curled mustard. Planted in late February, along with turnips, the young greens were savored raw as a salad green before they "roughed out." The basal leaves were picked for cooking greens and successive plantings until May supplied greens throughout summer. A second cycle of planting beginning in late September supplied greens into the holiday season.

The method of cooking was simple: it could be prepared as a stand-alone such as turnip greens and spinach with water and salt, and probably a hog jowl or bacon strip, or it could be intermingled with other greens in an amalgam, again with cured pork, although modern vegan variations have become popular using mushroom stock. Here's an encouragement: "mustard greens gently laved in spring water if it is to be had, put on to boil in an iron kettle with a generous portion of hog's jowl to bubble and froth along with the simmering goodness, arise to that state of perfection that few other edibles are capable of attaining" (1930). Naturally sharp in flavor, with a sprightly vegetal tang, mustard needs a touch of salt and the mellowness of fat to come into a harmonious fullness of flavor.

In the South Carolina version of the West Indian classic pepper pot soup, mustard greens took the place of callaloo. While the dish is so multifaceted that it cannot be reduced to a single formula, there are certain features common to most renditions.

Pepper Pot

There is a meat component that can include tripe, veal knuckle, calf's foot, beef, and/or ham

There is a greens component that can include spinach (Sarah Rutledge), mustard (most early twentieth-century versions), or any green that is ready to hand

There are root vegetables—potatoes, sweet
potatoes, carrots

There are peppers—2 fresh cayenne and pickled
bell peppers

There is often seafood—crabs, lobsters, cray-
fish, sometimes shrimp.

Canned mustard greens became gener-
ally available in groceries in 1931, but they had
a blander flavor than fresh greens from the
garden or produce stand. The canned greens,
however, did lead to experimentation by home
cooks with combing pre-cooked greens with
other ingredients. One such combination, mustard greens with lady peas (any of the family
of light colored cowpea, such as White Acres,
Conch Peas, Rice Peas, Lady Finger peas),
would become an established summertime
vegetable dish, often served without pork.

Some final thoughts about mustard: a
portion of our population is genetically pre-
disposed to a hypersensitivity to bitterness; in
South Carolina, the hotter the weather, the
sharper the flavor of the mustard. Mustard
lovers relish the bite. But to those who find
the bitterness off-putting, the Savannah
Hybrid Mustard presents a milder option.
The traditional Southern Curled Giant and
the Florida Broadleaf remain standard choices
for field and table. If one wishes a different
visual dimension to dinner, the Garnet Red
variety should be your first choice. In the past
decade, inspired by Asian vegetable pickling
techniques, some southern cooks have been
pickling greens. If you are inclined to these
sorts of experiments, the Tendergreen variety
is your choice.

~ Okra ~

Clemson spineless okra, the single most famous green vegetable bred in South Carolina, long the dominant variety in commercial production. David S. Shields.

Abelmoschus esculentus. Sometimes called lady fingers or ochrois, okra (*Abelmoschus esculentus* is a southern food that is both revered and hated. The plant is related to cotton and hibiscus. Brought to the New World by slave traders on the middle passage to keep enslaved Africans nourished, it has become the most famous of the African diaspora foods.

Even as a young boy in New Jersey, I (Kevin) knew okra well. It was a common vegetable cooked in my home, stewed with onions and tomatoes served over rice. Unlike other southern ingredients, okra has few fans outside the South. People object to the slimy texture when boiled. Yet okra mucilage has long been prized as a natural thickener for soup, specifically the most famous New Orleans dish, gumbo, and also the highly popular okra soup served with rice in Charleston.

The evidence of okra in southern parts of the Western Hemisphere dates back to 1648. In that year, Dutch naturalist William Piso published the *Historia Naturalis Brasiliae*,

identifying the plant on a trip through Brazil in 1637. Culinary historian Michael Twitty believes that okra arrived in North America at the start of the eighteenth century in South Carolina and Louisiana, and that Charleston and New Orleans were the main locales where it was grown. He notes that "Thomas Jefferson lauded it as one of Virginia's esteemed garden plants in the 1780s, and references to okra can be found in garden records and maps across the early Mid-Atlantic, Chesapeake and Lower South." Englishman Robert Squibb traveled to Charleston, leasing a plot of land on Meeting Street that became a nursery. By 1787, he published *The Gardener's Calendar* and directed that okra be sown in the months of March and April. Some years later, recipes containing okra began appearing in several cookbooks, most notably *The Virginia House-Wife* by Mary Randolph in 1824.

So versatile is this vegetable that it can be prepared in many ways: pickled, roasted, stewed, fried, and fermented. There are recipes for okra kimchi and okra marshmallows. The flowers can be used in teas and leaves cooked like greens, resembling beet or dandelion greens in texture.

One important part of the okra plant is the seed. Okra seed can be pressed for oil. In 1874, the *Cincinnati Gazette* proclaimed, "a fine oil has lately been discovered in the seeds of the ochra plant, of quality equal to olive oil." The seeds have also been dried and milled into flour. These include whole okra grain flour, dehulled okra grain flour, and okra seed grain. Oliver Farms Artisan Oils of Pitts Georgia currently offers both okra oil and flour for sale. Though the okra is highly versatile, its most frequent application is in soup. Of the many recipes on record we have included two below:

Okra Soup

"Communications,
Charleston July 25, 1831"

I take one peck of okra pods, which must be very tender . . . cut them across into very thin slices, not exceeding 1/8 in. in thickness. . . . To this quantity of okra add about one third of a peck of tomatoes, which are first peeled and cut into pieces. . . . A coarse piece of beef, (a shin is generally made use of) is placed into a digester [an early form of pressure cooker] with about two and a half gallons of water and a very small quantity of salt. It is permitted to boil for a few moments, when the scum is taken off and the okra and tomatoes thrown in. These are all the ingredients that are absolutely necessary,

and the soup made is remarkably fine. We however usually add some corn cut off from the tender roasting ears, (the grain from three ears will be enough for the above quantity). We also add sometimes about a half pint of Lima or civie beans, both of these improve the soup, but not so much as to make them indispensables. . . . The most material thing to be attended to is the boiling; and the excellence of the soup depends almost entirely on this being faithfully done; for if it be not enough, however well the ingredients may have been selected, the soup will be very inferior, and give but little idea of the delightful flavor it possesses when properly done. . . . Should there be no digester, then an earthenware pot should be prepared, but on no account make use of an iron one as it would turn the wholesome soup perfectly black. The proper color being green, colored with the rich yellow of the tomatoes. The time which is usually occupied in boiling okra soup is five hours. . . . By the time it is taken off, it will be reduced to about one half. . . . I will state the criterion by which this is judged of— the meat separates entirely from the bone, being 'done to rags.' The whole appears as one homogenous mass, in which none of the ingredients are seen distinct; the object of this long being thus to incorporate them. Its consistency should be about that of milk and porridge.

Okra Soup

Michael Twitty, adapted from Mary Randolph's
The Virginia House-Wife (1824) and Mrs. B. C.
Howard's *Fifty Years in a Maryland Kitchen* (1881)

4 tablespoons butter

1 tablespoon lard or olive oil (use
olive oil to keep kosher)

1 small onion, diced and dusted
with flour

1 clove garlic, minced

2 tablespoons finely chopped flat
leaf parsley

1 sprig fresh thyme

1 teaspoon salt

½ teaspoon black pepper

½ teaspoon red pepper flakes

4 cups beef, chicken or vegetable
broth

3 cups water

28 ounces canned tomatoes with
juice (or 3½ cups fresh tomatoes, peeled and diced)

2 cups fresh young okra cut into
small, thin pieces or frozen
okra pieces

2 cups cooked rice, kept hot or
warm (optional)

In a Dutch oven, heat the butter and
lard or olive oil until melted. Add the
onion and finely chopped parsley and
gently cook until onion is translucent and soft. Add the garlic and cook
for a minute more till fragrant. Add
the thyme, salt, black pepper and red
pepper flakes and cook for another
minute or so. Add the broth, water
and tomatoes and cook on a medium
simmer for 30 minutes. Add the okra
and cook for another 20 to 25 minutes,
or until tender. Ladle into bowls over
¼ cup lump of warm rice each. Serve.

The most revered variety in the hearts
and minds of South Carolinians is Clemson
Spineless Okra. Rupert A. McGinty (1861–1951)
served as Vice-Director of the South Carolina
Experimental Station from 1936 until his death
in 1951. An avid vegetable breeder, from 1934 to
1936 he was acting dean of Clemson's School of
Agriculture. It was during these years that he
and his three assistants wrested T. H. Davis's
landrace okra into the Clemson Spineless,
the plant for which he became famous. The
Clemson spineless okra descended from a landrace okra patch maintained by Thomas Davis
in Lancaster, South Carolina from 1880 to 1929.
For almost a half century it remained a private
population manifesting extraordinary diversity,
including the trait of spinelessness. Davis's okra
"included a mixture of strains, several of which
have now been segregated including types with
tall, medium, and dwarf plants having pods
ranging from almost white to dark green in
color" (1937). The extraordinary diversity and
the spinelessness trait were noticed by Mrs. Dora
D. Walker, a Clemson extension agent, who
brought it to the notice of the South Carolina
Experimental Station south of Charleston.
From 1930 to 1937, R. A. McGinty, assisted at the
station by F. S. Andrews, J. A. Martin, and L. E.
Scott, selected and perfected the plant until its
traits stabilized. They adopted the Perkin's long
pod, the most popular early twentieth-century
variety, as the ideal form to which to shape the
landrace. They achieved this in 1937. In 1939, the
Clemson Spineless Okra won the All-American
Silver Medal, making its national reputation. It
has remained the most widely cultivated variety
in the world since that time.

"The houses have piazzas, and are often beautifully shaded with trees. Orange and fig trees abound."

The Northern Traveller, 1832

On February 7, 1835, an arctic vortex swept over the Lowcountry, dipping as far south as St. Augustine. Temperatures plunged to 2 degrees Fahrenheit and remained in the single digits for days. From South Carolina to Florida, orange trees, some dating to the Spanish occupancy of the region, died. Charleston's yards, until that winter, abounded in orange trees. Indeed, the orange, not the water oak, mulberry, or pride of India tree was the city's dominant shade tree. So thickly did they grow—both the sweet and sour varieties—that the Charleston City Council in 1832 entertained a motion for "hewing down the shade trees of the city" in order to make "the pavements last long." While the editor of the *Charleston City Gazette* endorsed the removal of the pride of India trees from the cityscape because "the excessive hugeness of its limbs, calling for frequent trimming, yields but little shade," he despaired of the loss of the orange trees "which yield the most admirable shade and shelter, from the heats of our Southern sun." The orange trees yielded benefits more than shade.

Colonists found the sour orange tree growing on Charles Towne neck when they laid out the city in 1680. They thought the tree indigenous, but it was a naturalized Seville Orange that had been brought by the Spanish to St. Augustine in the mid-1500s, taken by the Native peoples into the sea islands from North Florida to South Carolina. Tempering the orange's sourness, settlers married it with sugar

and spice in marmalade, the first important recipe in the orange repertoire. It appears in the first cookbook to be published in the state:

Orange Marmalade

The Carolina Receipt Book (1832)

Rasp the oranges, cut out the pulp, then boil the rinds very tender, and pound fine in marble mortar. Boil three pounds of loaf sugar in a pint of water, skim it, add a pound of rind; boil it fast till the syrup is very thick, but stir it carefully; then put a pint of the pulp and juice, the seeds having been removed; boil all gently until well jellied, which it will be in about half an hour.

Assured that oranges flourished in the city, ambitious gardeners imported sweet Chinese orange trees. Professional arborist John Watson kept a nursery on the corner of Queen and Archdale Streets. Throughout the 1780s and 90s, ads appeared in the city newspapers alerting the citizenry that "any person taking a quantity of trees will have them reasonably" (1795). Many took Watson up on the offer—so many that Charleston became an urban orange grove until the fateful winter of 1835.

Oranges shipped from the groves along the St. John's River in the Florida Lowcountry made the Charleston market a citrus wonderland from November through winter. They were eaten fresh, juiced, candied (peels and pulp), fermented, infused in creams, added

Cousins: orange pie sits front plate, lemon meringue back plate. The latter won the glory in the twentieth century, but South Carolina has long kept the less celebrated orange pie in its heart. David S. Shields.

into baked goods and fritters, rendered into preserves, and mixed into shrub (orange juice, sugar, and vinegar—a favorite old tonic). The blossoms of the wild sour orange were distilled into orange water and used as a flavoring agent in confections and a household perfume. Vintners began making wine from sour oranges in 1851, and for a generation it became commercially available from New Orleans to Baltimore.

Varietal stability in oranges occurred in the 1870s, when growers abandoned seedling groves in favor or propagation by cuttings. The Florida citrus of the 1880s and 1890s— the Homossasa Orange, the Magnum Bonum, the Parson Brown, and the Pineapple—were

American creations that competed with the European Temple, Mediterranean Sweet, Majorca, Jaffa, Navel, and Malta Blood.

Orange juice is now how most oranges are consumed in South Carolina. Despite the fact that Charleston exported barrels of orange juice to Great Britain in the mid-eighteenth century, the juice of oranges was employed mostly in sauces and was not something consumed fresh-squeezed until the mid 1880s. Then it became a medical fad, as physical culturists became convinced that orange juice energized one's system. It began being offered at Florida resorts shortly thereafter and Charleston hotels in the 1890s. The Specialty Company of Savannah distributed orange juice to South Carolina at the end of the nineteenth century. It quickly became a morning breakfast fixture. Nehi Orange Soda, created in Columbus, Georgia, in 1924, became a fixture in the late 1920s.

One of the Lowcountry's distinctive dishes is orange pie, sometimes called orange pudding. While lemon meringue pie became a national dish, its cousin, orange pie remained local. It is an open-faced pie upon which meringue may or may not be added. Often shreds of peel are incorporated into the pudding to intensify the flavor.

Orange Pie

Abbeville Press and Banner (May 11, 1905)

Grated rind and juice of two oranges, four eggs, four tablespoonfuls of sugar and one of butter, and one pint of milk. Bake with only one crust and meringue for the top (4).

Of all the traditional preparations—candied peel, sour orange marmalade, orange jelly, and orange fritters—only the last has become unfamiliar. In 1913, a midlands gourmand observed, "Orange Fritters are as delicious an accompaniment to broiled or fried ham as apple sauce to spare rib." There were two ways of making it. Peeling and sectioning the orange, extracting seeds without destroying the integrity of the sections, dipping them in a wheat flour batter, and deep frying them crispy brown. The second method peeled the orange and cut it into transverse slices which were battered and browned. Dusting the fritters with powdered sugar was optional.

Oysters

The southern soft-lipped oyster on the half shell. David S. Shields.

Plump, iridescent, supple, and savory, the oyster was the reward of winter to its devotees. Yet there have always been a minority who looked askance at slurping a raw mollusk straight from the shell, or impaling a poached oyster from a bowl of stew. Adored by many, avoided by the squeamish, the oyster gave rise to a wide array of preparations: raw of course, or roasted, stewed, fried in cornmeal, cracker or bread crumbs, deviled in a mustard sauce, scalloped, baked in a pie or in ramekins, pickled, or dried. In December 1897, the Grand Lodge of the Ancient Freemasons inaugurated the tradition of public oyster roasts in Charleston. Quickly, the roast became a winter-time rite throughout the state.

Oysters flourish in their millions along the coast of South Carolina, skirting the margins of creeks, clumping in concretions of shells. Carolina's oysters belong to the "soft lipped" tribe of oysters, not the hard lipped oysters of northern New England. Into the coastal waters each bivalve releases a plentitude of seed. Once fertilized, the swimming spat fix upon a hard anchor and grow into full maturity in four years. While much has been made of the courage of the first human to eat an oyster, any early human would have noticed the avidity with which raccoons and other animals feasted on creek oysters. All of the coastal Native communities depended upon oysters for sustenance, and shell mounds memorialize their consumption. The Sewee Shell Mound near Awendaw is perhaps the most famous of these remains in South Carolina.

Early in colonial times, oysters were the most reliable protein source in the Lowcountry. Because they were encased in durable shells, they proved ideal for shipping, and so barrels of oysters, sometimes buffered with seaweed, traveled by cart, boat, and rail into the American interior, the most portable and least perishable of the coast's sea foods aside from live turtles.

Eaten raw, roasted, and even dried and powdered to be reconstituted in hot water for a thick soup, the Native methods of preparations persisted in the settlement period. European colonists, if they were coastal dwellers, were all familiar with oysters and abided by the traditional wisdom, consuming oysters only from September through April (in the warm month oysters are reproducing and reduce in size). Customarily, October 1 opened the harvest season in South Carolina. Besides being a food source, the oyster contributed its shell to processing: fired, crushed, and mixed with water, it formed "lime" concrete for tabby building or was used as substrate for coastal roads.

Individuals began harvesting intertidal oysters on a small scale, provisioning households and supplying local markets. An organized oyster fishery began in 1869 with the creation of the Charleston Oyster Company, which harvested the marsh on the east side of the city until development filled the lands during the 1870s. Commercial harvesting reactivated in 1889, when the state Legislature by special act granted bottom leases to what would become the Bull Bay and Edisto Fish and Oyster Companies. The Bull Bay Company hired John D. Battle to undertake the first systematic survey of intertidal and subtidal oyster beds. The industry grew explosively and undertook extensive harvesting until 1908 when the bushel count began to decline. Because of a failure to manage the oyster population, or police the harvest, and because of the resistance of oystermen to interact with government conservation agents, the oyster industry plodded over much of the twentieth century. Articles on oyster farming in Long Island and the waters of Connecticut had appeared in Carolina papers from the 1880s onward. While the state engaged in replenishment of reefs and oyster rocks throughout the first half of the twentieth century, farming by private lease holders was virtually non-existent until the 1960s, despite a model oyster farm developed by the state in Beaufort in 1940. A dependency on hand labor for harvesting and processing and the low wage paid to laborers institutionalized chronic under-capacity. Twenty-six commercial producers held leases in 1972 and their economic viability was not at all clear. Efforts at expanding beds by dumping tons of shell on the bottoms (clutch) to supply anchors for oyster colonies brightened prospects for the industry, but declining water quality and the proliferation of diseases in warming waters have posed new challenges for some parts of the coast. Nevertheless, the waters of South Carolina have sufficiently supplied local needs throughout their history.

In the twenty-first century, clammer Dave Bellinger undertook the sort of careful management of beds practiced in Virginia, creating the "Capers Blades" brand of oyster, a form distinctive enough to win a following from southern restaurants. Yet recently he has expressed distress at the toll climate change is exerting on the seafood resources in coastal waters.

The development of triploid oysters that do not reproduce in the summer gave rise to populations that could be harvested in those months that lack an "R," so one can find oysters on the menu of seafood restaurants during the peak beach months.

Oyster cookery has made a virtue of simplicity—when stewing oysters, their own liquor was the heated medium and cream and mace and salt added; when frying, they were dunked in egg wash and rolled in cracker or meal and quick fried in hot lard or vegetable oil. One preparation that appears repeatedly in manuscript cookbooks of the 1800s and therefore suggests a general need for solid instructions was pickled oysters. It appears in the first published cookbook in the state:

To Pickle Oysters

A Lady of Charleston,
The Carolina Receipt Book (1832)

Have the quantity you intend to pickle, opened very nicely; put into the best white wine vinegar, a few blades of mace, a table-spoonful of black pepper, give the vinegar a boil and pour over the oysters. They should be kept in small jars and tied close, or the air will spoil them.

Palmetto Pickle

The state tree of South Carolina, the cabbage palmetto (*Sabal palmetto*), can be processed into one of the distinctive prepared foods of the Lowcountry, palmetto pickle, a relish made of the crown, or cabbage, and heart of the palmetto. "This cabbage is the terminal bud, or heart, and consists of the thin, white, succulent, embryonic leaves, which overlap each other in brittle flakes sweet to the taste and having the delicate flavor of almonds. After boiling in soft water until quite tender, it is dressed with olive oil or melted butter, or with a rich, velvety mayonnaise, and constitutes a dish which no epicure would scorn. Cut in cross sections of an inch in thickness, or in fancy shapes, and treated with a good vinegar and spices, it makes a delicious pickle" (1911).

While Palmetto dishes had been a constant of Lowcountry cookery from its beginning, palmetto pickle enjoyed a boom in the period 1915 to 1918 when Pearl Napier, a USDA home demonstrator at Rockville, South Carolina, interested women's groups in the region to take up bottling the pickle as a home industry. Napier had come to Rockville at the invitation of Mrs. G. H. Townsend, who was convinced that the local delicacy, long a homemade product on Wadmalaw Island, might be converted into an industry. Napier was an expert in organizing such start-up home industries. Townsend and Napier banked on the local mystique of the rare pickle and were gratified to see the initial issue of one thousand jars snapped up by the Charleston market. The success of the venture can be judged by the ramp up in price per jar from 1916 to 1917 at Welch & Eason's grocery in Charleston—what sold for fifteen cents per pint soon retailed for forty cents. It had gained a brand name in the meantime, "Palmer Palmetto Pickle," although it was still "made and packed at Rockville, S. C."

The Rockville enterprise was directed by the Townsend family—Mr. and Mrs. George Horry Townsend—using palmetto cabbages procured from fields being cleared on Wadmalaw Island and new truck farming fields on John's island. Yet the manufacturers were conscious of the public anxiety about the loss of the trees. Cutting off the cabbage top from a palmetto would kill it. Newspapers published reassurances such as "Palmetto Pickle—claimed New Industry does not Threaten Extinction of Trees" (May 1917). Palmetto hearts were only being harvested from trees already uprooted for regional development.

Palmetto Pickle remained a fixture on Lowcountry shelves well into the 1930s. Now it survives as a homemade local pickle among landowners with ample stands of palmetto. Yet the clearing out of many of the palmetto forests of the Lowcountry by developers in the twentieth century contributed to the pickle's commercial demise. While harvesting palmettos is not illegal in South Carolina, the extensive cutting of the coastal forest falls afoul of federal and state environmental restrictions. Palmetto pickle will be a private pleasure for the foreseeable future.

Peaches

The first peaches appear at the South Carolina State Farmer's Market on the second or third week in May and are awaited with acute anticipation. The early peaches are all cling varieties and usually yellow fleshed. David S. Shields.

Ripe peaches, heavy on the branch, warmed by the sun, picked and eaten in an orchard or yard, rank as the finest pleasure a South Carolinian can have with fresh fruit. Since the eighteenth century, the peach has stood foremost in the affection of Carolina eaters of all fruits, higher than pears, cherries, apples, oranges, and mulberries. Before Charles Towne was settled, the Guale People near Beaufort enjoyed the Blood Peach, brought to America by the Spanish and cultivated by Native peoples from Mexico northward.

When Martha Laurens and the other great gardeners in Charleston imported stone fruits from Europe and Asia in the 1760s, peach trees inspired the greatest envy among rival growers. Laurens imported one of the great peaches of American history, the Lemon Cling Peach, shortly before the American Revolution. Scion wood from her tree would propagate the Lemon Cling on a national scale, to New York City and Thomas Jefferson's Monticello. By the end of the nineteenth century, it would dominate the groves of California and become the major canning peach of the early twentieth century. Indeed, the Lemon Cling was central to the first three eras of American peach consumption: the brandy era from 1750 to 1830, the preserves era from 1825 to 1900, and the canning era from 1885 to 1930.

While Georgia in the 1870s became nationally identified with peach growing, largely due to the success of the Elberta Peach and the Belle of Georgia White Peach, South Carolina eclipsed Georgia in the production of peaches over the course of the twentieth century. If truth be told, Georgia's innovations in breeding would not have occurred if Henry Lyons of Columbia, South Carolina had not, in 1840, secured from China a tree of the fabled Shanghai Honey Nectar Cling Peach, which would be crossed to create the Elberta and, in South Carolina, the Honey and Amelia peaches. Commercial-scale planting of peaches first took pace in the state in the 1910s, with McLeod Farms of McBee and Watsonia Farms of Monetta establishing extensive plantings. They would be followed Abbott Farms, Belue Farms, Titan Farms, Chappell Farms, Clinton Sease Farms, and Big Smile South Carolina Peaches.

Because a host of insects and diseases afflict peaches, breeders have labored to create new resistant varieties. Very few orchards retain the old varieties because of their vulnerability to brown rot, scab, Phytophthora,

ring nematodes, powdery mildew, and bacterial spot. But one orchard that does retain the storied Elberta, Blood, and Honey varieties is Hyder Farms in Landrum. Charleston's chapter of Slow Food has made the repatriation of the Lemon Cling Peach a project for the 2020s. So, if you need to taste the peaches of legend, there remain places in the state where you can secure the varieties.

In the 1950s, Lexington County launched a festival, held on the grounds of the High School in Gilbert each July 4th to honor the state's favorite fruit. It remains a lively celebration of the fruit, featuring peach ice cream, peach pies, peach marmalade, peach salsa, and just plain peaches. The winning recipes for a host of peach preparations appear annually in the state's newspapers in July and constitute a course in superlative peach cookery.

Few peach recipes are absolutely distinctive to South Carolina: peach pie, peach cobbler, peach preserves, peach sherbet, peach ice cream, peach marmalade, peach cake, fried peach pies, and peach pudding are pretty much the same around the South. But there are four preparations that have distinctive Carolina connections: peaches in brandy, spiced peaches, pickled peaches, and peach leather (see following entry). Peaches in brandy often nested the fruit in peach brandy, the favorite spirit distilled from fruit throughout the South. Merchant grocer Alexander Ballund made a name vending his own house-made peach brandy. But in 1841 a great French distiller moved into Charleston and made peach brandy his specialty: Francis Joseph Charlon. Charlon's brandy became the standard until the Civil War disrupted distilling. Peach brandy is now undergoing a revival in South Carolina with High Wire Distillery in Charleston releasing a peach Brandy in November, 2020.

Peaches in Brandy

A Lady of Charleston,
The Carolina Receipt Book (1832)

Wipe, weigh, and pick the fruit, and have ready a quarter of the weight of fine sugar in fine powder. Put the fruit into a saucepan, that shuts very close, throw the sugar over it, and then cover the fruit with brandy. Between the top and the cover of the saucepan, put a piece of double cap-paper. Set the saucepan into a pot of water till the brandy be as hot as you can possibly bear to put your finger in, but it must not boil. Put the fruit into a jar, and pour the brandy on it. When cold, put a bladder over, and tie it down tight.

Spiced Peaches

Sarah Rutledge,
The Carolina Housewife (1847)

Seven pounds of peaches, pared and cut in half; three pounds of good brown sugar; one quart of vinegar; one tea-spoonful of powdered cloves; one, tea-spoonful of powdered cinnamon. Boil the spice, sugar, and vinegar together for fifteen minutes; then add the fruit, and boil until soft.

To Pickle Peaches

Sarah Rutledge,
The Carolina Housewife (1847)

Gather your peaches when they are at their full growth, and just before they begin to ripen; be sure they are not bruised. Then take soft water, as much as you think will cover them; make it salt enough to bear an egg, with equal quantities of bay and common salt; then put in your peaches, and put a weight upon them, to keep them under water; let them stand three days; then take them out, wipe them carefully with a soft cloth, and lay them in your jar. Take as much white wine vinegar as will fill your jar, and to every gallon put one pint of the best (well mixed) mustard, two or three heads of garlic, a good deal of green ginger (sliced), half an ounce of cloves, half an ounce of mace, half an ounce of nutmeg. Mix your pickle well together, and pour it over your peaches; put them into jars, and cover them with bladder or leather, carefully tied. They will be fit for use in two months. The peaches may be cut across, the stones taken out, and their places filled with mustard-seed, garlic, horse-radish and ginger; the pieces are then tied together.

Peach Leather

Of all the foods that became signatures of South Carolina peach leather was that most deviled by fakelore. The sweet dried sheet of pureed peaches became a household treat in the fruit country of Piedmont Virginia, North Carolina, and South Carolina in the 1820s. Sarah Rutledge included a recipe in *The Carolina Housewife* of 1847. A century later, Charleston ladies seized upon it as one of the city's signature foods and presented it as a survival of the treats served by plantation mistresses of the pre-Revolutionary period.

Miriam B. Wilson (1879–1959) contributed greatly to the fantasy surrounding this confection. An entrepreneurial Ohioan, she came to Charleston in the 1920s when the city's Preservation Movement vied with Virginia's Association for the Preservation of Virginia Antiquities in envisioning a colonial glory in need of refurbishing. Wilson's archival instincts served her colonial fantasies. She became a pioneering collector of materials manufactured by slaves—pots, quilts, iron objects, clothes—and she sold confections made from "old recipes" in her "Colonial Belle Kitchen" in Charleston. One of them was peach leather. In 1938, she purchased the Old Slave Mart and made it a tourist destination and museum, selling her candies from there. The building's connection with African Americans made Wilson expanded her repertoire of candies to include the trio of famous black street sweets: groundnut cakes, monkey meat (molasses & coconut candy), and benne brittle. She incorporated the Slave Recipes Company and developed a national clientele for her confections. The big seller of her line was peach leather, "an old plantation favorite of the colonial days." The

publicity generated by these sweet strips of dried sweetened peach pulp was such to get food processing companies interested, so from the 1960s until the launch of Fruit Roll-Ups in the 1980s, waves of fruit leather products appeared in American stores.

What is the true story of peach leather? Probably this—Native cooks likely used their method of preserving persimmon meat as flattened "leather" to peaches after their introduction by Europeans. Originally peach leather like persimmon leather was not sweetened.

The creation of peach leather as we know it had to await the cheapening of sugar to a point where it became a preservative and not a luxury good. This happened in 1825 when the price of sugar dropped to the point that one could preserve the annual fruit crop with it. The later 1820s in America was the golden age of preserves, jellies, jams, and fruit leather.

In peach growing states peach leather became, in the 1830s, a standard form of preserved peaches. Upstate Carolina growers and householders considered it their own. But it was practiced as much in the coastal zone where lemon cling and other peaches flourished until Phytophthora began killing the orchards after the Civil War.

Peach leather became a signature Charleston dish a generation after peaches ceased being grown in the city. In 1924, peach leather became a Christmas treat featured at the Lady Baltimore Tea Room in Charleston. Almost immediately a second tea room—The Spinning Wheel at 250 King Street—began featuring it. In the following year the Charleston Junior League adopted it alongside the traditional cakes as a featured item in their annual fund-raising food sale. In 1927, Miriam Wilson adopted the confection as the signature treat of her Anchorage Antique Store at the Pirates House at 38 Queen. She also served "benne cream." The invention of a tradition could be said to have been complete in 1929 when the Junior League advertised the chief attractions of its "gift store: "Real Charleston Peach Leather, homemade beaten biscuits, crisp cookies, creamy chocolate candy, and clear apple jelly." It took five years for a commercial novelty to be installed as a Charleston signature. Blanche Rhett included a recipe in her 1930 cookbook *200 Years of Charleston Cooking,* hailing it as the "most famous confection of old plantation days." (The recipe was borrowed from Sarah Rutledge's *The Carolina Housewife*).

The Anchorage sold so many sweets in 1930 that it rebranded as the Colonial Belle Kitchen. In 1932, Wilson alluded to a mysterious 1764 manuscript that supplied the recipes for her "benne and peach leather products." But the paper was bogus. The earliest surviving recipes for peach leather did not call for cooking the peach mash and sugaring was optional. Miriam Wilson's version was that found in Sarah Rutledge's *The Carolina Housewife* (1847), in which the pulp and granulated sugar are brought to a "boil for two minutes." By 1940 peach leather had become one of the tourist "must haves" of Charleston, available in the Lobelle Gift Shop, in the lobby of The Sumter Hotel, at the Slave Market, and even in the City Market. In 1950, peach leather had its New York moment, when food archon Clementine Paddleford wrote it up in "Food Flashers" column in *Gourmet Magazine.*

Peach leather remained one of the advertised attractions of Onslow's Candy and Harold's Cabin through the 1970s, then in the 1980s, the decade of the Fruit Roll-Up, it lost its mystique. While the benne wafer retained its iconic status as a Charleston treat, peach leather lost its special association. Was it no longer sufficiently rare and local? Was the quality of the peaches being employed in the leather declining?

Though most of the South now regards the pecan (*Carya illinoioinensis*) as a "home" nut and pecan pie as a pan-southern dessert, in reality the Native range of the pecan was limited to a rather constricted region of the Gulf coast from East Texas into Mississippi and up the Mississippi River Valley. The commercial cultivation of pecans dates from 1876 when the Centennial pecan began to be planted in groves as far east as Georgia and northwest into Oklahoma.

Barrels of pecans first appear in advertisements in the Charleston newspapers in 1832. With each subsequent year, the quantity being imported increased. They came from Texas where people foraged the wild trees, cured the nuts, and shipped them in barrels out of Galveston or New Orleans to ports on the East Coast and Europe. In Charleston it stood second among the exotic imported nuts that merchants advertised: almonds, pecans, Brazil nuts, English Walnuts, filberts (hazelnuts), and butternuts.

In the 1840s, John Horlbeck experimented with pecans at Boone Hall Plantation north of Charleston, planting in-shell nuts imported from Texas. A straggle of slow-growing pecan trees flanked the great oak alley in the 1850s. John Horlbeck's grandson, Major John S. Horlbeck, loved eating the nuts from these few trees. He saw the explosion of commercial groves taking place in the deep South after the Bayview Pecan Company of Mississippi introduced the Stuart pecan variety. In 1892, he began planting extensive groves. The old plantation trees had produced numerous seedlings on the grounds; the most vigorous and quickest growing of these were selected to

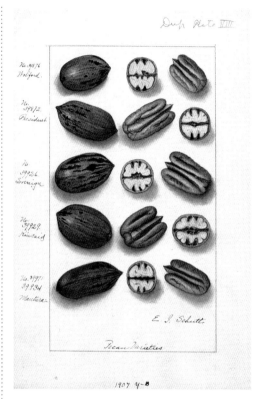

Ellen I. Schutt, "Pecan Varieties, 1907," USDA Pomological Watercolor Collection, Beltsville, MD.

be the stock of the first planting. On these he grafted cuttings of the Stuart variety. Finally, he experimented with the very thin-shelled Schley pecan.

The scale of Major Horlbeck's planting was astonishing. A decade after beginning the project, Boone Hall boasted fifteen thousand trees, the largest pecan grove in the world. It occupied nearly a square mile of land, radiating on either side of the oak alley and extending throughout the four thousand plus–acre tract. In October, workers would assault the trees with long poles, knocking the branches until the nuts fell, where a second crew gathered the nutfall on sheets. The local demand was enormous—sufficient to purchase the entire yearly crop. But Horlbeck always reserved a portion of the crop, the largest nuts, for sale in New York to confectioners. In 1912 medical difficulties prompted Horlbeck to sell the major part of the grove to the South Atlantic Pecan Company, a corporation organized by pecan pomologist Judson P. Welsh of Rutgers University. In 1914, the company harvested thirty-two tons of pecans from the Boone Hall groves.

Pecan candy came into the Carolinas by way of Texas, where Mexican street hucksters sold pecan candy made with roasted nuts and boiled brown sugar. The earliest recipe appears in *Mrs. Elliott's Housewife,* a North Carolina boardinghouse manual, of 1870. The recipe differs somewhat from New Orleans praline recipes in that lemon juice (or sometimes vinegar) is added to the sugar and butter melt rather than milk. White granulated sugar was Elliott's preference over brown. The molten sugar matrix is spooned over the pecans.

Pecan pie was invented in Texas in the 1880s. It was first mentioned in print in 1886 in the Austin paper, *Texas Siftings.* And from the first it was framed as "a real state pie," that is, a dish intended to be a signature of a place's ingredients and skills (1886). The pecans were boiled in milk and added to a custard pie. These were eggier, and creamier than later pie fillings, with half as much sugar. What happened was that the filling of the pie became more sugary—or more accurately—more syrupy shortly after the turn of the twentieth century. This syrupy filling more resembles Mississippi cane sugar pie with nuts added than an old southern Chess pie with nuts added. Seeing this style of pie emerge in the early decades of the century makes one realize why Karo syrup seized upon the pie as the vehicle for getting placed in the southern housewife's pantry in the 1930s.

Spiced pecans—sugar crusted and dusted with cinnamon, sometimes salted—now dominate the holiday confection shelves. This treatment was first introduced by Vantine's candies of Charleston in 1910. Vantine's was a cosmopolitan mail order house that traded in oriental and exotic goods. The treat did not become popular enough to inspire home cooks to make them until the post–World War II period.

❧ *Persimmon* ❧

American persimmon
(Diospyros virginiana).
Henri-Joseph Redouté in
François-André Michaux,
Histoire des arbres
forestiers de l'Amérique
septentrionale, *vol. 2*
(*Paris: Imprimerie de L.*
Haussmann, *1812*).

The persimmon, the paw paw, the red mulberry, and the Chickasaw plum were the major fruit trees native to South Carolina. Each made a contribution to culinary culture—plum jelly, mulberry wine, and paw paw custard each have old fan bases. But persimmon grew to be the most cherished of the native fruits. Persimmon pudding was the finale of many a fine home meal; persimmon beer was Carolina's country refreshment; dried persimmons were a standard Christmas stocking stuffer before oranges and bananas became common in the 1890s. Home bakers crafted persimmon breads and persimmon cakes during the holiday season. Confectioners churned persimmon ice cream. The soft ripe fruit, shaken from the tree, warmed by the sun, and eaten in the open air was the favorite forage of hunters and hikers.

Getting a friend to bite a green persimmon and suffer its astringent pucker ranked high among the classic childhood pranks.

Legend held that the fruit wouldn't turn sugary and unctuous until the first frost; but that was nonsense. Many trees ripen entirely, dropping fruits and seeds well before the first frost comes. The tell-tale sign of ripeness is the appearance of wildlife. When deer and possum collect around the local trees, then you harvest. The avidity of deer for the fruit was such that old time farmsteads ringed their corn fields with persimmon trees, hoping that they would distract the animals from ears drying on the stalks. You still find many old persimmon trees growing on the margins of fields upstate.

In the 1870s, Rev. Henry Loomis of California shipped Japanese Kaki persimmons to the United States to establish orchards. While most of the experiments in kaki culture took place on the West Coast, the introduction of the orange-colored, acorn-shaped Hachiya persimmon captured the attention of nurseryman G. L. Taber in the Florida Lowcountry. Fruit of the Hachiya might weigh up to a pound. The Hachiya tree was conveniently shorter than the American persimmon. From 1900 onward the Japanese persimmon had a following in the South, and when the Fuyu, a variety that entirely lacked astringency, appeared in the late 1920s American breeders ceased trying to make the American persimmon a mass market fruit.

All of the classic recipes of Carolina persimmon cookery were formed with the American persimmon as the subject. Now many of these formulae employ the Kaki persimmons since they are more readily available at the grocery. The most ancient of these recipes were Native in origin: persimmon leather and dried persimmons. Mashed, pressed, and dried persimmon leather is more toothy than

sweet; when granulated sugar became available cheaply after 1825, loaf sugar was added to the mash, making it more like the fresh ripe fruit in taste. Sliced, dried persimmons remain a holiday season treat, though now Fuyu persimmons are those that are sliced, dried, and bagged for the consumer.

Standing foremost among the persimmon treats was pudding, a dish that sprang into being sometime in the second quarter of the nineteenth century. The standard dish was made with persimmons exclusively, but if one did not have enough, the cheat was to add boiled mashed sweet potato. The following family recipe has a classic shape:

Persimmon Pudding

J., *The Rural Carolinian* (1872)

Pick all over, rejecting the unripe ones. Force through a sieve in order to separate from the seeds. All a little sugar, and flavor to your taste. Add three eggs to every pound and make as thin as you wish with milk. Put in shallow wans with crusts, and bake slowly.

How did one flavor to taste? Usually by adding cinnamon, nutmeg, and ginger; some substituted buttermilk for milk. Baking time? 50 minutes in a 350°F oven.

Persimmon beer was a southern brew from the colonial era that survives as a home concoction from Maryland to Texas. The old method, cited by Thomas Jefferson, had the brewer baking loaves of smashed ripe persimmons until hard, drying them, and smashing them to powder and putting them in water, letting wild yeast setting the mix to ferment. Later versions tended be simpler, but no less flavorful.

Persimmon Beer

Francis D. Winston,
Raleigh Farmer & Mechanic
(December 5, 1911)

Get you a molasses barrel, scald it out with hot water, take some corn stalks and place them in the bottom of the barrel, in a space occupying about a foot and a half square. Then you put on this half a dozen small pine limbs; not over a foot long; then you add a dozen roots of white sassafras; and around this you place a dozen pones of well baked corn bread, and a dozen well done sweet potatoes; add to the half a dozen leaves of the bay tree. Put in a peck of ripe locusts [locust tree pods]. And add two bushels of very ripe, frost bitten persimmons. Cover this with enough warm water to fill the barrel, and in a week or ten days draw out at the spigot all of the water and pour it back in the barrel. In four or five days you can begin to taste the beer. . . . If you like you may add a quart of black molasses at first. This gives the beer a beautiful amber color.

Adding locust pods to persimmon pulp may be a Native procedure for brewing persimmon beer. The pine twigs harbor the yeast that starts the ferment. The sassafras roots and sweet potato remind us that persimmon beer was the alcoholic cousin of the root beers being concocted at pharmacies and early soda fountains.

When the 1919 Volstead Act prohibited the public commerce in alcohol in the United States, home brewing enjoyed a revival. Persimmon beer was a favorite daily tipple. Most was mildly alcoholic, a shade north of 3.2% alcohol but rarely topping 6.4%. In 1922, a midsummer hail storm knocked most of the green persimmons off the trees in South Carolina, leading to a greatly lamented drought of persimmon beer in autumn of that year. The repeal of prohibition led to the return of persimmon beer to its old status as a folk beverage of the southern countryside.

Pickling in South Carolina has been a means of preserving vegetables, fruits, nuts, meat, and seafood in vinegar, usually with an admixture of spice. While Carolinians of German descent fermented cabbage in salt, making sauerkraut, the usual means of preserving items was acetic acid—malt vinegar, cider vinegar, wine vinegar, and cane sugar vinegar. Vinegar making took place on farms and plantations in the early 1800s, but over the course of the nineteenth century it declined as vinegar became one of the commodities purchased at the grocery store. At the end of the nineteenth century and into the twentieth, R. M. Hughes's Monograph Apple Vinegar from Louisville was the cook's choice in South Carolina. Today Bragg Apple Cider Vinegar inspires the most admiration among serious picklers.

In the era before effective refrigeration, pickling was one of the favored modes of food preservation. It was cheaper than sugar preserving or brandying fruit and altered the shape and texture of food less than drying and jerking. The range of edibles that responded well to immersion in acid was great, ranging from shellfish to fruit, from corn to beans. Having a crisp green okra to sample in February, a half year past harvest, was a heartening thing, preventing the winter from becoming a monotony of root vegetables and collard greens. Yet there were those who found the sharpness of acetic acid overwhelming. England's leading cooking expert in the early 1800s, William Kitchiner, attacked pickles, calling them "Sponges of Vinegar often very Indigestible, especially in the crisp state in which they are most admired." To mediate the acid, cooks added the important third dimension of pickles—the salt, sugar, and spice.

The nineteenth century became the heyday of the pickle in the United States precisely because all three components of the pickle—the vegetables, the vinegar, and the spices—enjoyed an extraordinary elaboration from the 1820s through the 1880s. Botanical experiments exploded the number of fruits and vegetables in cultivation. American trade, particularly with Asia, India, and South America, procured an apothecary's chest of novel spices and herbs. Cheap sugar prompted an explosion of fruit wines and fruit wine vinegars, extending the flavor range beyond apple cider and malt.

The earliest spices and flavorings were pepper, mustard, sugar, ginger, horseradish, and garlic. The end of the eighteenth century saw the addition of mace, cloves, cinnamon, turmeric, curry powder, and cayenne. The nineteenth century saw allspice and celery seed added to the pickling pot.

These flavoring agents were applied to a wide range of fruits and vegetables. Indeed, there were several extremely popular kinds of pickles in the 1800s that have become exceedingly rare or non-existent: pickled nasturtiums, walnuts, cantaloupe (which were then called mangoes), lemons, and martynias (a vegetable pod with a tip that looks like the curled-up toe of an elf shoe). A trio of sweet-sour spice pickles became favorite relishes in the early days of the United States: Chow-Chow, Piccalilli, and the closely related Atjar Pickle. Vegetable pickles tended to twin into sweet and sour, with sugar dominating the former and salt the latter. Jerusalem artichoke, cabbage, cucumber, okra, onions, pimento peppers, green tomato, and watermelon rind stood foremost in popularity, although pickled corn, beets, green beans, and watermelon rind appeared regularly in state fair judgings over the past two centuries. Pickled peaches were a pantry staple, with spicy hot marking one horizon of flavor and syrup sweet the other. Pickled shrimp and oysters were important and widespread.

Cucumber Pickles

In 1973, Dr. W. Carroll Barnes (1908–1973), head of Clemson's Agricultural Research station in Charleston during the 1940s to the 1960s, introduced the great southern pickling cucumber, Sumter. It was widely adopted and is still in cultivation in commercial fields and home gardens because of its great disease resistance. You have all seen Sumter, that square, boxy, compact cuke immersed in brine or vinegar in the pickle jar. If you love whole dill pickles, this is your choice.

Cabbage Pickles

While sauerkraut was the most popular home method for preserving cabbage by fermentation, the use of vinegar as a preservative also had a large following. There were two varieties of cabbage employed more often than others for pickling: the drumhead and the purple headed. The former went for boiled yellow cabbage pickle, colored with mustard and turmeric, the latter for a sweet-sour pickle:

Pickled Purple Cabbage

The Unrivalled Cook-Book (1886)

Shred the cabbage, lay in a wooden tray, sprinkle thickly with salt, and set in the cellar until the next day; drain off the brine, wipe dry, lay in the sun two hours, and cover with cold vinegar for twelve; to enough vinegar to cover the cabbage add a cupful of sugar for every gallon, a teaspoonful of celery seed for every pint, and equal quantities of mace, cloves, and whole white peppers; pack the cabbage in a stone jar, boil the vinegar and spice five minutes and pour on hot cover, and set away in a cool, dry place; it must stand six weeks.

OKRA PICKLES: Emerging as a pantry item after the Civil War, a jar of okra pickles received honorable mention at the 1871 Harvest Fair of the Anderson Farmer's Association, with a regret that a recipe was not submitted with the sample jar. A fashion for okra pickles began in 1963 when women began trading recipes in the state's newspapers. The vogue may have been sparked by Ladybird Johnson serving pickled okra in the White House as a Texas treat. *The Beaufort Cook Book* (1965) offered a basic plan for preparation, noteworthy for not slicing the pods but pickling them whole with salty vinegar, garlic, sugar, and lots of dill. A hot pepper was optional.

PICKLED PEACHES: Prior to the advent of canning in the middle of the nineteenth century, the widespread embrace of peach pickles, both whole, sliced, and even mashed, prompted a love of the jarred fruit that has endured since 1820. Certain old peaches gained a reputation as picklers—the Indian Blood, the Oldmixon freestone, and the Elberta. A good part of their appeal is visual—whole fruit suspended in clear liquid in a sparking glass mason jar (see recipe in Peaches entry).

GREEN TOMATO: In the 1850s, sugaring ripe tomatoes (called tomato figs) was a favorite way of preserving them. Because ripe tomatoes often had a soft, loose consistency then, pickling the heart of a ripe tomato did not supply an aesthetic product. But unripe green tomatoes made ideal pickles because of their firm flesh.

Green Tomato Pickle

Mrs. Hill's Southern
Practical Cookery (1872)

One peck of green tomatoes sliced; one dozen onions sliced; sprinkle with salt, and let them stand until the next day; then drain them. Use the following spices: one box of mustard, half an ounce of black pepper, one ounce of whole cloves, and one ounce of white mustard seed. Alternate layers of tomatoes, onions, and spices. Cover with vinegar. Wet the mustard before putting it in. Boil the whole twenty minutes.

At the pinnacle of South Carolina pickling stood the spice pickles, Chow Chow, Atjar and its relative Piccalilli. All are South Asian in their spicing and origins and date from the eighteenth century. They are sweet-sour pickles with the vinegar playing against sugar and usually mustard. The vegetables incorporated

in the pickles varies somewhat; indeed, an improvisational latitude came to characterize all three preparations, and a family's jar of pickles became a distinctive signature.

CHOW CHOW: Grocer Henry Bennett offered jars of Chow Chow for sale at his store at 10 Tradd Street in Charleston in 1795, along with piccalilli, pickled lemons, and cabbage pickles. Recipes hail from every part of the South, and Virginia repeatedly claims a priority in its manufacture. The Heinz company began the mass production of Chow Chow in the 1890s, so it was available in any first rank grocery in the eastern United States from that time. All Chow Chow has a yellowish tinge, because every recipe calls for mustard in the mix, and some call for turmeric. Yet until the turmeric boom of the twenty-first century, this spice was an exotic, often not available in a grocery, and consequently not found in country versions of the recipe. This 1890 recipe from Camden is a classic example of the mustard, not turmeric, form once common in South Carolina:

Chow Chow

"Pickles Sweet and Pickles Sour,"
Camden Journal (October 9, 1890)

One head of cauliflower separated into tiny sprays; one quart of sliced cucumbers; one pint of small onions, cut in half; one quart of green tomatoes slices; four green peppers sliced; five pints of vinegar, two cups of granulated sugar, one teaspoonful each of ground cinnamon, cloves, mace and celery seeds, and four tablespoonfuls of ground mustard. Mix all the condiments together except the mustard, and tie them in two small muslin bags. Place these and the vegetables in a preserving kettle and pour over them the cold vinegar, into which has been stirred the sugar and mustard. Bring to the scalding point, boil for half an hour, and then set away in glass jars or bottles.

ATS JAAR PICKLES: Ats Jaar Pickles are one of the Dutch colonial recipes conveyed through the world imperial trade networks from Indonesia to North America. The first form of a family of pickles we now recognize under the name Piccalilli, it incorporated a wide range of vegetables into the mix but adhered to a fixed approach to seasoning the pickling medium. One of the oldest recipes from South Carolina describes its contents and method, coming from kitchen manuscript of Harriot Pinckney Horry, and dates from 1770. The key seasonings—ginger, garlic, red pepper, salt, mustard, and turmeric—were sometimes supplemented with mace and cinnamon by adventurous cooks in the 1800s, but sugar never entered the formula. Every sort of vegetable could be incorporated into the matrix except okra.

Ats Jaar, or Pucholilla

The Receipt Book of
Harriott Pinckney Horry (1770)

Take Ginger one Pound, let it lie in Salt and Water one Night, then scrape it and cut it in thin slices, and put it in a Bottle with dry Salt and let it stand till the Rest of the Ingredients are ready. Take one Pound of Garlick divide it in Cloves and Past it. Take small

Sticks of about two or three Inches long and Run them through the Cloves of Garlick. Salt them for three days, then wash them, and salt them again and let them stand three Day's longer then salt them and Put them in the Sun to Dry. Take Cabbages cut them in Quarters and Salt them for three Day's then press the Water out of them and put them in the Sun to Dry. Take long Pepper Salt it and dry it in the Sun take ½ a pint of Mustard Seed, Wash it very Clean, and lay it to Dry, When it is very Dry bruise half of it in a Mortar take an Ounce of Termarick bruised very Fine, put all these Ingredients into a Stone Jar, and put one Quart of the strongest Vinegar to 3 Qts. Of small. Fill the Jar 3 Quarters full and supply it as often as you see Occasion. After the same Manner you may do Cucumbers, Mellons, Plumbs, apples, Carrots, or anything of that sort. They are to be put all together, and you need never empty the Jar, but as the Season comes in dry the things and put them in and fill them up in Vinegar. Be Carefull, no Rain or Damp comes to them for that will make them Rott.

PICCALILLI: Piccalilli, or mixed India pickle, differed from Ats Jaar originally in its addition of curry powder into the seasoning mixture. It was a sour relish that incorporated anything from cabbage to sliced fruit. But in the 1880s, some people began incorporating sugar into the pickling mixture, so the twentieth century Piccalilli became a pickle whose flavor stood half way between that of Chow Chow and Ats Jaar.

Pilau

Pilau belongs to a family of world rice dishes (Risotto is a close relative, and Paella even closer) in which rice is cooked in a water-based stock of some ingredient from which it derives flavor. If salted water is the medium in which boiled or steamed rice is cooked, a stock made of boiling meat, fowls, or vegetables is what cooks pilau.

Throughout the nineteenth century, magazine writers reminded readers that pilau (or pilaf) was a dish that originated the Middle East and migrated to Anglo-American tables. In 1834 the Charleston-based *Southern Agriculturist* observed that rice "can be delightfully boiled in the liquor of beef, pork, or fowl, thus saving fresh water and salt seasoning. With the addition of black or red pepper and a little saffron, it makes the favorite dish of what Turks call "pilau." The more orientalist the account of the pilau, the more ingredients were listed in the mix—nuts, fruits, vegetables, spices. Carolina pilaus tended to be simpler—with one focal ingredient (or two in the case of tomato okra pilau) supplying the base flavor.

In South Carolina six forms of pilau enjoyed great popularity: chicken, shrimp, rice, okra, tomato (red rice), and Hoppin' John. Of vegetable pilaus, green pepper, eggplant, butterbean, green pea, and summer squash inspired followings. Meat was important in oriental pilaus, but the beef, pork, and sausage pilaus of South Carolina were decidedly secondary in the rice kitchen, and Old World mutton pilau is never mentioned in accounts of Carolina cookery. Much more popular are the "bird pilaus"—dove, duck, giblet, rice bird, turkey, and egg pilaus. While oyster pilau graced many a Lowcountry table, clam did not. A special regard was given to turtle pilaus, made from either the salt water terrapin or the fresh water cooter. They required extraordinary prep work to secure the turtle meat needed to flavor the rice.

Some have suggested that early in the twentieth century the variety of pilau preparations and the special knowledge of ingredients was diminishing. In 1912, Mrs. L. B. observed, "Young chicken does not make good pilau. The old-time cooks on the coast certainly knew how to cook okra, tomato, green pea pilau, as they did 'Hoppin' John' to a finish, moist, thoroughly done yet grainy." Mrs. L. B. spoke in the moment when a group of food processing companies (Maggi, Oxo, Knorr) were industrializing the dry "portable soups" of ship pantries into the modern bouillon cube. In the 1920s, chicken bouillon cubes begin cropping up in recipes for chicken and vegetable pilaus. Carolina pilaus invariably used Carolina Gold Rice until it became unavailable in 1918. Then long-grained, non-aromatic white rice took its place. With the restoration of Carolina Gold a decade ago, it has become again the default for Carolina pilaus. Its great advantage is its starch quality—wholesome but not so soluble as to become too sticky or mushy—and its muted hazelnut flavor serves as an ideal matrix upon which to marry flavors. As Mrs. L. B. indicates, the ideal texture combines moisture with firm grain structure. Indeed bogs (such as chicken bog and sausage bog) were distinguished from pilaus by their decidedly more liquid consistency.

One matter of interest is the general lack of fish pilaus in South Carolina. The one part of the Lowcountry in which such dishes are recorded is Florida. In Carolina, the closest dishes to a fish and rice mélange are adaptations of Indian kedgeree—a mixture of fish (baked, canned or smoked) broken into flakes, cooked rice, and eggs. Some recipes incorporated the eggs in hard-boiled form, chopped and added to the fish and rice, while other recipes mixed the rice and fish and then added the raw eggs to the mixture while it cooked in a saucepan. An April 19, 1895 issue of the *Union Times* contains a fine recipe of the latter form of kedgeree.

Two kinds of pilau receive repeated and positive mention in the historical record, yet lack any surviving recipe from South Carolina or the contiguous states: squirrel pilau and rice bird pilau. The latter probably differed from the dove and squab pilaus listed below in that the plucked birds were roasted for a short time before being boiled.

Chicken Pilau

Ladies Home Journal (November 1892), 32

Carve the fowl into joints, as for frying; put it into a stew-pan, with a few slices of pickled pork, or fresh pig cut in thin slices. Season highly with red and black pepper; salt to taste. Cover the fowl with water. Let it stew gently; skim until the water looks clear. Have ready a pint of rice washed and soaked. Stir this slowly to the stew. Fifteen minutes will complete the cooking after the rice is added. When the rice is nearly done, should there be too much gravy, leave off the cover until it is sufficiently reduced. This dish should only be moist. No gravy is required; make it rich with butter.

The fowl, if a full-grown one, is sometimes left whole. The rice is first put into the dish, and the chicken laid upon the top.

Crab Pilau

Ladies Home Journal
(November 1892)

Boil, for ten minutes, twelve large crabs, salting the water thoroughly. When cold, remove the flesh from body and claws, mix with tablespoonfuls of butter, several parsley leaves finely chopped, large pinch of black pepper. Have ready some hot ham fat in saucepan, slip in the mixture, stirring well. Pour in three points of boiling water, one pint of prepared rice. Serve with parsley.

Dove Pilau

"Pilau of Birds,"
Charleston News and Courier (July 11, 1937)

Boil half a dozen small birds with a pound of bacon in water enough to cover well. Season with salt. When tender take them out into the remainder put 2 pounds of clean washed rice. Cook until done, keeping closely covered. Stir into it a cup of butter, and salt to taste. Put a layer of the rice in a deep dish. On this lay the birds with the bacon in the middle. Add the liquor, if any. Then cover them all with the rice. Smooth and spread over it the beaten yolks of 2 eggs. Cover with a plate or baking dish cover. Bake 15 or 20 minutes in a moderate over. Without the eggs, this pilau may be cooked in a rice steamer or pot on top of stove.

Duck Pilau

Harry Hampton, "Woods and Waters," *The State* (January 9, 1940)

After the specimen was picked and singed it was hung on a knot on a live oak overnight to 'cure'. Next night it was rinsed in brackish water from the river and liberally rubbed with salt. The pot was put on to boil in the meantime and when hot the duck was dunked and left to stew up. . . . Onion will draw the fishy flavor of birds. . . . Soon a fine gravy began to form from the butter fat little duck and the air around became permeated with a noble aroma. When we figured the duck was near enough done, we put in a cup full of rice and sat back once more. . . . When the rice was tender between the teeth we dragged off the pot.

Egg Pilau

Susan Myrick, *Macon Telegraph* (October 24, 1934)

Cook 2 cupfuls of rice in the contents of four cans of chicken broth. Add a teaspoon of salt to the mixture and cook with the cover on the saucepan. The rice will absorb all the liquid by the time it is done (about 20 minutes).

As soon as the rice is done, stir in six eggs and a little black pepper. Add ¼ cup of butter, or more, according to your desires. The heat of the rice will melt the butter and cook the eggs sufficiently without returning it to the fire.

Fish Kedgeree

Union Times (April 19, 1895)

Put one-half cup of rice into two quarts of boiling water. Boil rapidly for thirty minutes and drain. Turn into a saucepan with one-half box of shredded codfish, stir till the codfish is thoroughly hot, add a tablespoonful of butter, one-fourth teaspoonful of salt, a saltspoonful of pepper, break over two whole eggs, stir quickly, turn into a hot dish, and serve.

Fish Pilau

Tampa Tribune (May 14, 1927)

Spread a buttered casserole dish with a layer of cooked rice. Add a layer of cooked, flaked fish and, another layer of rice. Steam an hour and serve with tomato sauce.

Green Pea Pilau

The Garden Club of Charleston Newsletter (April 1923)

Shell and boil your garden peas. When nearly done, take the peas out and use the water to cook 2 cups of washed white rice—about 20 minutes. Sautee the peas lightly in salted butter and mint leaves. When rice has been steamed to the grains, pour off excess water. Mix in peas and butter. Bake from five to ten minutes. The best peas are the smooth English garden peas—the wrinkled can be too sweet.

Guinea Squash Pilau

The State (August 9, 1908)

Take one large or two small egg-plants, pare and cut in one-inch dice. Put in a bowl, sprinkle well with salt, cover with boiling water and let it stand for ten minutes then drain. Chop fine two moderate sized on-ions and fry light brown in one table-spoonful of butter. When well colored skin and place in a saucepan. Dry the diced egg plant and fry in the but-ter, adding more if necessary. Turn all into the saucepan, add one quart of hot water and one pink of stock, season to taste and bring slowly to the boiling point. Add two cupfuls of well-washed rice and boil slowly until all the liquid has been absorbed, then place at the side of the fire, where it can not possibly burn, for 15 minutes. Turn out on a very hot dish.

Hopping John

Sarah Rutledge,
The Carolina Housewife (1847)

One pound of bacon, one pint of red peas, one pint of rice. First put on the peas, and when half boiled add the bacon; when the peas are well boiled, throw in the rice, which must first be washed and gravelled. When the rice has been boiling half an hour, take the pot off the fire, and put it on coals to steam, as in boiling rice alone. Put a quart of water on the peas at first, and if it boils away too much, add a little more hot water. Season with salt and pepper, and, if liked, a sprig of green mint. In serving up, put the rice and peas first on the dish, and the bacon on the top.

Limping Susan
[Tomato Okra Pilau]
Charleston News and Courier
(March 31, 1965)

2 slices bacon
1 small onion
2 cups stewed tomatoes
2 cups thinly sliced okra
2 quarts water
1 teaspoon salt
Pepper to taste
2 cups rice

Cook chopped bacon in deep frying pan until brown; remove bacon and fry onion in bacon fat until brown Add tomatoes and okra and let them cook, stirring occasionally; add salt and pepper. Cook rice in 2 quarts of water with 1 teaspoon salt added; after 12 minutes, drain, and mix with to-mato mixture and put in top of double boiler. Let steam for 15 or 20 minutes; add bacon just before serving.

Mushroom Pilau

Charleston News and Courier

(March 30, 1972)

3 to 4 cups hot cooked rice, cook in
    beef [mushroom] stock
½ cup diced pimento
½ cup chopped onions
1 can sliced mushrooms drained
    [1 package fresh Baby Bella
    mushrooms sliced]
1 tablespoon butter
1 cup of brown gravy
2 tablespoons dry white wine
½ cup sour cream
½ teaspoon salt
¼ teaspoon pepper

Toss rice lightly with pimiento. Pack into a lightly buttered 1 quart ring mold. Cover and keep warm until serving time. Saute onions and mushrooms in butter about 5 minutes. Stir in gravy, wine. Heat to boiling. Add sour cream and seasonings but do not allow to boil again. Turn rice ring onto a heated platter. Fill center with creamed mushrooms.

Okra Pilau

Charleston News and Courier

(November 29, 1930), 8

2 slices bacon, cut in dice
1 cup rice
1 cup okra
2 cups water

Brown the bacon, and remove it from the fat. Cut the okra in small pieces and fry in the bacon drippings until its stops stringing. The fire should be low during this process, since over too hot a flame the okra burns very easily. Add the rice and cold water, cover and let steam until done (about 40 minutes). Add the bacon dice and serve. This will serve four.

Oyster Pilau

The State (October 16, 1936)

One cup rice, washed, one medium-sized onion, one stalk celery cut in small pieces, one teaspoon parsley, chopped, one-eighth teaspoon thyme leaves, one pint oysters, drained, on sweet green pepper, one teaspoon salt, one hot red pepper, cut in small pieces, three medium slices salt pork. Put salt pork through food chopper or cut in very small pieces and render out in pan or vessel in which the pilau is to be cooked; add onion chopped in small pieces, together with green pepper, celery, parsley, thyme leaves and hot pepper. Cover and allow to simmer gently, but not brown. When tender, add rice and two cups water, and salt. Cover and cook 20 minutes over a moderate heat or until rice grains are tender. . . . Never stir rice as it breaks the grain and causes dish to be soggy.

Shrimp Pilau prepared by Kevin Mitchell. Rhonda L. Wilson.

Pilau of Rabbit

J. W. Ellis, *What Shall We Eat* (1868)

Cut up the rabbit; pound an onion in mortar, extract the juice, and mix it with a saltspoon of ground ginger, a teaspoonful of salt, and the juice of a lemon. Rub this into the meat; cut up 2 onions in slices, and fry them in ¼ lb. of butter; when brown take them out, put in the rabbit, and let them stew together. Have ½ lb. rice half boiled in broth; put the meat and all into a jar [casserole dish], with ½ pint milk, whole pepper, ¼ doz. cloves and a little salt. . . . [Cover] and bake until done, adding a little broth to moisten if necessary.

Shrimp Pilau

Parker Family Papers

Take 1 pint of Rice, boil grainey, while hot add 1 heaping tablespoonful of Butter, 1 pint of milk, mace, pepper

& salt to taste; have 2 plates of picked shrimps, put alternate layers of rice and shrimps, letting the first and last layers be of rice. Beat up the yolks of an egg, put it over the rice & bake.

Shrimp Pilau

Mrs. J. G. Giaffis,
The State (January 2, 1955)

2 lbs. fresh shrimp (uncooked)
2 cups rice
1 can tomato paste
1 medium onion
2 stalks celery
1 stick margarine [butter]
1 teaspoon sugar
Salt & pepper to taste

In a large skillet, which may be covered later, melt margarine at low heat, add chopped onion and simmer slowly for 5 minutes. Add chopped celery. 1 can tomato paste and 3 cans of water. Add salt and pepper to taste and 1 teaspoon sugar. Then add shrimp which have been shelled and veined, but not cooked. Bring mixture to a boil, and then turn immediately to low heat, cooking 15 minutes and stirring occasionally. Meanwhile wash rice and boil until not quite done. Wash rice again to remove excess starch and add to shrimp mixture. Stir thoroughly. Bring to quick boil and then turn off heat, place lid on pan and allow to stand on stove for ¼ hour. Reheat, if necessary, before serving.

Squab Pilau

Helen Woodward, "Spice & Rice,
The Pilau," *Arkansas Gazette Magazine*
(December 8, 1929)

3 Squabs
2 cups rice
6 tablespoons butter
4 onions chopped fine
4 cups stock
2 teaspoons salt
3 cups canned tomatoes and juice
1 small can pimentos
2 tablespoons Worcestershire sauce
2 teaspoon black pepper
Dash of cayenne
Paprika to redden slightly

Put the squabs in cold water as if preparing soup. Let cook until the meat is tender but not quite ready to fall off the bones. Measure the stock and if necessary add enough hot water to make four cupfuls. Cook the chopped onion in the butter until it is tender and yellow. Add the onion to the boiling tomato juice, and add the mixture to the kettle in which the stock and fowl and cooking. Wash the rice well and add to the pot, along with the seasonings and the pimento, cut in small pieces. Allow the mixture to cook, slowly, until the rice is done and the whole is a gorgeous gooey substance, the meat of the fowl falling loose from the bones and being mixed with the rice mixture. During the latter half hour of cooking, it is necessary to stir often to prevent sticking and if the liquid is cooked down too quickly, add more hot water to finish the cooking. But the mixture should be thick enough that it is not at all 'runny' when the rice is done. Too long cooking injures the flavor of the pilau. The larger bones may be lifted out during the latter part of the cooking.

Summer Squash Pilau

Charleston News and Courier

(June 6, 1974)

Toast ½ cup sunflower seeds in low oven for 15 minutes, stirring occasionally until lightly browned. Cook 3 yellow squash, sliced thin, [in boiling water] for 2 minutes. Drain well. Combine squash, 3 cups cooked and cooled rice, 3 thinly slice green onions and toasted sunflower seeds, being careful not to break up the squash. Combine ½ cup garlic flavored wine vinegar, 2 teaspoons dillweed, ½ teaspoon of salt and pepper, 1 tablespoon of olive oil, and 2 tablespoons corn oi. Pour over rice mixture and toss gently until well blended. Chill.

A few words need to be said about our final listing, tomato pilau, or as it is better known in the Lowcountry, red rice. In 1968, the Savannah Chamber of Commerce began a campaign "Some People Come 500 Miles for Our Red Rice," asserting a proprietary claim on this standard dish of the Lowcountry rice lands. South Carolina has, on the basis of print records, a stronger claim to its genesis. Mary Washington, the African American cook who was one of Blanche Rhett's chief informants in *200 Years of Charleston Cooking* (1930), supplied the classic formulation—bacon, rice, chicken stock, tomatoes, pepper, and salt. When the Francis Marion Hotel determined to feature local Charleston dishes on its menu in the late 1940s, this is what they announced: "She Crab Soup . . . Charleston Shrimp Pie . . . Red Rice . . . Hoppin' John . . . Awendaw Corn Bread . . . Potato Pone" (1949).

Red Rice, or Tomato Pilau

Evening Star (March 20, 1913)

Put one and a half pounds of ripe tomatoes into a mortar and press them to extract their juice, which strain through a fine sieve and pour into a saucepan with an equal quantity of broth. Peel and chop fine two onions and fry them in butter till well browned Drain the onions, put them in the tomato juice, add a pinch of salt and place the saucepan over the fire. When the liquor boils put in one pound of washed rice and allow the whole to simmer at the side of the fire till all the moisture is absorbed. Now heat four ounces of butter, stir it in with the rice, put the lid on the saucepan again, and let the dish stand on the side of the stove for twenty minutes. Turn the pilau on to a hot dish, sprinkle over a little pepper and serve while very hot.

Pine Bark Stew

From the 1830s to the present day, outdoor political rallies, fund raisers, civic anniversaries, family reunions, camp meetings, and parties had their own repertoire of dishes and a class of specialist caterers capable of handling on site cooking over open fires and propane rigs. Event cooks tended to go in one of three directions: barbecue, fish fry, or oyster roast. The fish fry was the most complex of these because it was never restricted to fried fillets or planked shad; there was inevitably a stew, either catfish or pine bark, often a chicken bog or perloo, and sometimes mullet or shad roe, plus sides.

Pine Bark Stew came into being near Darlington sometime during the final decades of the nineteenth century. It was a true stew, not a chowder; this meant milk was not and is not its liquid component. Nor for that matter is pine bark, despite a legend promoted in the 1960s by Dr. Chapman J. Milling, insisting that "one famous outdoor cook of Darlington failed to obtain fish for his stew and used pine bark instead, making it so hot that either nobody could eat it or nobody knew the difference" (1967). A perverse minority insist on putting a chunk of pine bark into the stew pot to give the stew a touch of resin, but the truth of the matter was that the iron cauldrons were cooked on a quick hot fire, usually fed by chunks of pine bark. The chief ingredient of pine bark stew, Milling's legend suggests, is fish—bream, medium sized bass, catfish, or red breast. Because of its boniness, the red horse was a controversial addition to the pot. One laid the fish on onions fried in bacon grease or rendered side meat. Water, tomato ketchup, Worcestershire sauce, red pepper, and salt made up the rest of the stew.

Pine Bark Stew is red. Its proper home is an iron kettle in the open air. More liquid than chicken bog or catfish stew, this kettle at the Pee Dee Shad Festival has an hour of cooking to go before being served. David S. Shields.

During the twentieth century, pine bark stew spread from the Pee Dee through the Lowcountry from Wilmington to Savannah, prepared outdoors. In 1909, when President Howard Taft visited South Carolina, the citizens of Florence treated him to a pine bark stew and Henry S. Rose's recipe appeared in the papers. Rose prepared the stew in large "wash pots"—cast iron cauldrons used on plantations for boiling water for laundry. Taft's feast led to the first popularization of the stew outside of the Pee Dee.

Pine Bark Stew

Charleston News and Courier

(November 9, 1909)

Fish, after being thoroughly cleaned, are salted. The first thing put in is bacon, which is fried and the grease left in the pot, the various ingredients consisting of tomatoes, tomato sauce, Cayenne pepper, Worcester sauce. Onions are boiled for a half-hour, the fish are then put into the pot, and boiled for thirty-five minutes. They are then taken off and allowed to cool for a few moments, served with pure South Carolina rice. Of course, there is sufficient water put in to make ample soup, which is the 'feature' of the stew. The fish that were used this evening were caught with cook and line the Little Pee-Dee and Lumber River on the border of Eastern Carolina, and are of the finest variety of brims, red bellies and speckled trout. These are said to be the best fish in the world. (1–2)

In spring, the stew might be made out of "trout, jack, bream, and other fine fish." A skillet of fried fish was prepared on the side for those who did not savor stew. While typically an open-air communal dish, regional restaurants adopted pine bark stew as a menu item, particularly for club banquets early in the twentieth century. James' Restaurant in Darlington made it a fixture well before Taft's visit popularized the stew to the larger world.

In the 1920s, a canned version was introduced by the USDA network of canning clubs, as part of a campaign to make available regional stews and soups. This version contained "Onions, tomatoes, celery, pimento and fish . . . cooked slowly in vegetable oil . . . and poured over 'southern style' rice." The varieties of fish employed were not specified.

In the 1930s and 1940s, the stew became a local fixture, prepared by specialists such as Patsy Watson of the Otranto Club. When *Charleston Receipts* was published in 1950, New York's food oracle Clementine Paddleford came to Charleston, sampled Watson's stew, and celebrated its mystical savor in *This Week*. The national exposure led to a resurgence in the dish, albeit with home cooks scaling it down to kitchen dimensions and dinner party consumption. Since the 1950s, pine bark stew has remained a fixture both as an event dish and as a party sideboard dish. The 1960s saw a multitude of newspaper recipe versions scaled to family consumption, often framed by nonsensical claims that it was a dish from the colonial era or concocted in the swampy lairs of "the Swamp Fox" Francis Marion during the American Revolution. Since tomato ketchup was not widely available prior to the second quarter of the nineteenth century, these fanciful legends seem curiously divorced from history.

Porgy

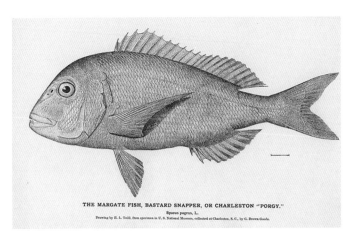

THE MARGATE FISH, BASTARD SNAPPER, OR CHARLESTON "PORGY."
Sparus pagrus, L.
Drawing by H. L. Todd, from specimen in U. S. National Museum, collected at Charleston, S. C., by G. Brown Goode.

H. L. Todd, "Charleston Porgy," G. Brown Goode, Fishes and Fisheries of the United States *(Washington, DC: Government Printing Office, 1887).*

In the days when "sport fisherman" cruised out to the banks near the oceanic shelf on excursion boats to catch blackfish, they demeaned the anglers who could not afford buy a place on a fishing vessel and were forced to cast off piers and docks. The low-class fisherman no doubt sought a low-class fish. As a 1904 sport remarked, "the porgy is essentially the poor angler's fish." Sometimes this class attitude got mixed up with a race attitude. Dubose Heyward captured the old prejudice when he named the crippled black street vendor in his famous play and opera Porgy. For all the mental baggage surrounding the porgy it has some distinct virtues. It is large boned, so is an ideal pan fish. It was prolific, so it was good protein cheaply obtained. When African American entrepreneurs made the fish sandwich the popular dish at the lunch rooms on Market Street after the turn of the twentieth century, the porgy was the chief fish employed in them.

What Americans called a porgy differed in New England and the South. From Maine to Connecticut, the Atlantic menhaden (*Brevoortia tyrranus*) was the porgy. In New York and New Jersey, the scup was the porgy. But the porgy known to the southeastern coast is the red porgy (*Pagrus pagrus*), or the common sea bream. The Latin name pagrus morphed into porgy among English speakers early in the colonial era. Although the name suggests the fish would be red, pinkish silver is a more accurate description of the tints of its upper body and dorsal fin. They grow on average a foot to a foot and a half in length, and tend to weigh over eight pounds when adult. They school over reefs and eat crustaceans, mollusks, and small fish. The flesh is not oily. It fillets readily and suits the frying pan.

Joe Cole, Charleston's most famous seafood huckster, created a song about the porgy whose chorus became a folk lyric known to all from 1890 to 1920:

> Porgy walk en porgy talk
> Porgy eat wid de knife and fork.
> Pooor Geeee!

The hucksters made morning rounds of the city—at the crack of dawn with shrimp for breakfast, and during the forenoon with strings of fish laid out in a head basket. The typical string had eight fish on it, a substantial meal for a family. Porgy was also sold at the fish market on Bay at Market Street. C. C. Leslie was the first to stock porgy regularly in the market it in the 1870s. It has been a presence ever since at fish markets around the city.

For the nineteenth and twentieth centuries there was no limit on the number of porgies an individual could catch in a day. Now regulations restrict the catch to three per person per day. In the nineteenth century, schools of porgy were netted and processed in fish oil plants to supply a base for paint; often porgy oil was sold as linseed oil. Porgy when prepared as a meal tended to be baked or fried. Here are two classic preparations found in deluxe cook books of the Gilded Age:

Fried Porgies, Tartar Sauce

Felix Déliée,
Franco-American Cookery (1884)

Pare off the fins, cleanse, and dress four pounds of porgies; wipe them dry, make slight incisions on each side, toss them in a napkin with a handful of flour, shake the superfluous flour off, plunge the half at a time in plenty of very hot fat, and fry slightly crisp and of a very nice color; drain on a cloth, salt, range on a folded napkin with a handful of fried parsley, and serve with a tartar sauce in a sauce-bowl.

Stuffed Porgy, Corsican Style

Adolphe Meyer,
Post Graduate Cookery Book (1903)

Split open the porgies and remove the spinal bone. Stuff it with fish forcemeat, to which add chopped olives and fillets of anchovies, 1 tablespoonful of each to 1 quart of forcemeat.

Tie the porgies with string and place them over sliced carrots and onions, moisten with half fish stock and half port wine, add a faggot [bundle] of herbs, and cook in a moderate oven, basting the fish constantly. When done, drain it and dress it on a dish; strain the fish stock and reduce it with brown sauce to a good consistency, season to taste, and finish with a pat of butter and lemon juice.

Pot Likker

The savory liquid left in the pot after cooking greens. You can even have pot likker after you cook a pot of green beans. It is known for being nutritious since it contains essential vitamins and minerals including iron and vitamin C and high amounts of vitamin K known for its blood clotting capabilities.

It is important to remember that not just any greens can go into a pot to make pot likker. For the most part you need collard, mustard and turnip greens. The *Macon Telegraph* on August 8, 1906 called for pot likker being made with cabbage when collards are not in season. Weaker greens such as spinach or chard are never included in the pot. No matter the green, the recipe stays the same: greens, water, onion, and some sort of smoked meat product.

The history of pot likker goes back to slavery. Slaveholders would eat the greens from the pot, leaving behind the likker left over for the enslaved to eat, not knowing the nutritional value it possessed. After slavery both poor Whites and Blacks lived off pot likker to sustain themselves. John T. Edge in the *Pot Likker Papers* quotes Richard Wright, "I lived on what I did not eat . . . . Perhaps the sunshine, the fresh air and the pot likker from greens kept me going."

So beloved is pot likker, former Governor and U.S. Senator Zell Miller of Georgia defended the traditional spelling "potlikker" in *The New York Times.* "[T]he juice that remains in a pot after greens or other vegetables are boiled with proper seasoning. The best seasoning is a piece of salt fat pork, commonly referred to as "dry salt meat" or "side meat." If a pot be partly filled with well-cleaned turnip greens and turnips (which should be cut up), with a half-pound piece of the salt pork and then with water and boiled until the greens and turnips are cooked reasonably tender, then the juice remaining in the pot is the delicious, invigorating, soul-and-body sustaining potlikker . . . which should be taken as any other soup and the greens eaten as any other food . . . . Most people crumble cornpone (corn meal mixed with a little salt and water, made into a pattie and baked until it is hard) into the potlikker" (1982).

Growing up as a young boy in New Jersey, I (Kevin) learned the art of dunking/dipping corn bread in pot likker from my grandmother Doris, who would make a fresh pot of collard greens after laboriously cleaning them and then finally sitting down at the table to eat with golden brown pieces of corn bread. Today, pot likker has taken on new forms. Chefs are using it to poach fish in, taking it to the white tablecloth. Chef Todd Richards of Atlanta has turned it into ramen. Chefs are also using other ingredients to make the pot likker, such as the likker gained from boiling peanuts.

Pumpkin

Americans—even southern Americans—tend to associate pumpkins with New England, New England's pumpkin pie (the rival of sweet potato pie at the Thanksgiving table), and Halloween jack-o-lanterns. But the Native peoples of the southeast grew a number of varieties of what we now call pumpkin—*Cucurbita pepo, Cucurbita mixta, Cucurbita maxima, Cucurbita moschata.* Several old forms of pumpkins have come down to us, along with a rather distinctive set of pumpkin foodways: the Seminole pumpkin, The Tennessee Sweet Potato Pumpkin, and South Carolina's own Dutch Fork Pumpkin.

Several qualities recommended pumpkins: they tended to keep without rotting several months in cold weather, they grew to ample size, their often substantial rinds prevented easy depredation from critters, they were loved by livestock who fed on them voraciously, they could be dried and reconstituted with water, and they proved hardy in the face of pest and disease pressures, the banes of southern field cultivation.

Dutch Fork

(*Cucurbita moschata v. Dutch Fork*)

A tan-colored lobed pumpkin grown in the Dutch Fork area around Newberry since the early nineteenth century, this ancient vegetable has the diversity of shape, size and color (it sometimes shows a yellow skin) that attests a Native origin. Circumstantial evidence suggests this is the descendent of the Cherokee pumpkin grown in the early eighteenth century in the Pumpkintown area of Pickens County. The multitudes of pumpkin vines skirting the Oolenoy River there, planted by the Cherokee living at UWharrie village, gave rise to the name. When the Cherokee were dispossessed of this land in 1791 as punishment for their alliance with Great Britain during the American Revolution, land speculator Cornelius Keith settled and named Pumpkintown. He is, perhaps, responsible for the spread of pumpkin seeds into the midlands of South Carolina, for he was a trader as well as a land shark.

Several features of the pumpkins won favor with settlers in the Dutch Fork. Livestock loved the flavor, making them a valuable source of winter feed for cattle, hogs, and fowl. They grew plentifully, robustly, and attained a good size, making them an ample food source. Reports of as many as thirty-one pumpkins growing on a single vine (eight to ten pounders) appeared in the Bamberg and Newberry papers in the 1910s and 1920s. The pumpkin hulls were so sturdy they could be stored much of the winter without spoiling. Finally, they had a mild agreeable sweetness that appealed to human taste buds and a texture that lacked the stringiness of some squashes and pumpkins. It proved to be a splendid local variety for pies

Dutch Fork Pumpkin. Kevin Mitchell.

[139]

and baking. "Usually a small, hard-shelled, fine-grained and dry pumpkin makes the best pie," observed the editor of the *Newberry Herald and News* in 1914.

After 1820, South Carolina farmers often purchased vegetable seeds imported by local seed brokers from overseas (cabbages and certain grains) or from the North (garden vegetables). Cheese pumpkins from Long Island and Connecticut field pumpkins made their ways into South Carolina, the latter because of their great size, a feature that would win prizes in fairs and notice in local newspapers. But northern pumpkins, having been shaped for decades to prosper in the colder climates of the North, did not thrive during the tropical heats of Carolina summers. The Dutch Fork Pumpkin and the Seminole Pumpkins of Florida had been bred to grow in hot humid country. Their reliability won them local admirers.

The important keeper of Dutch Fork Pumpkin seed from the 1850s into the twentieth century was Thomas Watland Holloway (1829–1903) of Pomaria. He improved the pumpkin by selecting seed to give it regular shape and tan coloration. In 1878, he won the first premium at the South Carolina State Fair for pumpkins. His preeminence as an agriculturist thereafter was recognized by his becoming the receiver of entries for the State Fair. He distributed his seed regularly in the region from the 1860s onward. A circle of seed savers in the Dutch Fork kept the pumpkin viable into the twenty-first century. Strains were maintained by the Eleazer, Wicker, Kibler, Fulmer, and Epting families. Seed may be purchased from Sow True Seed of Ashville, North Carolina. Nat Bradford of Sumter, South Carolina grows the pumpkin as produce along with the Cherokee candy roaster squash (North Georgia variety).

In the 1800s, the leaves of the pumpkin were dried and thrown into a hot fire to drive flies from an area with its smoke. There is a collection of dishes that process pumpkin elaborately. And, of course, there are simpler preparations rarely if ever recorded in writing because they were so elementary: dried pumpkin, baked pumpkin, boiled pumpkin. Of all pumpkin recipes associated with South Carolina, one stands foremost in its locality, its popularity, and its frequency of appearance in home recipe collections, the formula for preserved pumpkins called "pumpkin chips." Here are two recipes about sixty years apart.

Pumpkin Chips
Mrs. S. W. Boone (1855)

Take a good dry pumpkin, cut it up in large pieces, then plane or cut them into very thin and small. Squeeze the juice of one Lemon to every pound of the chips, put the juice on the chips, and let them lay one night. Boil the lemon skins until they are soft, and all the bitter out, then cut them into slips. Put one pound of sugar to one pound of chips. Boil the lemon skins in two waters, take the last water and boil it with the sugar until it makes a syrup, then put the chips and skins with the syrup and boil until crisp.

Pumpkins Chips
Kingstree County Record
(October 4, 1917)

Pare and scrape the pumpkin, cut into small squares about as thick as a knife blade, and after covering with its weight in granulated sugar, let it stand all night. There will be a syrup in the morning. Boil it all slowly until nearly tender, then add one lemon slice thin for each pound of pumpkin; cook until the pumpkin is clear; remove from the syrup and when the latter has boiled until it is thick pour it over the pumpkin and cool. [In the 1910s when fresh ginger became more available in the South Carolina markets, slices were added to the final mixture.]

Pumpkin Bread

Southern Gardener & Receipt Book (1860)

The pumpkin is first deprived of the rind, and afterward cut up into slices and boiled; when soft enough it is strained in a colander and mashed up very fine. In this state it may be used in pieces, or mixed with flour for pudding, cake, &c. If it be intended for bread, you may add a third or half as much wheat flour as pumpkins. The sponge must be first set in the ordinary way with yeast in the flour, and the pumpkin worked in as it begins to rise; use enough pumpkin as will bring the dough to a proper degree of stiffness without water. Care should be taken that the pumpkin is not so hot as to scald the leaven. It requires more baking than bread made entirely of wheat.

Pumpkin Pudding

Port Royal Standard & Commercial
(May 16, 1876)

Pare the pumpkin and put it down to stew, strain it through a colander; two pounds of pumpkin to one of butter, one pound of sugar, and eight eggs; beat to a froth; half wine; glass of rose water, one teaspoonful of mace, cinnamon, and nutmeg all together.

Southern Pumpkin Pie

Southern Gardener & Receipt Book (1860)

Take a brown earthen pan, grease it, and sift Indian-meal over it, about the thickness of a quarter of an inch. Prepare the [cooked] pumpkin in good new milk, sweeten to the taste, and add a little ground rice instead of eggs, with a little ginger. Bake.

Pumpkin Soup

Abbeville Press and Banner
(December 16, 1885)

Take three pounds of pumpkin; peel it and cut it into small pieces. Put it in a saucepan with water enough to cover it, adding a little salt; boil gently until it is soft, drain it and pass it through a fine colander, for it must not be watery. Put three pints of milk in a stewpan and mix with it the strained pumpkin; let it come to a boil; add a very little white sugar and salt and pepper to taste, and serve.

Punch

The social bowl—the centerpiece of the reception, the club celebration, the anniversary, the ball. Always iced, always sweetened with sugar or syrup, always brightened with the acid kiss of citrus, punch became a fixture in South Carolina entertainment during the colonial era. Each association had its own formula, and each formula called for one or another rare ingredients from around the globe that came into the port of Charleston. The Winyah Indigo Society was formed around a punch bowl in 1755, and its constitution required that the members partake at every club meeting. An early poem on punch elucidates this truth:

> Let me send him a formula, simple and
>   true,
> But requiring a genuine artist to brew.
> Batavian Arrack, of bottles take one;
> It has ripened and strengthened right
>   under the sun.
> Curacao of the Dutchman a small glass
>   put in,
> (As strong and as sweet and as subtle
>   as sin,)
> Of Claret six bottles, of Cognac take
>   two,
> And two pounds of sugar (about that)
>   will do.
> Let a fragment of ice ascend like a spire,
> That the strife elemental of cold and
>   of fire
> May go on in the bowl to add to the zest
> Lis a passionate soul in delightful
>   unrest!

After some debate about this formula, a supplement is suggested:

> I think you should put in some orange
>   in slices,
> And the rind of a lemon which also
>   quite nice is. (1866)

The theory of punch is simple: combine as many drugs as one can in one bowl: alcohol, sucrose, fructose, spice, caffeine (note the ubiquitous presence of tea in recipes before the Civil War). The nineteenth century added carbonation. Though Joseph Priestly discovered a method of carbonating water artificially in 1767, no Charleston supplier existed before Louis Y. Chupein in 1824. Carbonation was considered a drug for a long period of time because persons noted that a carbonated mixer got one drunk quicker than a non-carbonated mixer: "The Champagne Effect." They thought it was the chemistry—but the truth of the matter is that the gas in one's stomach builds pressure that forces alcohol into the bloodstream more rapidly.

In the earliest period of punch making, brandy and rum dominated the bowl. Whiskey and Champagne began to make inroads in the 1840s. Bourbon was the primary ingredient in classic Christmas punch, a holiday fixture by the 1860s, but in few other punches until the twentieth century.

Prior to the rise of the cocktail in the last decades of the antebellum period, punch was the most alcoholic amalgam of ingredients calculated for ready ingestion. Because it "went down easy" it gathered a particularly toxic reputation among temperance reformers in the nineteenth century. Consequently, great effort was expended to fashion non-alcoholic punches that might be consumed as substitutes on social occasions (sweet tea with lemon might be considered one of these). But well before Prohibition, sparkling grape juice punches found their way onto wedding reception tables. Ginger ale and ginger beer often provided the piquancy of these bowls.

Of the classic alcoholic punches, a number gained potent reputations: Charleston Light Dragoons Punch, Champagne Punch, Christmas Punch, St. Cecilia's Punch, West Indian Rum Punch (sometimes called Roman Punch), and Chatham Light Artillery Punch from Savannah. With the southern culinary revival of the 2010s, the Dragoon's Punch became a fixture at restaurants and cocktail bars, while St. Cecilia's Punch enjoyed popularity as an event bowl. The revivals tend to alter and "update" the old recipes, but the original should be mastered if one aspires to be an expert mixologist. Louis F. Sloan, steward of the Charleston Light Dragoons, prepared the punch from the end of the Civil War to the turn of the twentieth century. This was his formulation. It would have been based on brandy in the era before the war.

Charleston Light Dragoons Punch

Jacqueline Harrison Smith,
Famous Old Receipts (1908)

One and one half gallons (6 quarts) whiskey, 8 qts. Apollinaris, 2 lbs. sugar, 1 jar or 1 can Maraschino cherries, ½ doz. lemons, 1 can sliced pineapple, 1 small tumbler raspberry cordial. To mix these, first squeeze out the lemons and strain the pulp, and then put in about a quart of water, then 2 tumblers of sugar, stir thoroughly until the sugar is dissolved, then add the whiskey, then the cherries, then 2 pt. of "Jamaica rum," then add 5 qts. of Apollinaris. The other 3 qts. of Apollinaris add just before serving to produce an effervescent effect. It is necessary to stir the mixture the whole time it is being made, so it will blend properly. Throw 2 lemons thinly sliced on top of punch just before serving. Place a cube of ice in the bowl.

The recipe below is from *Charleston Receipts* (1950), but dates from before prohibition. No written copy of this recipe predates the twentieth century. The featuring of Champagne in the formula argues that its initial formulation postdates 1840.

St. Cecilia's Punch

The Junior League of Charleston,
Charleston Receipts (1950)

6 lemons, 1 quart brandy, 1 pineapple, 1½ pounds sugar, 1 quart green tea, 1 pint dark rum, 1 quart peach brandy, 4 quarts of champagne, 2 quarts carbonated Water. Slice lemons and cover with regular brandy, letting them steep for a day. An hour before serving slice and add to the brandied lemons. Then add sugar, rum, tea and peach brandy. When ready to service, fill bowl with ice, pour in carbonated water and champagne into your mixture.

Red Chicken Stew

Sumter is famous among lovers of South Carolina food as being the home of the Bradford Watermelon. It also boasts a second distinction, a one pot dish that proved the best alternative to chicken bog for people who did not like their chicken immersed in rice—red chicken stew. It, like chicken bog, could be cooked in the open air for events, but did just as well as a home dinner dish. It was popularized in the early twentieth century by barbecue master Yank Blanding (active 1910–1955), but was probably created earlier by George McKagen, both of Sumter.

Yank Blanding's Red Chicken Stew

McClellanville, S.C., Favorite Recipes (1956)

Take one fat hen, about 4 or 5 pounds, dressed (cut in pieces as if you were going to fry) and boil slowly, together with 3 or 4 large onions, cut fine, until meat leaves bones. Cool and remove bones. Add 3 or 4 hard cooked eggs, chopped fine, 3 or 4 Irish potatoes (cooked previously), 1 bottle catsup, salt and pepper to taste. Add above ingredients to cooked chicken and onions about ½ hour before serving and let come to a boil.

It should be observed that ketchup in the twenty-first century is substantially sweeter than it was early in the twentieth century, so you might substitute tomato paste for a portion of the ketchup bottle. Worcestershire sauce had become standard in Carolina stews by 1900, yet Blanding omits it from his version of the stew, a version that hews closely to the McKagen original. Blanding does add the detail that the hard-boiled eggs are to be chopped before being incorporated into the mix. Sumter native Nat Bradford told us, "this stew is unquestionably the food highlight of my childhood. It's what all my kids come home for." In 2015, Nat cooked a vat for the National Society of Landscape Architecture at its Chicago meeting. It created a sensation.

Red Horse Bread

The WPA Guide to Florida popularized the name hush puppy for a cornmeal fritter popular in the South. From the 1950s onward, the old Carolina name for the fritter—red horse bread—faded as newspaper reporters and roadside eateries embraced the story of barking dogs bribed to silence with deep fried corn batter bread. The problem with the old name was that it seemed a misnomer to begin with; there was nothing equine in its origins. Red horse bread had been named after a fresh water sucker fish nicknamed the red horse that was frequently fried, along with catfish and bream, at barbecues and fish fries. By mid-century, the red horse fish was already scarce in Carolina waters. It is now protected. Red horse bread was fried in the same cauldrons of boiling lard or peanut oil cooking the fish. It was served piping hot alongside the fish it had accompanied in the boiling fat.

There were distinctive features of the South Carolina version of the cornmeal fritter: it incorporated a great deal of black pepper; it was invariably made with white cornmeal mixed with wheat flour in a 2 to 1 ratio. Chopped cooked onion—and in the late twentieth century, bell pepper—was incorporated into the batter. Buttermilk became the liquid of choice to freshen the cornmeal batter.

The idea of a fritter composed of cornmeal and deep fried in lard was early American. Originally called "Indian Meal Fritters," recipes circulated in the 1800s century from Maine to Alabama. Christian Isobel Johnstone's recipe from 1847 provides a classic formula:

Indian Meal Fritters

Christian Isobel Johnston,
Treatise on Domestic Brewing (1847)

Beat four eggs very well, and mix with a pint of milk, into which stir gradually ten spoonsful of Indian meal. Work the mixture well till it is a smooth batter, when drop a ladleful at a time into half a pound of boiling lard in a deep frying pan. Lift out the fritters, when done, one by one with a perforated skimmer, and drain and serve hot and hot.

An eggless version using yellow cornmeal became significant in the period after the Civil War:

Corn Meal Fritters, without Eggs

Mrs. T. J. Crown,
American Lady's System of Cookery (1860)

Take a pint bowl of yellow corn meal, put to it a tablespoon of sweet butter, and a teaspoon of salt. Stir gradually into it enough boiling milk to make a thick batter; put a tablespoonful of sweet lard with a saltspoonful of salt, into a frying pan, let it become boiling hot, put in the batter by the tablespoonful, flatten it out to an even thickness, and let it fry gently until one side is a rich brown, then turn the other; when both are done, take them on a dish, and serve with a bit of butter and syrup or sugar over.

These traditional eastern recipes would be particularized in the late nineteenth century in South Carolina by event cooks such as Matt Brooks. In their hands, the addition of onion, black pepper, and in the 1930s, diced bell pepper made red horse bread distinctive. The preference of white cornmeal over yellow, the addition of flour to the formula, and eventually the adding of the egg and substitution of buttermilk for milk resulted in a fried bread of greater finesse than the old "yella meal" breads of the 1860s and 1870s.

Red Horse Bread

*Winter Cover Crop Experiments
at the Pee Dee Experiment Station (1933)*

2 cups enriched corn meal
1 tablespoon enriched flour [later
   recipes called for 1 cup of flour]

1 teaspoon soda
1 teaspoon baking powder
1 tablespoon salt
1 egg
6 tablespoons chopped onion
2 cups buttermilk

Mix all dry ingredients, add chopped onion, then milk and egg. Drop spoonfuls into deep hot grease where fish are cooking. When done they will float. Put on brown paper to drain.

While true red horse bread is still served at events in the Pee Dee in South Carolina, served by fish guides such as Furman Casey, it has given way to hush puppies in barbecue joints and southern family restaurants. What's the difference? The restaurants avoid the expense of the original red horse bread: instead of white cornmeal and buttermilk, they use yellow corn bread mix and boiling water or plain milk. Pepper is eliminated and sugar sometimes substituted.

Rice Bird

L. Prang & Co. "Bobolink or Rice-bird. Dolichonyx oryzivora. *1. Male in summer. 2. Male in winter. 3. Female.*" https://www.loc.gov/item/2003664028/.

Of the trio of migratory fowl that stood at the pinnacle of gastronomic glory for South Carolinians—the canvasback duck, the sora rail, and the rice bird—only the last cannot now be hunted. If one were to ask which lost food of our state is the most to be regretted, the answer must be the rice bird. Market gunning, greed, and the decline of the rice culture imperiled the population. Now the rice bird is an endangered and protected species.

Rice birds (Bobolinks) were the bane and glory of the Lowcountry rice plantation. Every September, clouds would congregate over the ripening fields of Carolina Gold Rice, descend, and fatten on the grain in preparation for their migration flight to South America. After they had gorged, they were among the tastiest of all birds. Whether baked in a pie or basted in butter and broiled on a spit, the rice bird was the delight of the autumn Charleston table.

The clouds of birds arrived in the rice fields of the Lowcountry on August 21. They would feed on ripening grains of Carolina Gold in the milk stage, building stores of fat. The last of the flocks would depart southward to the West Indies and South America in the third week of October. Planters always exaggerated the destruction wrought by the birds, claiming 50% loss of a crop. The maximum loss was probably around 30%, which was nevertheless substantial. After the Civil War, a class of Gullah hunter, called "minders," emerged. These were gunner-guardians of the rice fields. Armed with a musket, later a shotgun, and #10 shot, they fired into the flocks, killing as many as sixty birds per discharge. "Outside hunters are not permitted in the fields because the destruction of rice by careless walking would be too great. . . . A negro, knee-deep in mud and water, will make his way through the rice to the edge of a vast flock of the little birds which have descended like a cloud upon the grain, bending it down. The gunner is prohibited from shooting at the birds on the rice, for the shot cuts the stalks" (1896). The gunner shouts, the birds fly up, and he aims for the densest concentration above him, firing. The birds rain around him, easily spotted and picked up. These are turned over to the field owner, with payment pro-rated to the number of birds killed. Up until the 1880s, the bulk of the harvest was consumed locally.

Early birds were not "ripe"—for they had not fattened completely on the grain. It was the taste of the late September and October birds that became the stuff of legend. Gastronomes from the North reading rhapsodies about ripe rice birds from Carolina authors demanded to taste the bird. Here is a sample of the prose that sent northerners' gastric juices percolating: "The little rascal has such a richness

and delicacy of taste—he melts away in your mouth, so easily and satisfactorily, he is so juicy and nice, and his little bones offer so slight resistance to your masticating molars that if you are no planter, you forget his robberies" (1853).

Northern demand gave rise to two developments: the emergence of entrepreneurs such as Dan Crowley of Georgetown who organized the harvest and processing of birds, and the harvesting of birds by "pot hunting." No New York diner at Delmonico's wished to bite into a broiled rice bird and encounter lead shot. Crowley and others hired fleets of Gullah huntsmen to canoe through the rice fields at night, two men to a boat, one man bearing a torch and the other a bag. Stunned by the light and torpid with a day of feeding, the birds could be picked off the stalks where they roosted, necks wrung, and popped into a sack. Another method had the building of a fire on the verge of a field, the erection of banks of nets, and a group of noise-making "drivers" rouse a flock at night into flight; they would fly toward the light and get tangled in nets.

"The rice bird is justly famed as the most toothsome delicacy of the coast. Its fame is by no means confined to the coast country either, and no first-class restaurant in any large city thinks the bill of fare complete at this season of the years without the familiar announcement of 'rice birds on toast" (1894). How was this prepared? A devotee supplied a description in 1859 in the famous sportsman journal, *The Spirit of the Age:* "I know of no more recherché mode of cooking them than to place them in rows strung up before a moderate fire, and under them a dripping pan, well supplied with slices of toasted bread, to receive the rich and luscious drippings which flow and exude from them. Allow them to cook thus gently, occasionally turning, so as to have them not over-roasted, as to one's taste a small pinch of salt and of black pepper should be put into each bird." Another favorite dish was rice bird pie. The birds were placed in a pie pan with ½ pint of rice, ½ pint of milk, the yolks of two eggs, and seasonings. It was baked slowly over moderate heat until done.

At the dawn of the twentieth century Nicholas Sottile's Washington Square Café on the corner of Meeting and Chalmers streets in Charleston made broiled rice birds its signature dish. The favorite haunt of the city's politicians, Sottile's café dispensed untold thousands of birds during that heyday of market gunning. For those who lived in rice country, a tradition of rice bird feasts marked rice harvest season. The description of F. E. Johnstone's feast of 1902 on the Santee River, prepared by Gullah cook Susy Taylor and assistant Willis Small, tells of a culinary glory no longer to be had in the Lowcountry: "Here is the menu: rice, grown on the place, beat and cooked on the premises; sweet potatoes fried in rice bird oil; rice birds, fat, juicy and crisp; pure old rye, forty years old; port and sherry wine; segars [cigars] from Havana" (1952).

The decline of the rice birds was precipitous in the early twentieth century. Market gunning decimated populations. (In 1902, Dan Cowley, mentioned above, shipped six thousand dozen rice birds on ice to New York City and Philadelphia.) The mechanical mowing of hayfields in Canada where the birds nested wrought destruction as well. Finally, the decline and then collapse of commercial rice farming in South Carolina in the 1910s eliminated the food source upon which the migratory flocks depend. The birds still came, but fell on oats and other crops instead. The Audubon Society engineered a prohibition of shooting the rice bird on the eve of World War I. In 1919, permission was given to shoot but not sell the birds. This led to a strong resistance among old order planters and hunters, habituated to seeing the bird as the enemy of rice, and profiting from selling the birds on the eastern game market. They did not see that they were killing the golden goose. And as in so many cases regulation came too late. Historical circumstances also intervened. The automobile eclipsed the horse in the 1920s and horses became a surplus creation; their population dwindled. Less hay was needed to feed them. Fewer hayfields were planted. Fewer nest sites existed for the rice bird.

The rice bird is now a protected creature. When Carolina Gold began being grown again in the Lowcountry, it wasn't until 2009 when the first flock appeared, hovering over a ripening field, ready to feast. They have appeared regularly since that time.

Rice Bread

Loaf of rice bread prepared by baker Justin Cherry, Half Crown Bakehouse, Summerville, SC. This has the tradition four to one wheat flour and cooked rice mixture. David S. Shields.

What began as a matter of economy became in the course of time a matter of preference—the incorporation of cooked rice or rice flour into wheat flour breads. In the Lowcountry, rice bread stood foremost among the loaves at the table. It ruled from the dawn of the nineteenth century through the 1920s when the failure of the local rice plantations halted the local surplus of rice. As baker Michael Kalanty has shown, Carolina's famous rice bread had three ages and three recipes. The earliest, dominating the antebellum period, incorporated well-cooked rice middlins (broken rice, an offshoot of milling) into a wheat dough so that the rice composed approximately ¼ of the total mass; yeast would work on this dough and it would bake into a fine grained light loaf thought ideal for toasting. The following historical recipe captures the first kind of rice bread. It skips the step incorporating yeast into the dough to make the sponge.

Rice Bread

Charleston Courier (January 7, 1812)

As the article of bread is now a serious object in housekeeping, it may be acceptable piece of information to the public to learn, that many families have adopted the use of rice in making bread, in the proportion of one-fourth.—The rice is previously boiled for ten or twelve minutes in three times its weight in water, which is put to it cold. Thus ten pounds and half of flour, the quantity needed in three quarter loaves, when made into dough, with what the bakers call sponge, will knead up with 3½ pounds of whole rice so prepared, and produce will be six loaves, instead of three—herby a saving will be made of twopence in the quarten loaf valuing; the rice at sixpence per pound after paying the baker amply for trouble, the consumption of the corn will be reduced nearly one half. The bread is very palatable, and lighter and white than wheaten bread.

The second phase of rice bread replaced boiled rice with rice flour. Rice flour became an important item of commerce in the second quarter of the nineteenth century, esteemed particularly for crème de riz, out of which the French made refined sauces. Its lightness as a crust in fried fish and vegetables led to experiments with rice flour batters and the rice flour fritter—the puff—became fashionable. Once South Carolina mills began manufacturing it in quantity, experimental bakers such as John

C. H. Clausen attempted to formulate a more elegant form of rice bread using rice flour instead of boiled rice grains. The matrons of the Philadelphia Cooking School picked up these innovations and were teaching enrollees rice-flour bread through the 1850s and 1860s:

Superior Rice Bread

Mrs. Goodfellow's Cookery
as it Should Be (1865)

One quart of rice flour moistened with warm water; when well moistened, to prevent its being lumping, pour in two quarts of boiling water, and stir it while it boils; when quite cool add half a pint of good yeast, and one pint of new milk; if in summer the milk is always better boiled, to prevent it becoming sour; add a half teaspoonful of salt, then as much wheat flour as will make it the consistency for bread; set it to rise, when risen add a small quantity of sifted wheat flour. Bake in ordinary sized loaves, but be careful it is not too soft, as the bread will then be hollow.

The third phase of rice bread development took place in the latter half of the nineteenth century. Throughout the South, farmers grew soft winter wheat, not the hard wheats that stood at the head of European bread baking. Hence southerners developed a marked preference for the lighter texture quick breads and pastries than to the classic "wheaten loaf." Because the greatest innovation in baking goods with soft winter wheat during the century was the employment of chemical leavens—first salaeratus or baking soda—after 1856, baking powder—it was inevitable that fancy bakers began substituting quick rise agents for yeast in the rice flour/wheat flour rice breads. The matriarch of American cookbook writers in the antebellum period, Eliza Leslie, formulated a version of "Rice-Flour Bread" using rise agents:

Rice-Flour Bread

Miss Leslie's New Receipts (1854)

Sift into a pan a pint and a half of rice-flour, and a pint and a half of fine wheat-flour. Add two large table-spoonfuls of fresh butter, or lard; and mix in a pint and a half of milk. Beat four eggs, very light, and then stir them, gradually, into the mixture. When the whole has been well-mixed, add, at the last, a small tea-spoonful of soda, or sal-eratus, dissolved in as much warm water as will cover it. Put the whole into a buttered tin pan; set it, immediately, into a quick oven, and bake it well. It is best when eaten fresh. Slice and butter it.

In the 1800s, rice bread generated as many recipes as any food preparation in southern print and manuscript, except custard. By 1925, it had evaporated from the home keeping columns of newspapers and magazines. In part the disappearance of rice bread can be viewed as an off-shoot of the nationalization of milling in the United States, when roller mills processing Midwestern hard wheat made white bread cheap and plentiful. This began in the 1890s and amplified with the rise of chain groceries selling national brands in the early twentieth century. Rice was local, even parochial in the eyes of grocery Moghuls.

When the Carolina Gold Rice Foundation organized in 2005, a major culinary goal of its restoration of Carolina Gold was the revival of Rice Bread. Only since 2015 have bakers taken up the staple of Carolina tables making it available again.

Rye

Rye (*Secale sereale*), one of the four settler grains—the others are wheat, oats, and barley—conveyed from Europe to the Carolina colony in the seventeenth century, could grow on the poorest soil, and had the surest chance of making a crop. Sand dominated the coastal plain and much of the hill country in the midlands; wheat, barley, and most varieties of oats would not grow on ex-dunes. Rye would.

The rye varieties that came over from England and Europe in the colonial era derived from strains in Northern Europe. They were originally summer crops harvested in autumn. In the American South their cold tolerance enabled them to be grown as winter cover crops. Several varieties of rye came over prior to the founding of the United States, and two established themselves in South Carolina. In the mountain west a white tall growing rye dominated—"mammoth white rye." Along the coast a black seed variety prevailed. "Mountain rye" or "white rye" was the original whiskey rye of the American South. During Prohibition it became functionally extinct and was supplanted by Abruzzi Rye, a productive, robust variety found by USDA plant hunters in Italy in 1900 and promoted extensively by the Coker Seed Company of Hartsville, South Carolina. Black seed rye survived because it tolerated heat better than Abruzzi and became the favorite forage of piney woods and cracker cattle, hogs, and goats along the southeast coast.

In most parts of North America, rye bread would have been the chief preparation for eating the grain. In South Carolina, however, rye bread stood fourth behind rice bread, corn bread, and wheat bread in the preferences of the population. It was prepared at home by the German Americans of Orangeburg, the Dutch Fork, and in Charleston, and throughout the nineteenth century at least one baker in every city in the state offered rye bread. Sarah Rutledge included two recipes in *The Carolina Housewife* (1847), both containing sugar as an ingredient to counter the sour. If rye bread did not excite the generality of the population, there were other rye preparations that did: rye crackers, rye porridge, rye griddle cakes, and rye crust apple pie. The last became particularly cherished by some Carolinians. The crust was simple—an amalgam of rye flour and lard, three parts flour to one part lard, moistened with a little water and seasoned with salt.

Though rye pancakes are generally reckoned a Swedish preparation, they enjoyed a vogue in South Carolina, particularly in the Dutch Fork. Here is a Dutch Fork recipe:

Rye Pancakes
Abbeville Press and Banner
(January 18, 1888)

One cup of sour milk, one cup of flour, one cup of rye meal, four tablespoonfuls of molasses, one egg, and one small teaspoonful of saleratus; [baking soda]; drop from a spoon into hot lard, and fry like doughnuts.

Sarah Rutledge included a somewhat different formula for the pancakes in *The Carolina Housewife*: "Five spoonfuls of rye flour, three of wheat flour, two of corn flour, a very large spoonful of brown sugar, three eggs beaten

[153]

very light; mix into these milk enough to form a thin batter. Bake on a griddle, turning each. Butter while hot" (1847). She also included a popular and basic cracker recipe under the name 'rye wafers:' "Four spoonfuls of rye flour, one spoonful of butter, made into a very thin batter with water. Bake in the wafer iron. The same mixture, with the batter a little thicker makes nice waffles."

All of these dishes were formulated for South Carolina's signature rye, Seashore Black Seed Rye. Seashore Black Seed Rye has been part of planting schemes since 1831 when the *Charleston City* Gazette first advertised Carolina Seed Rye for sale in its pages. It had always been grown in modest amounts for winter grazing, for home milling, and for windbreaks. Both heat and cold tolerant, the grain was early maturing, coming to harvest in five months when it stood six feet high. Its stiff straw and tall habit made it an ideal windbreak planting for vegetable plots—tomatoes, strawberries, eggplants—that suffered from sandblasting near the coast where winds picked up particles from the beach. When the boll weevil made its march through the cotton lands in 1910, Seashore Black Seed Rye became the ideal rotation cover crop to repress the weevils. More productive than the other rye landraces, it could not produce as much as Abruzzi, or modern varieties. Its flavor, however, became particularly savored by cracker cattle and hogs in the southeast.

The preservation of the variety through late nineteenth and early twentieth centuries lay largely in the hands of two Carolina seedsmen: Alfred Jouannet (1861–1935), the French horticulturist and truck farmer who came to South Carolina in 1882, and William H. Mixson (1865–1933), founder of the Southern Fruit Company, and later Mixson Seed Company, one of the largest southern seed companies, operating wholesale and retail. Recent revival of interest in rye by millers and brewers can be attributed to Greg Johnsman of Marsh Hen Mill in Johns Island. It has been boarded on the Slow Food Ark of Taste, and is now used by bakers, restaurateurs, distillers, and brewers. On good land it produced about fifteen bushels of grain per acre. When introduced, Abruzzi could produce double the amount, but it did not prosper in the coastal zone where temperature change could be quick and extreme.

Rye berries from Greg Johnsman, Johns Island, SC. David S. Shields.

Scuppernong Grape

Scuppernongs and Muscadines are sold as single grapes, not in clusters. They appear at the end of July or the first week of August in produce stands across the state. David S. Shields, Cayce Farmer's Market, August 2018.

The beloved native grape of the Carolinas, the scuppernong, is sweet, large, round, aromatic, and chock full of seeds. Its thick skin, a liability in most grapes, was turned into a virtue by making it the substance of "hull pie." Ripening in the last week of July, the large globular fruit are easily plucked, making it the favorite native grape to hunt and pick by children. As a wine grape, it is sweet and fruity, rarely subtle when fermented, but when Prohibition was instituted in 1919, it became the widely used resource of home wine makers. Scuppernong wine retains a strong local following, particularly as a chilled summer glass. In the twenty-first century, the scuppernong's several culinary uses were supplemented by its

employment in cosmetics thanks to research by Clemson University.

Native to eastern North Carolina, the Scuppernong differed from its relative to the west, the muscadine, in the color of its berries—light, rather than dark like the muscadine. Both were strains of the *Vitis rotundifolia*, distinctive for its large round berries that do not cluster. Sweet and thick-skinned, the scuppernongs had been a Native staple and a resource for wildlife before settlers tried rendering it into wine, jelly, and pie. It was mentioned in the accounts of Sir Walter Raleigh's colony on the outer banks in the 1580s. The name derives from that of a river in Tyrell County, North Carolina, where the

A slice of hull pie, the traditional midlands pie made of scuppernong/muscadine grapes. Pie made by Wendy Eleazer of Elgin, SC. David S. Shields.

light-colored round grapes grow wild. It was the first native American grape to undergo formal cultivation.

In the 1870s, J. Van Buren supplied some pointers for identifying scuppernongs by their vines. "The wood or bark of the Scuppernong is of an ashy gray color, with numerous small specks of russet of a lighter color; the bark is smooth, and does not peel off in strips, as is the case with the other varieties of the grape; the wood is hard, and divided into joints from one to three inches in length; the growth is very rampant, but the shoots are small and wiry." Because of the difficulty of propagating Scuppernongs from vine cuttings, the vines were layered and the rooted segments trimmed off and transplanted. Seedlings from Scuppernongs tended to be varicolored.

In the wild, the berries grew to ¾ to 1¼ inches in diameter. Their form is invariably round, and their color dull yellow-green, spattered with russet dots. The skin tends to be both thick and tough, and the berry must be allowed to ripen fully, else it will be pulpy.

[156]

When ripening, the grapes exude a honeyed perfume that can make walking through a planting a heady experience.

Because scuppernongs and muscadines thrived in South Carolina, the State Agricultural commissioners were convinced that it would be the source of fortune to the state, promoting its employment in wine making particularly. After Ben Tillman instituted state control of alcohol with the Dispensary Bill of 1894, the state produced and distributed scuppernong wine. Grafton Vineyards outside of Columbia broke the state monopoly in 1898 by producing sweet scuppernong wine. Bear's scuppernong wine was the most popular brand in South Carolina in the early twentieth century, available in most cities and towns until Prohibition. It hailed from Wilmington, North Carolina. During this period, South Carolina grapes were shipped as far as Missouri for wine making. As of 2020, several Carolina vineyards offer scuppernong wine: Deep Water Vineyard in Charleston uses the Tara variety to make a "smooth white wine"; Three Star Vineyard in Johnston uses very sweet scuppernongs; Victoria Valley winery in Cleveland, South Carolina makes wine in which the sweetness is not overwhelming; and Hyman Vineyards in the Pee Dee makes wine from muscadines, sharing its light bronze color.

Hull Pie became a signature dish of the South Carolina midlands in the 1890s. Made with a bottom crust and a lattice top, it employed both the skins (hulls) and seeded pulp of two cups of scuppernong grapes. The skins are usually simmered in water for 10 minutes; the pulp is boiled for half that time, drained, and mashed. The hulls and pulp are then mixed with sugar—¼ cup minimum (some use more), ½ tablespoon of butter, cinnamon, and salt. Those who like really tart pie add 1½ teaspoons of lemon juice. Into this mixture add 2 tablespoons of cornstarch and enough water to give supply some thickness. Pour onto a pie crust, put lattice on top, and bake at 400°F for 25 minutes.

Even more popular than Hull Pie was scuppernong jelly, which became such an iconic state dish that it was a category in the jellies and preserves judging in the South Carolina State Fair in 1880 and has remained a fair fixture up to 2020.

Shad

"The difference between shad and oysters is marked. As a rule the oyster carries his bones outside of himself. The shad's boneyard is within." (1887)

Along the East Coast, the shad run was an annual event in every river system from Florida to New England. The plentitude of fish supported many coastal Native communities with a spring supply of protein. During the colonial era of settlement, it was the most dependable fish run of the year, and a recurring source of sustenance and profit. While cod may have propped up New England, shad supplied the entire eastern seaboard.

Each region had its favorite shad preparations: planked shad, baked shad, poached shad, and from South Carolina to Virginia, corned shad. Shad Roe was universally craved. The fish's popularity led to protective legislation shortly after the Civil War prohibiting the stretching of gill nets blocking the entire expanse of a river preventing their spawning upstream. Fisherman colluded, however, to circumvent the law. In 1904, the South Carolina legislature threatened to shut down the fishery at Georgetown on the Santee because of its penchant for taking every fish in the river. In the 1870s, the Geechee fisherman on the Savannah faced a similar threat of state action in Georgia. The first experiments in running a shad nursery using live roe shad date from 1878 because of the decline on the Savannah and associated rivers. From ancient days roe shad commanded higher prices than buck shad.

The American shad (*Alosa sapidissima*) is a notoriously boney and flavorful fish. Weighing from three to eight pounds when running, these members of the herring family school in the ocean and run into the rivers of the East Coast to spawn in winter. Those in northern rivers can survive breeding, return to the ocean, and breed several times. The southern shad, not so. Running shad can travel great distances upstream provided there are few encumbrances. Caught Commercially in nets, sportsmen pursue the fish with rod, line, and spoon. There are few winter sights so humorous on the southern rivers than a pelican scooping up a shad and trying to control its thrashing in its bill pouch.

Boning shad is an art. The inability of fish handlers to debone shad resulted in decades of waste in the industry in the early and mid-twentieth century when buck shad were discarded and roe shad split, the roes removed, and the meat handed over to the fertilizer industry. Attempts to dissolve the bones by vinegar baking or salt crusting the fish only accomplish the degradation of the skeleton by cooking the fish to dissolution—not the most elegant treatment. If you have a fishmonger with a talented boner or have trained yourself by following online videos and purchasing thin flexible boning knives, you can enjoy the splendid taste of filleted shad.

Shad has a distinctively piquant flavor that has long stimulated the imaginations of chefs up and down the eastern seaboard. The Lowcountry had one preparation that the chefs at the Astor Hotel, Sherry's, and Delmonico's

[158]

TASTE THE STATE

Planked shad roasting beside open fire at the Pee Dee Shad festival, 2019. David S. Shields.

never attempted, and it may the best tasting of all shad preparations—corned shad. Boned fillets are salted, sugared, and peppered, left in the refrigerator overnight to cure, and broiled the next day. Here is a classic recipe from Mrs. Sarah Elliott, a boardinghouse keeper in Oxford, North Carolina:

Corned Shad

Mrs. Elliott's Housewife (1870)

Clean and split open a fresh shad, mix one teaspoonful of cayenne pepper and one of brown sugar, lay the shad open on a flat dish and rub it gently on the inside with the pepper and sugar. Next morning broil it nicely and put bits of butter on it.

Baked Shad with Roes

Felix Déliée,
Franco-American Cookery (1884)

Procure one roe-shad and the roe of another; scale, pare, and cleanse nicely; bestrew a buttered baking-dish with chopped onions and parsley; make a lengthwise, deep incision on each side of the fish, put in the dish with the second roe, and add more chopped onion and parsley, salt, pepper, two glasses of white wine, half a pint of white broth, and small bits of butter; put in a moderately heated oven, baste the fish once in a while, and cook for half an hour; drain and thicken the gravy with a tablespoonful of flour kneed with butter; slit the second roe and put it lengthwise on the fish; pour the sauce over, besprinkle with fine bread-crumbs, and small bits of butter on top and bake fifteen minutes longer, till slightly browned; press the juice of a lemon over, and serve in the baking-dish.

Fried Shad

A Lady of Philadelphia,
The National Cook Book (1856)

Cut your shad in half, wash it and wipe it dry, score it and season with cayenne pepper and salte, dredge flour over it, and fry it in hot lard. When done, put the two halves together, that it may assume the appearance of a whole fish.

While kitchen preparations were all well and good, most favored shad prepared in the open air, nailed to planks and tilted before an open fire. The method was Native, learned by Carolinians from the Santee people in the seventeenth century. Families or communities or associations convened in March or early April on the banks of rivers, holding a "shad bake." The shad bake remains a spring tradition in the Pee Dee in South Carolina. The accompaniments to the fish are rice, pickles, and red horse bread/hush puppies.

She-Crab Soup

Before we discuss this famous Charleston soup, we must understand what a she-crab is. It is a female crab that is carrying an abundance of eggs or roe. When incorporated into a dish, crab roe makes a noticeable difference in richness and flavor from a dish made exclusively of crab meat. Roe is seasonal and may be difficult to get.

She-crab soup resembles a bisque, which classically was thickened with pureed, cooked rice. It is made of milk, crab or fish stock, crab meat of course, and the unique, defining ingredient, the roe of female crabs. The soup is finished with a splash of sherry or madeira. Some recipes include mace, shallots, or onions. Originally a Lowcountry dish, its popularity has spread to Tidewater Virginia and Maryland.

William Deas, one of "the great cooks of the world," created she-crab soup early in the twentieth century while working as a butler and cook for the Goodwyn Rhett family. According to legend, he fashioned it in the spur of the moment while preparing a meal for President Taft during his tour of South Carolina in 1909. It became a fixture at Rhett's dinner parties, served to visiting celebrities and most of Rhett's neighbors South of Broad. Helen Woodward, who gathered recipes for the Rhett family cookbook, writes that Deas could be heard in the streets of Charleston singing about his soup. Because Deas was one of two African American informants for Blanche Rhett when she compiled *200 Years of Charleston Cooking* (1930), the recipe appeared in that famous collection.

After leaving the service of the Rhett family shortly before the Second World War, Deas became chef at Everett's restaurant. In 1951 to 1952, owner Everett C. Presson launched a publicity campaign highlighting Deas and his soup. It would be the first time since the death of William Barron in 1900 that an African American restaurant chef would be celebrated in the Charleston press. The campaign made the soup a signature of Charleston cuisine. He would continue to prepare it at the restaurant until his death in 1961. The soup has remained in the repertoire of Carolina cooks and spread throughout the South.

Anyone making the soup today would benefit by using prepicked canned crabmeat, though the joy in making the soup comes from picking the meat fresh after boiling a great big pot of crab. You can also find a popular canned variety from the Blue Crab Bay Co. This is a condensed soup brand that contains the she-crab roe in it. Another popular brand amongst southerners was Boone's Foods Harris She-Crab Soup, but unfortunately it is no longer in production.

She-Crab Soup

KEVIN MITCHELL

6 tablespoons butter

1 cup minced celery (see note)

1 cup minced onion (see note)

1 cup minced fennel (see note)

1 cup all-purpose flour

2 cups clam juice, room temperature

2 cups crab stock (if not available use clam juice or seafood stock)

4 cups milk, room temperature

1 tablespoon fresh lemon juice

1 bay leaf

3 ounces dry sherry, or to taste

½ teaspoon ground nutmeg

¼ cup heavy cream

¾ cup blue crab roe, picked over to remove cartilage, shell, or other matter

1 pound lump crabmeat, gently picked over for shell and drained

Salt to taste

White pepper to taste

2 tablespoons sliced chives or chopped parsley to garnish

Heat the butter in a heavy-bottomed saucepan over medium heat without browning. Add the onions and celery and cook for 1 to 2 minutes, or until the onion is translucent. Sprinkle in the flour while stirring to make a roux. Cook over low heat for 2 to 3 minutes to cook out some of the starchy flavor of the flour.

Whisk the crab stock or clam juice, if not using crab stock, into the warm roux. Increase the heat to medium-high. Whisk vigorously as the clam juice thickens and is smooth. Run a rubber spatula around the inside corners of the saucepan to release any lumps of roux. Whisk in the milk, and allow the mixture to re-thicken, whisking until smooth again. Simmer 1 to 2 minutes. Add the lemon juice, bay leaves, sherry, nutmeg, and cream. Let simmer lightly for 10 to 15 minutes, stirring occasionally. Remove the bay leaves and discard. Add the roe and crabmeat just before service. Leave crab as lumpy as possible. Add the salt and white pepper to taste.

Ladle the bisque into warmed bowls and garnish with chives or parsley and a few additional drops of sherry.

Note: Mince the onion, celery, and fennel by pulsing in a food processor with a steel blade. Be careful not to overchop them, which will result in mush. I add fennel to the classic recipe because it gives the soup a balanced flavor and goes well with sherry.

Sheepshead

Black fish was the money fish. Whiting was the breakfast fish. Grouper was the stew fish. And sheepshead was the dinner fish. It was curious in habit and appearance—oval-bodied, striped vertically with six bars, and equipped with four incisor-like teeth used to nibble barnacles and crunch crustacean shells. It could grow to over two feet in length, but adults averaged a shade over a foot long. It haunted the coasts, congregating at pilings and jetties. It could be found up brackish estuaries, feeding at oyster rocks and piers. In the early twentieth century, poles were erected at creek mouths, called sheepshead racks, to attract the fish. It became a favorite catch for city anglers. Not a schooling fish, they sometime aggregated in small groups, but were mostly solitary. Fiddler crabs were the traditional bait and long bamboo poles that could drop the bait over jetty rocks were crafted by Gullah watermen in the nineteenth century.

In the early twentieth century, Charleston postmaster Joseph M. Poulnot became an angling legend for his ingenuity in hooking sheepshead. He would imbed the hook into the claw of his live fiddler crab bait and train the crabs to brandish the claw to hook the fish (1916). In 1915, he and two companions caught twenty-eight Sheepshead averaging over two feet in length from a boat on the front beach of Sullivan's Island in the course of three hours.

Not a migratory fish, Sheepshead is present in Carolina's waters year round, and so is the highest quality local protein that could be put on the table any day of the year. Needless to say, a well-developed repertoire of sheepshead dishes arose in the state. One of the oldest dishes had the sheepshead poached in a tomato and cayenne tinged broth. Sheepshead was battered and crisp fried in lard, or sautéed in butter. The heads were low boiled to a gelatinous texture and use to suspend poached pieces of

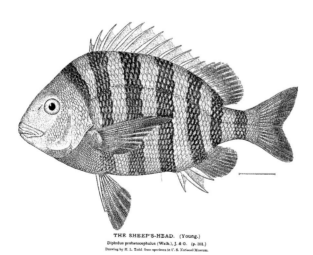

THE SHEEP'S-HEAD. (Young.)
Diplodus probatocephalus (Walb.), J. & G. (p. 381.)
Drawing by H. L. Todd from specimen in U. S. National Museum.

H. L. Todd, engraving of the Sheepshead from vol. 2 [illustrations] of George Brown Goode, The Fishes and Fishery Industries of the United States *(Washington, DC: GPO, 1887).*

the fillets. At the hotels it was served with cardinal sauce and with a cream sauce. Here is a recipe associated with Charleston's great French chef Francois Beylot of the Pavilion Hotel in the 1880s: "Poach a cleaned sheepshead in mirepoix stock. Adorn with steamed shrimp and poached oysters. Add tomato puree to béchamel sauce, add salt, cayenne, and lemon juice, dress with tarragon." (n.d., private collection)

During the same decade, the fish gained admirers among the haute cuisine chefs in New York. It appeared regularly on the menus of Delmonico's, Sherry's, and the major hotels. Felix Déliée, in his 1884 classic *Franco-American Cookery*, offered versions that reflected the treatments characteristic of: Carolina; Georgia; Mobile, Alabama; and Louisiana. The Mobile version used garlic, a fish broth, wine, sweet chili pepper, and a white sauce. The Georgia version used tomatoes, onion instead of garlic, a plethora of green peppers, and Espagnole sauce. Louisiana employed a creole sauce. Here is the Carolinian method according to Déliée.

Sheep's-Head a la Caroline

Felix Déliée,
Franco-American Cookery (1884)

Select a large and thick sheep's head; cleanse, pare off the fins, make a deep lengthwise incision to the bone on each side; place on a buttered dish-pan with salt, pepper, chopped shallot, green pepper, a bunch of parsley, two ounces of butter, a half pint of white wine, and a pint of water or light broth; cover with a buttered paper, boil, and cook in a moderate over for forty minutes, taking care to baste often with the liquid; strain the liquid in a saucepan, thicken with an ounce of flour kneaded in butter, boil five minutes, finish with four ounces of butter, lemon-juice, and chopped parsley; slide the fish on a dish, pour the sauce over, surround with a dozen tomatoes stuffed a la Carolina, and serve. The Carolinian style tomatoes are stuffed with rice, seasoned and baked.

Sheepshead remains a staple of the local seafood menu. Because it is difficult to catch, it has not suffered from the overfishing that has diminished the populations of many food fish. If you are an angler, it remains the best challenge you can have pier fishing at Folly Beach or winter fishing on the blackfish banks. The current catch limit in South Carolina is ten per person or fourteen per boat, per day. Fish larger than fourteen inches must be returned to the sea.

Shrimp and Grits

Shrimp and grits, while originating in the Reconstruction era in the Lowcountry, has become a southern dish. Freezing and speedy transportation have made shrimp widely available. Every region of the South grows and processes grits corn. Consequently, local variants of the dish have proliferated everywhere in the South. The range of preparations is well registered in Nathalie Dupree and Marion Sullivan's 2014 cookbook, *Shrimp and Grits*. The original dish was simple: a bed of white grits, and peeled boiled shrimps laid upon it, napped with shrimp gravy (see gravy entry for recipe). Originally it was breakfast. Nowadays it can be any meal, but most frequently it appears on the lunch and dinner menus.

Shrimp and grits is the name used since Bill Neal, chef of Crook's Corner restaurant in Chapel Hill, North Carolina repurposed the old Lowcountry breakfast as an entrée in the 1980s. *New York Times* critic Craig Claiborne's 1985 write up of the dish ignited interest for the old Lowcountry breakfast dish shrimp and hominy. The printed recipe revealed that Neal had switched out the old pristine white flint hominy grits with a mid-twentieth century favorite, cheese grits. In Charleston, where memories are long and no senior diner would abide cheese in their shrimp and hominy, Donald Barickman restored the classic white hominy grits base but borrowed the idea of serving the dish for dinner and Neal's name for it to make "Shrimp and Grits" the signature dish of Magnolias Restaurant, the eating establishment that heralded the revival of Charleston's dining scene after hurricane Hugo in 1989.

How did the dish originate? There is no documentation, but one can surmise that it developed from the earlier dish, shrimp and rice with shrimp gravy (the Lowcountry version of Shrimp Creole), with a substitution of the Lowcountry's second most popular milled grain (corn) for its first most popular (rice). It may be that the disruption of rice production during the Civil War occasioned this substitution, for corn requires less labor and attention to grow than rice. At any rate, the first mentions of shrimp and hominy are all post–Civil War. (See Hominy Grits for more.)

Prior to the First World War, the shrimp was purchased from ambulatory vendors who roamed the streets of cities at daybreak, crying out the availability of shrimp. Some of these hucksters became celebrities—Joe Cole "The Shrimp Fiend" sang his famous song in an earth-rattling bass voice:

> Swimmy, swimmy, swimp,
> Raw, Raw, swimp.
> want you all to member.
> We'se got tell September.
> So come and get yo raw, raw swimp.
> Raw, raw, sprawn, wid shooger een he
>   hawn.

Cole secured shrimp freshly offloaded from the night fishing shrimpers at the docks, arrayed them on a tray perched on his head, and called the cooks out of the house to buy a plate. There were three types of shrimp: chicken shrimp (small, cheap, and second rate), river shrimp (medium-sized, flavorful, and often preferred), and ocean shrimp (big, meaty, and robustly flavored).

An 1888 news article from the *Charleston News and Courier* indicates that in its original form, the boiled shrimp was prepared separately from the hominy grits and served on top of them at the table: "The long elliptical dish in the centre of the table, with its sides overrunning with the pretty little pink crescent-shaped fish is the cynosure of all eyes, and as the pater familias doles out the regulation amount for each plate of hominy the eyes of the children glisten and the death-like stillness that ensues bears witness to their love for their breakfast." An article two years earlier about the shrimp business in Charleston noted "the local partiality for hominy and shrimps" (1892).

Local pride in shrimp and hominy became pronounced in the 1880s. A newspaper commentator opined that the average Charlestonian startled awake by the raucous call of a 6:00 a.m. street vendor had a better morning ahead of him than a New York millionaire, for the Lowcountry citizen "will have a breakfast of hominy and shrimps and . . . even Vanderbilt and his $10,000 cook are in that one particular poorer than any man in Charleston, For neither Mr. Vanderbilt nor his $10,000 artist can get up a shrimp breakfast ("as she is cooked" in Charleston) at the frozen North. It is admitted that there are no shrimps in America at least that can compare with the Charleston shrimp in delicacy of flavor or in tenderness of flesh" (1888).

Shrimp and hominy were celebrated as iconic Charleston fare in Blanche Rhett's classic 1930 compendium, *200 Years of Charleston Cooking*. It supplied the first recipe to appear in print. Her version derived from the celebrated African American chef, William Deas. From 1930 until the 1980s, shrimp and hominy would be recalled as one of the old, cherished dishes, invariably prepared at home, never at an eatery. A curious irony is that shrimp fritters (shrimp deep fried in a batter made of hominy grits) made a regular appearance on restaurant menus.

Rare no longer, shrimp and grits ranked in the top five most frequently served southern restaurant dishes in 2020.

Shrimp Paste

A pâté of ground mashed shrimp has become a standard company dish of Lowcountry entertaining. Before Carolinians began making their own, they imported Dinsmore's Shrimp Paste, a British form of potted shrimp generally available in groceries from 1835 onward as a sandwich spread. S. H. Oppenheim's store on King Street opposite The Citadel (when it was on Marion Square) had it in stock during the antebellum period, albeit under its southern nickname "Dinmou's Shrimp Paste." In the post-bellum period, a second form, incorporating anchovy in the paste as well as shrimp, joined Dinmou's classic style.

Carolinians began making local versions as early as the 1840s. At first they called the preparation potted shrimp—there were two sorts, one in which whole small shrimps were boiled then preserved by pouring melted butter over them and letting it solidify. This version is no longer prepared. The second version is the ancestor of the southern entertainment dish and sandwich spread. It appears in Sarah Rutledge's *The Carolina Housewife* in 1847. We should observe that a parallel dish "Potted Crabs" appeared in the earlier *Carolina Receipt Book* of 1832. Crab paste has not survived as an entertainment staple.

To Pot Shrimp

Sarah Rutledge,
The Carolina Housewife (1847)

Pick the shrimps after they are boiled from the shells; beat them well in a mortar, and put as much melted butter to them as will make them of the proper consistence to be pressed compactly together; add pepper, salt, mace and nutmeg to the taste; put the mixture in small pans, and pour melted butter over them about quarter of an inch thick. If wanted for immediate use, grated bread may be added.

The evolution from potted shrimp to shrimp paste occurred when cooks realized that incorporating the butter into the paste had the same preservative effect and imparted a creamier texture to the pâté. During the Charleston Renaissance of the 1910s to 1920s, women decided that shrimp paste was a signature local dish. It went from an ordinary household item to part of the local culinary mystique. One of the Renaissance matrons, Minnie Pringle, supplied a recipe for the new form of paste:

Shrimp Paste

Minnie Pringle,
Charleston News and Courier
(February 15, 1929)

Pound to a fine paste one plate of boiled shrimps, rub in one half pound of butter, one grated nutmeg, dash of cayenne pepper and salt to taste. Mix thoroughly, cover with cracker crumbs and brown in oven if wanted cold, serve in slices.

[167]

The idea of spicing this paste with an entire nutmeg is unthinkable. Some groceries broke whole nutmegs into sections and one purchased fragments—as one did with mace if not ground. Perhaps Pringle meant one section of nutmeg.

Blanche Rhett's *200 Years of Charleston Cooking* (1930) included a different recipe, obtained from Mrs. C. Norwood Hastie, served as a cold entrée that added Worcestershire sauce, French mustard, vinegar, and red pepper to the mash. After World War II, Carolina Recipes Inc. began selling Charleston Shrimp Paste in glass jars. To promote the product, it advertised a $125 prize for the best suggestions about how to serve Charleston Shrimp Paste. Home cooks in the post-war period began experimenting with the addition of sherry or madeira into the shrimp matrix. The laced pastes were used exclusively for evening entertainment. The alcohol-free version was standard for club meetings and children's sandwiches.

Shrimp Pie

In 1894 a newspaperman asked what was Lowcounty cuisine? A colleague humorously recited the repertoire of dishes: "swimp pate, swimp salad, swimp au mayonnaise, swimp pilau, swimp au naturel, oyster on the half shell, clam chowder, broiled whiting, stone crab stew, baked drum, ragout de trotteir, baked bass, boiled sheephead." When shrimp came into season, it appeared at every meal on the coastal table. Whether the poor family who cast nets in the tidal creeks or a south-of-Broad aristocrat whose house servant purchased a plateful of heads on shrimp for 5 cents from a street vendor, the Lowcountry eater regularly consumed the crustaceans from the second week in May through October, and with luck, through November.

At breakfast, shrimp might appear in simple dress: boiled, headed, shelled, and served "with a sprinkling of pepper." Huguenot French Charlestonians had a method of stewing them with tomatoes or of serving them in a combination with bell peppers, an early manifestation of the classic *Vol-au-Vent de Chevrettes.*) But there was one shrimp dish that inspired more delight than shrimp and grits on the morning table—shrimp pie.

Shrimp pie once rivaled eggs and bacon as a breakfast staple. In old Charleston it was considered the "most important adjunct of the boarding houses of the city" (1877). Shrimp pie was the ideal morning dish since it could be prepared the night before and left unrefrigerated in a pantry for morning consumption. While appearing on city sideboards in Savannah and Charleston from the early republic, the dish appears to have been perfected as a banquet and event dish by the talented African American chef Nat Fuller, who featured it in his famous Charleston restaurant, the Bachelor's Retreat. During Reconstruction, Torck's Restaurant advertised it for lunch, serving it in conjunction with oyster or cooter soup, boiled mutton, and seasonal fried fish. The dish migrated from breakfast to lunch, dinner, and even banquet suppers during the latter half of the nineteenth century. The spicy Lowcountry pie perfected by Fuller diverged from the English shrimp pie found in many late eighteenth-century and nineteenth-century cookbooks, a pie that included anchovies and white wine. Fuller dispensed with both and decreased the amount of mace and nutmeg spicing the mixture. The "Shrimp Pie" found in the 1855 edition of *The Carolina Housewife* stood half-way between the London pie and Fuller's:

Shrimp Pie

Sarah Rutledge,
The Carolina Housewife (1855)

Have a large plate of picked shrimp; then take two large slices of bread, cut off the crust, and mash the crumb to a paste with two glasses of wine and a large spoonful of butter; add as much pepper, salt, nutmeg, and mace as you like; mix the shrimps with the bread, and bake in a dish or shells. The wine may be omitted, and the bred grated instead.

This pie would in the course of time transmute, with cooked rice supplanting the soaked bread, an addition of chopped onions, and individual flavoring with either bacon, hard-boiled eggs, or celery. Restaurateurs would in the latter portion of the twentieth century, add eggs to this basic pie formula. We can see the cooked rice and eggs approach in the *Charleston Receipts* recipe for "James Island Rice Pie."

A second version of the pie elaborated the Huguenot shrimp and tomatoes theme, adding the bell peppers, sometimes bacon, and thickening with catsup. Vinegar or lemon juice supplanted wine among those with temperance scruples. Cayenne took the place of mace and nutmeg. This Frenchified and Creolized version approximates that which Nat Fuller served. Immediately after the Civil War, Mrs. A. P. Hill published a version of this piece, which included macaroni as a novelty:

Shrimp Pie

*Mrs. Hill's Practical Cookery
and Receipt Book* (1872)

To two quarts of peeled shrimps add two tablespoonfuls of butter, half a pink of tomato catsup, half a tumbler of vinegar; season high with black and cayenne pepper; salt to taste; put into an earthen dish; strew grated biscuit or light bread crumbs very thickly over the top; bake slowly half an hour. This may be varied by using Irish potatoes boiled and mashed; in place of bread crumbs; or use a layer of shrimps, then macaroni, previously soaked in hot sweet milk.

A family of shrimp and corn pies grew up in the last half of the nineteenth century as new sweet corn varieties suited for southern cultivation became available. This family of pies often used an egg base, sometimes incorporated some cheese, and occasionally tomatoes.

Shrimp pie has always been a signature Lowcountry dish, and the number of versions that have developed attest to the firm grip it retains on the imaginations of the region's cooks.

Soft-Shelled Crabs

Coastal South Carolina enjoys the summer bounty of the Atlantic Blue Crab *Callinectes sapidus* and shares with Tidewater, the Outer Banks, and East Florida a rich set of foodways around this delectable crustacean. Some would put Daufuskie crab cakes up against the vaunted cakes of Crisfield and Baltimore, Maryland. The crab salad found on luncheon menus in Charleston's Hotels rivals that of any Richmond restaurant or DC seafood house. Perhaps the most distinctive dish to South Carolina is Crab Pilau (see recipe in entry on Pilau), which has enjoyed a resurgence of popularity in the restaurant world as Gullah Crab Rice.

Charleston does feature significantly in seafood history for one important development connected with crabs—Charles C. Leslie, the African American director of the Fish Market in the 1870s and 1880s, established the first southern "farm" for soft-shelled crabs in Mount Pleasant. In a salt-water enclosure he collected all of the peeler crabs brought in by the mosquito fleet, insuring that he had a constant supply for hotels, restaurants, and private customers during the period from March to June. He would wait until they molted their old shell and collected the vulnerable "softies" almost immediately.

Leslie was able to erect a workable soft crab nursery because he had the counsel of the foremost ichthyologists in the United States. For years he had supplied specimen fish to marine biologists for their study and hosted them on their expeditions to the southeastern coast, taking them out on his fishing vessel, the *Thomas R. Crocker.* Leslie's name appears in credit lines on specimen labels in many old,

established university and museum fish collections. In return for his specimens, service, and knowledge, the ichthyologists laid out the design and method for a successful soft-shelled crab nursery, and Leslie brought it into being in spring 1886.

Early on, consumers realized that it did not do one's stomach any favors to eat a soft-shelled crab that was long dead. Until the perfection of freezer technology in the 1950s, it was a product that was kept alive, if at all possible, until the moment of cooking. If blue crabs were cooked by tossing them live into boiling water, the soft-shelled crab was washed in batter and cooked in boiling fat, or hot butter. The habit in seasoning the soft crab was to employ a good deal of pepper. Folk wisdom said that one did not drink milk after eating fried soft-shelled crabs.

At various times during the twentieth century, no organized soft-shelled crab nursery existed in the state, and the major restaurants had to depend upon out-of-state supply. William H. Magwood provided a reliable supply in the 1930s. In 1979, John Reynolds and Jim Llewellyn established a nursery on Bohicket Creek that supplied McCabe's, Rast's, and other Charleston area seafood houses of the early 1980s. Crosby's Seafood pioneered the selling of frozen and fresh soft-shelled crabs in that same decade.

At the mid-twentieth century seafood houses the methods of preparation tended to be simple: one could batter dip and deep fry the crabs (a rice flour and beer batter vied with cornmeal and buttermilk batter), one could season and pan fry them in butter or lard with batter, or plain with seasoning, and one could grill the crabs with a coating of oil, salt, and pepper. Home cooks tended to use an egg and bread crumb or cracker crumb coating before pan frying in lard or butter. One Gullah tweak on frying is to add a small amount of pickle juice to the pan liquids to bump up the flavor.

There are a few rules about prepping soft-shelled crabs at home. One must trim out the gills "dead man fingers" on both sides of the apron. They are easily accessed once one has removed the underside flap. One must wash the crabs carefully before cooking. One must discard any that have died and are producing an odor. If you are using frozen crab, lay it in warm water while still in its saran wrap covering until it has begun to defrost.

The "softies" that appear on the Carolina markets in mid-March stay on restaurant menus all over the Lowcountry and in inland cities until mid-June. If restaurants are serving soft-shelled crabs at other times of the year, they most likely are using frozen product.

Sugar sorghum came to South Carolina in 1853 when Governor James Henry Hammond planted fifteen strains of this cousin of sugarcane at Redcliffe plantation. The seed had been brought by Lawrence Wray from Natal, South Africa. More cold tolerant than sugar, these tall juicy grasses promised to grow well in the upstate of Carolina where even robust Purple Ribbon sugarcane failed because of freezes. All fifteen strains prospered and his distribution of sorghum seed assisted in rehabilitating his reputation in the state, tarnished by his sexual abuse of four teenage nieces. The sap of the sorghum, boiled down, produced a dulcet syrup; but its chemistry inhibited the refinement of the juice into granular sucrose. Hence sorghum syrup would be the end product of sorghum processing ever after, particularly when sugar beets were found to generate granular sucrose without great difficulty.

The Civil War turned sorghum from a niche product to a commodity crop. After the secession of the Confederate states, the North lost access to cheap sugar. Sugarcane was not cold tolerant. Sorghum could grow as far North as southern Michigan. In 1863, Louisiana sugar was cut off from the rest of the South. Everyone began planting sorghum in the North and the South. Its versatility as a commodity became apparent after mass planting. The leaves could be used for forage. The grain could be milled for flour or used as fowl feed. Certain of the fifteen varieties (the White African "enyama imphee" for instance) had grain of such quality that it could be boiled and consumed like millet—a preparation known as Guinea Corn in the Lowcountry and the West Indies. Sorghum beer and sorghum whiskey

(called sucrat) sprang into being. The seeds were roasted and ground to make a not-too-savory form of coffee (okra seeds did better). All of the range of applications were pushed into practice by the Civil War. A reporter revealed how wartime conditions fueled the mass adoption of sorghum.

> At home and abroad, sorghum came to take the place of the vanished sugar. The children at home ate it in their ginger cakes, and the soldiers in camp drank it in their rye-coffee. The molasses and sugar of Louisiana were procurable in degree till the fall of Vicksburg; but the spirit of independence was rife, and each State desired and determined to rely as much as possible on its own products. The theory of State sovereignty was extended even to sorghum; and its introduction was hailed everywhere as one of the greatest boons of a beneficent Providence. The juice of the cane, extracted in a primitive fashion by crushing the stalks between wooden rollers revolving upon wooden cogs and impelled by horse power, was caught in an ordinary trough, boiled down into proper consistency in preserving kettles, kitchen pots, or whatever might be utilized for the purpose, and barreled for use as sorghum molasses. The syrup thus produced was quite a palatable one, with a slightly acidulous and not disagreeable flavor (1886).

The flavor was so agreeable that when sugar became available once more after the Civil War, farmers kept growing sorghum for fodder and syrup. Biscuits sweetened with

Joe Trapp of Blythewood, one of the expert sorghum boilers of the state, crushing Honey Drip and Dale cane for juice. The juice will be boiled, skimmed, and reduced to syrup over several hours. David S. Shields, Hopkins, SC, 2015.

sorghum became a homey food and the autumn sorghum boil became a neighborhood occasion. The favorite strains for syrup—Amber and Honeydrip—were improved forms of Hammond's original fifteen strains. White African was grown too for its grain as well as its syrup. While the twenty-first century has made grain sorghum the focus of agriculture—whether for biomass fuel production or feed—a handful of syrup makers have kept the foodways alive. Joe Trapp of Blythewood, James Helm of Carolina Bay Farm in Hopkins, and Four Oaks Farm in Lexington all produce annual batches, but a number of people across the state conduct private boils, and jars of syrup are precious gifts to friends. Home brewers often use large iron cauldrons for their boil, a mid-nineteenth-century practice. Persons brewing syrup for commercial product use

evaporator pans that enable more uniform heating. During the boil starches frothing on the surface of the heated juice are skimmed off. Expert syrup makers can tell when the batch is done by how it drips from the back of a spoon.

Sorghum Cake

Edgefield Advertiser (January 29, 1896)

Mix together one cup of sorghum [syrup], one tablespoonful of lard, one teaspoonful of salt, two teaspoonfuls of ginger, and two cups of flour. Add one cup of boiling water into which one teaspoonful of soda has been stirred. Pour into a greased pan and bake in a moderately hot oven.

Spoonbread

OWENDAW

The lightest form of corn bread, custardy and airy like a soufflé, spoonbread became the signature of hotel southern dining in the mid-twentieth century. Yet it was nineteenth century in origin, reflecting the abundance of eggs, milk, and butter on larger farms, and the popularization of chemical leavens in the 1840s. While corn bread was Native in its genesis, spoonbread was settler food. It took the traditional Native American porridge sappawn and turned it into a baked dish by the admixture of milk, eggs, and baking soda. In Sarah Rutledge's *The Carolina Hous-Wife* a series of recipes—"Camp Corn Bread," "Owendaw Corn Bread," and "Chicora Corn Bread"—lay out the evolution of the dish. The first is the Native original, and the second a plantation development increasing the eggs (4), butter (very large spoonful), and milk (pint) content of the batter. Finally, Chicora Corn Bread reveals a full-blown experimental mentality with its admixtures of baking soda, brown sugar, and a tablespoon of wheat flour. The classic South Carolina spoonbread, however, was the Owendaw bread with the admixture of baking soda. Indeed, the faith in the power of chemical risers in baking grew so great in the South that it was eventually added to the basic corn bread recipe as well.

Much of the last part of the twentieth century in southern cookery was spent elaborating spoonbread, making it more like a soufflé by adding flavor additives such as cheese, bacon, or garlic. In the early part of the twentieth century the substitution of buttermilk for milk and the incorporation of cooked rice had been the two principle emendations of the classic form.

The quality of spoonbread depends in some measure on the corn used. Heirloom cornmeal (white corn was traditional—Cocke's Prolific, Hickory King, Sea Island White Flint-but yellow corn was favored in parts of the midlands) imparts depth of flavor, indeed so profound a taste that no extra ingredients are needed.

There are tricks to Owendaw spoonbread. You must cook the cornmeal in milk in a saucepan over modest heat, stirring it until it has a thick smooth consistency. Then add butter. One of the things that happened in the twentieth century was to bump up the amount of butter in the mix to the point where some were doing a 1 to 1 proportion with the meal—that is if you use two cups of milk and ½ cup of cornmeal, you stir in ½ cup of unsalted butter. The butter is added while the cornmeal mixture is still hot, so that it melts in. The 4 eggs are added after the mixture has cooled down, as are the baking powder and salt. Those who go the soufflé

Spoonbread, or Owendaw, made of Cocke's Prolific corn, the white dent variety preserved by Manning Farmer of Landrum, SC. David S. Shields.

route add the yolks first, then beat the whites and fold those in. It is baked in a dish at 350°F for 45 to 50 minutes.

Similar recipes exist from various parts of the South. In Virginia it was known as batter bread until the twentieth century. The designation "spoonbread" dates from early in the twentieth century in both Virginia and South Carolina, when newspaper writers determined that "Owendaw" and "batter bread" were too pedestrian a designation.

The dish went national shortly after World War II. Before that it was a regional offering in Richmond and Charleston and environs, sometimes found on a hotel menu, a boarding house staple, and something made at home. In 1922, the *Richmond Times Dispatch* held a contest for the best Old Virginia Batter Bread recipe. It was won by Mrs. P. H. Boisseau of Danville. But during the post-war peace,

the hotel chefs of the Old Dominion invited northern chefs and food writers to sample the local cuisine at a conclave in Fredericksburg. The one thing that set the northerners raving was spoonbread. It was served with cured herring roe (a traditional breakfast food). From that moment on it became a hotel staple served in urban centers and mountain resorts throughout the South, a dish that northern tourists requested during their vacation jaunts southward. Recipes began appearing in newspapers. The spoonbread boom was registered in South Carolina by the retiring of its old name, Owendaw (which had troubled some since the town came to be spelled Awendaw), and its replacement with spoonbread. The Fort Sumter Hotel's menus in the 1940s list spoonbread, and *Charleston Receipts* offers two recipes for spoonbread. It was an old friend, rebranded.

Strawberry Shortcake

Early settlers in South Carolina encountered beautiful wild strawberries. These were crossed with a Chilean strawberry to create the luscious fruits we know today. Sometime in the 1700s, the red, heart-shaped berry came into existence and was employed in one of the great spring desserts, strawberry shortcake. Even then it was an old dessert. A recipe appeared in an English recipe book in 1588—no doubt using the white Alpine strawberry native to Europe. Over the years, the principle changes in the recipe have to do with the amount of sugar used per each quart of berries. When sugar was scarce in the sixteenth and seventeenth centuries, the amount depended on the wealth of the household. It was usually measured in tablespoons. When sugar became plentiful in the United States in the 1820s, the formula ½ cup of sugar per quart of strawberries became standardized. The sweetness of this formulation was warranted by the kinds of strawberries that became standard in the 1800s. Plant breeders in Charleston created two varieties: the Nuenan's Prolific in the 1860s and its offspring, the Hoffman's Seedling, in the 1880s. Both were sub-acid, sour-sweet strawberries, exploding bright on the tongue and then mellowing to honey. These acid forward strawberries required more sugar to tame in a strawberry shortcake. Even when the sub-acid strawberries were supplanted by the low-acid, high-sugar Fairfax strawberry in the 1930s, cooks did not diminish the sugar in the mix. Eaters had become used to a lot of sweet with their strawberries.

Strawberry shortcake was originally made with circles or broken pieces of piecrust, macerated strawberries, sugar, and cream. Today

Most strawberry farms are u-pick operations and feature large berries to satisfy the children in picking families. Here, however, is sweet Charlie, a smaller variety that has some of the taste quality of the classic Fairfax strawberry. David S. Shields.

it is made with biscuits or sponge cake. The biscuit crust is more traditional. As early as 1905, newspaper complaints about the rise of the sponge cake contrasted the splendor of the old style: "They used a biscuit crust . . . not a sweet, crumbly characterless and incompatible foundation of cake, but a biscuit crust made pretty rich. And having baked a suitably large and tolerably thick dish of such crust, they split it open while it was still hot and buttered lightly the soft upper side of the bottom crust." In the early twentieth century, the basic strawberry shortcake was sometimes gussied up with a meringue cap on the cake over which

[177]

the macerated strawberries were spread, "but when the shortcake is to be eaten with cream, as is generally the case, this is better omitted" (1900).

Strawberry Shortcake

Barbara E. Shapleigh,
Charleston Evening Post (April 6, 1923)

Sift one pint of flour, four teaspoons of baking powder, one-half teaspoon of salt and two teaspoons of sugar together. Cut into the flour four tablespoons of but or three tablespoons of lard and moisten to a soft dough with about two-thirds of a cup of milk. Take onto a floured board and roll to one-half inch in thickness. Cut with a biscuit cutter. Place in a buttered pan and bake 15 minutes in a hot oven. Split, butter and fill with strawberries sweetened and slightly mashed. Place on top a spoonful of beaten cream.

Since the 1950s, U-Pick strawberry farms have made picking expeditions one of the great family pastimes of spring. Each section of the state has its go-to farm: Gurosik's Berry Plantation near Augusta, Dempsey Farms UPick near Charleston, Stewart Farms near Greenville, Cottle Farms near Columbia and Lake City, James R Sease Farms near Gilbert, Elliott Stawberry Farm near Cent, The Happy Berry, Inc. at Six Mile, and a half dozen more.

Summer Squash

There is a redundancy in the name summer squash, because in its earliest sixteenth and seventeenth century American usages the word squash by itself meant those soft-fleshed cucurbits eaten by humans in the summer. It was distinguished from hard-fleshed gourds and round pumpkins, associated with fall and winter, and the latter as much with stock feed as with human consumption. In the South, summer squash was used to categorize a group of squashes consumed over the summer—yellow crookneck, cymlings, zucchini—and to specify the flattened patty pan bush squash that was also called the cymling in the American colonies. There was a broadness to the name that verged on imprecision. There were squashes that were not reckoned summer squashes—late season, large vegetables such as the Cushaw, the Tennessee Sweet Potato Squash, the Cherokee Candy Roaster Squash—and the New England Hubbard and Winter Crook Necked Squashes. New Englanders repeatedly stated a preference for the winter squashes, while in South Carolina the cymling summer squash and the yellow crookneck enjoyed preference. The distinction? "The summer squash have thin skins and rather soft seeds and are tender and succulent, while the winter squash have heavy rinds, starchy and fibrous flesh, and heavy, large seeds" (1938). Until the 1930s, South Carolinians only recognized the cymling and the yellow crookneck as summer squashes. In the mid-1930s, the zucchini joined the category.

Mild-tasting, and capable of harmonizing with other flavors, the squash enjoyed a loyal group of devotees, yet several things could ruin the vegetable: being cooked in too much water for too long, and being left on the bush too long, leading to a woody-textured vegetable.

Cymlings–Patty Pan Squash

With its scalloped edge, blunt knobbed perimeter, shallow domed top, and deeper domed bottom, the cymling looks like a jelly fish flipped on its bottom. The diameters of the fruit when edible vary from mini-cymlings three inches across up to a fulsome eight inches. They are three to four inches deep. If left to mature, they will expand to a foot in diameter. Most are smooth-skinned; those that have warts crossed with the older form of yellow crookneck squash. Coloration can vary: yellow was the oldest strain, white next, pale green, and occasionally orange. Because insects—the pickle worm and the melon worm particularly—bedevil the growing plants, gardeners must be

Summer squashes: zucchinis, patty-pans, and yellow crook necks. David S. Shields.

[179]

vigilant in defending their squash. In most part of the state they grow robustly and prolifically.

There has been a major shift in the preparation of summer squash over the past two centuries. In the nineteenth century, many preparations called for the squash to be boiled, then mashed or extruded through a colander. Two traditional pan-southern dishes embody this approach particularly: cymling fritters and cymling pudding.

Cymling Fritters

Marion Cabell Tyree,
Housekeeping in Old Virginia (1879)

After boiling and running through a colander, mix with an egg, season with salt, pepper, and butter, make into cakes and fry a light brown.

Cymling Pudding

Marion Cabell Tyree,
Housekeeping in Old Virginia (1879)

Boil young cymlings, mash and run through a colander. Add one teacup of milk, three eggs, a large lump of butter, pepper and salt. Put in a buttered deep dish, and bake a light brown. For a change, you might line the dish with thin slices of buttered bread, pour in the cymling batter and put some pieces of butter and grated cracker on top.–Mrs. M. C. C.

In the twentieth century, the pendulum swung, and a penchant for preserving something of the texture of the cymling took

hold. There was a quite self-conscious effort to modernize the popular attitude toward the vegetable. Seed catalogs rejected the old names and began to call them "bush squash." In the kitchen, cooks cubed squash and (1) steamed or boiled it and dressed it with butter, salt, and pepper or a white sauce; or (2) fried it in bacon fat or oil with corn, tomatoes, and onions.

Yellow Crookneck Squash

The majority of yellow crookneck squashes grown in the South have mildly warty skins. They also have a familiar shape, a neck curved to one side with a blunt end, a tapering bulb for the body of the squash on the calyx end. This body forms a chamber for generating seeds. A giant form of this vegetable prevalent in the eighteenth century has given way to the familiar eight-inch-long squash.

Like the cymling, the yellow crookneck was usually mashed in its culinary preparations during the nineteenth century. In a widely republished remembrance of 1907, a Mr. Kilkinby, recalled the processing of the crookneck in his home kitchen. "Among all those preliminary smells and sounds none was more charming than the smothered pounding that indicated the smashing of the squash. Those little yellow crooknecks that we grew in our own garden, to be picked when they were precisely and exactly ripe, were now, having been duly cooked, smashed up in a wooden chopping bowl with a plate, and this was the sound that we heard, the sound of the edge of the plate when it went through the tender bright yellow squashes to bring up softly on the wood. And so they were smashed, smooth and fine, these freshly picked, delightful yellow crooknecks, to be duly seasoned with butter and salt in the course of the smashing; and then they were served hot and delicious."

Frying squash vied with boiling and mashing them in terms of popularity. Fried crookneck squash usually entailed slicing the squash crossways into a stack of coins.

Fried Squash

Raleigh Progressive Farmer (July 17, 1894)

Cut a crook neck squash in slices and soak them in cold salted water one hour. Wipe them dry, dip them in batter and fry brown in a little butter, or dip them in egg, roll in fine bread-crumbs and fry in boiling-hot fat.

In the early twentieth century a fashion for baking yellow crookneck squash developed in parts of the South. In terms of the dishes, the simpler, the better. The following recipe protected the quality of the vegetable admirably.

Crook-Neck Squash Baked in Cream

Rock Hill Herald (September 21, 1940)

One small yellow crook-neck squash, 3 tablespoons butter, ⅛ teaspoon pepper, ¼ teaspoon salt, ½ cup milk or top milk. Wash and slice squash in ¼ inch pieces. Spread both sides of slice with butter. Sprinkle with salt and butter. Bake in covered baking dish in moderate over (350 degrees F.) for 45 minutes. Then add cream or milk and bake uncovered for 15 minutes until lightly browned.

Zucchini

David G. Fairchild, the pioneering plant hunter, and his patron Barbour Lathrop encountered the zucchini and collected seed during his 1899 to 1900 global expedition. In his 1901 report of his findings, Fairchild noted "Zuccini from northern Italy; one of the most important vegetables of the Venetians and worthy serious consideration by our truck farmers." It took a quarter century before the prolific, green Italian squash was grown to the extent that it could be advertised in town newspapers. The break-through year was 1927. In 1928, H. F. wrote to the Macon Telegraph, "You mention a food in your weekly menus called zucchini. Will please explain what it is, as I have never heard of it before?" The editor answered: "Zucchini is a small Italian squash similar to the ordinary summer squash, and may be used freely as a non-starchy vegetable if cooked by boiling or baking." Half a century later it would be so common a home-grown vegetable that one dreaded a "gift" of surplus zucchini from a neighbor.

The zucchini's taste and texture was not so delicate as the other summer squashes, and so invited a latitude of treatment not found with the cymling or crookneck. Garlic and tomatoes, tomato and other sauces, bacon drippings (often expressly forbidden in recipes), were all welcome. Indeed, incorporating the zucchini into baked goods, particularly the 1970s classic, zucchini bread, did not occur with South Carolina's Native squashes. The Italian practice of stuffing and deep frying battered squash blossoms is first mentioned in the 1930s in southern newspapers, but the practice did not become widely advertised until 1973 to 1974.

Sweet Corn

One of the delights of summer, sweet corn appears at the top of the sign at roadside produce stands. There are names cherished above all others: Silver Queen! Country Gentleman! Stowell's Evergreen! And now bicolor sweet. While the very best field corns could become roasting ears on those first two days they reach the "milk stage," tasting sweet plucked from the fire, a sweet corn retained its sugar throughout maturity. In the colonial era there was no sweet corn in South Carolina. It only existed in three separate maize families in the Western Hemisphere: Chulpi in Peru, Maize Dulce in Mexico, and Papoon Corn in New York and Canada. The latter would be the ancestor of North American sweet corn.

A mutation had occurred in an Iroquois flour corn sometime in the 1750s, inhibiting the transformation of sugar into starch; the corn got stuck in the sweet phase. It came into settlers' hands in 1779, seized as a spoil of war by Lt. Richard Bagnal of Poor's Brigade during the American Revolution. It was sweet, rather soft, and wrinkled. The original strain had a red cob, though this was bred out of the North American sweets by 1800. An improved version became widely known as Old Colony corn. It was some version of this that came into South Carolina after 1822. The first local broker of sweet corn seed was Dawson & Blackmore at 17 Broad in the late 1840s. In the period after the Civil War, sweet corn proved not to be a truck crop, because the sweetness degraded over the time it took to transport it northward to New York City's markets. It wasn't until 1923, when farmers in Jasper and Beaufort began experimenting with a planting of sweet corn after the lettuce crop, that the idea of growing sweet corn for long-distance consumption took hold.

While most people preferred sweet corn roasted in the fire or in a cook stove and dressed with butter, pepper, and salt, unimaginative cooks cut it from the cob and boiled it—often too long, for it becomes tough and tasteless after boiling for half an hour. Fortunately, southerners devised a number of recipes that employed it in other ways: stewed corn, corn custard (an adaptation of the older 'green corn pudding' made with field corn in the milk stage), scalloped sweet corn, shrimp and corn pie, corn au gratin, sweet corn fritters, and spoonbread with sweet corn. In these latter preparations the kernels were cut from the cob before cooking and incorporated in the mixtures. One of the dishes that enjoyed the greatest local favor was fried corn. The preparation is simple: cut the grains from five ears of sweet corn and put them in a frying pan in which some bacon has been cooked. Remove the bacon and pour off some of the fat if there is too much to fry the corn in. Add salt and pepper to taste, cover closely, and fry over a slow fire and stir often for ten minutes or more.

Before canning sweet corn became commonplace in the 1890s, sweet corn was often parboiled and dried; this prevented the sweetness from degrading into starchiness (this happened when you simply dried sweet corn). Soaking in water reconstituted the corn, and it proved to be a versatile ingredient. Some Carolinians (particularly those who favored camp cookery) preferred dried corn to canned, and several family manuscript recipe collections contain instructions for dried corn soups.

In the late twentieth century, vegetable breeders introduced supersweet and sugar-extended corns, some of which could retain sweetness a week after pickings, others of which were thirty or more times more sugary than standard varieties such as Silver Queen (introduced by Rodgers Brothers in 1958). The supersweet corns have found favor among people who like sweet corn ice cream, and as roasting ears. Their sugar, however, disrupts the balance of the old recipes, such as corn pudding. So, demand for Silver Queen and other old sweet corns remains stable.

Sweet Potato Pie

Sapelo strawberry sweet potato, a rare white fleshed variety that works well as a pie sweet potato. David S. Shields.

There was a moment early in the twentieth century—1904 or so—when canned pumpkin pie filling from the North and its distribution through southern groceries set off the woe reflex in southerners. Writers to the papers began moaning about the disappearance of southern civilization. The native sweet potato pie was being cast aside in favor of Yankee pumpkin in the name of convenience (or laziness). A writer to the *Richmond Times Dispatch* observed, "We . . . have to lament that the potato pie is not as much in vogue as it was of old. The reason for this deplorable condition of things cannot be found in lack of public appreciation; no, not that. The explanation must be that so many canned goods for pie-making are ready to hand, or that the city housewife goes to the

baker for pies oftener than she did formerly. . . . Southerners do not show that loyalty to the sweet potato pie that Northerners do to the pumpkin pie" (1904).

Persons long resident in the south will recognize here the "poor mouth," that automatic elegy for a civilization gone with the wind or decaying like a family in a Tennessee Williams drama. But of course the sweet potato pie did not vanish into "times forgotten." It's still here in the South waging its eternal war against pumpkin pie (a.k.a. winter squash pie).

There have long been two varieties: the custard pies made of mashed sweet potatoes; and the slicer pies, with thin sections of yellow yam intermingled with butter and sugar. A maxim holds that anything important to a culture gathers a multitude of names. Such is the case here: "Sweet potato pie is a great favorite in the south, and the men come in asking, 'Got any tate pone?' Another name for sweet potato pie is 'poodle pie.' Everything is custard, too, in the pie line. Ordinary custard pie is called 'egg custard;' lemon pie is 'lemon custard,' potato pie is 'potato custard'" (1896). The last name applied exclusively to that species of pie made with mashed sweet potatoes. In pre-twentieth-century cookbooks the recipe appears as frequently under the rubric "custard" as it does "pie." Any open-faced pie (that is lacking a top crust) with a body whose smoothness is achieved by incorporating beaten eggs could be called a custard.

A hallmark of old school sweet potato custard pie was the incorporation of sherry or brandy into the pie filling. With the coming of Prohibition, the alcohol disappeared, leaving some variation of the following formula: One cup of sweet potatoes cooked, mashed, salted, and buttered, beaten and run through a sieve. One and a half cups of whole milk, or sour cream intermixed with the sweet potatoes. Spices—cinnamon, ginger, nutmeg at minimum. Four tablespoons of sugar (brown or white). Two eggs beaten into the mixture. Depending on the taste of the pie maker, the proportions of ingredients, the dryness of the pie, and the spice level might be altered. This would be poured over a crust in a pie plate and baked. Once finished the top may be sprinkled with sugar.

The sliced potato pie was a different animal; first, it had a top crust; second, it was substantially deeper than a custard pie; third, it took longer (an hour) to cook. The classic Lowcountry recipe occurred in *Mrs. Hill's Southern Practical Cookery*:

Sliced Potato Pie

Annabella Hill, *Mrs. Hill's Southern Practical Cookery* (1867)

For baking this, a plate deeper than the common pie-plate is necessary. Bake medium-sized sweet potatoes not quite done; yams are best. Line the plate with good paste; slice the potatoes; place a layer upon the bottom of the plate; over this sprinkle thickly a layer of good brown sugar; over this place thin slices of butter and sprinkle with flour, seasoning with spices to the taste. A heaped tablespoonful of butter and a heaped teaspoonful of flour will be sufficient for one pie. Put on another of potatoes, piled a little in the middle. Mix equal quantities of wine and water, lemon juice and water, or vinegar and water, and pour in enough to half fill the pie; sprinkle over the potato a little flour, and place on the upper crust, pinching the edges carefully together. Cut a slit in the centre, and bake slowly for one hour.

Particularly noteworthy is Hill's designation of a category of sweet potato to employ: the yam (the yellow-orange fleshed sweet potato, not the true *Dioscorea scorea* yam of West Africa). In the early 1920s, when agronomists began promoting the canning of sweet potato pie filling, comparative tastings were held by the National Canners Association to determine the tastiest varieties for pie making. "The Gold Skin was again unanimously awarded first place, and the Porto Rico, Nancy Hall, and Vineless Pumpkin Yam of the moist-fleshed group, and the Big-Stem Jersey, Improved Big Stem, Yellow Strasburg, and Triumph of the firmer flesh types, in about the order given, received favorable comment" (1922). The Association had tested forty-three varieties. A testament to the conservatism of pie-makers' tastes is the fact that in 2014 all four of the first named sweet varieties survive, under the names "Yellow Jersey," "Porto Rican," "Nancy Hall," and "Georgia Pumpkin Yam." To these classic varieties, the Jewel and the Garnet, have been added as first rank pie potatoes.

The Georgia Pumpkin Yam's name suggests how the reputation of that famous northern pie hovered above the sweet potato custard. Pumpkin pie's reputation during the 1800s became firmly fixed to the celebration of Thanksgiving, which became a national holiday by president Lincoln's decree in 1863.

Given its Yankee associations, Thanksgiving did not inspire celebrations in southern states until 1877 to 1878, when churches led people to its commemoration. By that time a northern bill of fare had become fixed, with pumpkin pie gracing the bottom of the bill. Southerners grew pumpkins (pigs loved them), but when it came to members of the squash family, favor ran to cushaw pies or candy roaster squash, after 1925 or so (It is ironic that some of what now passes for pumpkin pie filling is actually processed winter squash meat). Not until the Spanish American War did southerners buy into the national holiday in large number and embrace the menu as well. When they did, they had an abundant supply of canned pumpkin readily available. So, in the face of food nationalism and modernity, local devotees of the turn of the twentieth century had to reassert the virtues of the regional favorite.

~ Tanya Root ~

Once one of the signature root vegetables of the Lowcountry and still a morning staple in the Caribbean, the Tanya (the corm of the elephant ear) was boiled, roasted, and baked. It ceased to be a food vegetable in the 1910s during the USDA poison scares over taro root. David S. Shields.

Does the South lack for root vegetables? In the winter produce section of the groceries, the sweet potatoes, potatoes, turnips, rutabagas, carrots, and beets overflow their bins. But once the abundance was even greater. One has to go to an island produce market in the Caribbean to witness the profusion that existed in the markets of New Orleans, Mobile, Savannah, and Charleston in the 1870s. One will see piles of corms, tubers, and roots that Carolinians only read about: dasheen (the pink taro, *Colacassia esculante*), tanya or provision plant (the arrow leafed elephant ear *Xanthosoma sagittifolium*), eddoes (small taro), and even the true West African yam. In South Carolina and Georgia, throughout the eighteenth and nineteenth centuries, the first two roots were greatly popular and went under the name tannier (pre-1830) and tanya (post-1830). The dasheen was called the pink tanya and the arrow leaf elephant ear, the blue tanya. They were so popular in Charleston in the mid-nineteenth century that they were presented as gifts to new residents of the city.

The first surviving image of a tannier/ tanya growing in the South appears in volume 2 of Mark Catesby's famous *A Natural History of Carolina, Florida and the Bahama Islands* (1743). It appears in the background of the plate illustrating the Brown Viper. Indeed, Catesby spoke of the introduction of a variety of tannier during his residence in Carolina in the 1720s that lacked the acrid raw flavor that required much boiling. It could even be eaten raw "without offending throat or palate." It is difficult to fathom what root he meant since all of these roots contain chemicals that must be cooked or dissolved by water not to poison an eater.

The first published American instruction about cultivation occurred in the September 9, 1825 issue of the *American Farmer*. "They are planted in South Carolina, in the latter end of March, in small beds, or hills, three of four feet apart; the leaves are very large, from eighteen inches to two feet long, and from twelve to fifteen inches wide. For seed plants, the small fruit of the last year, or the larger fruit, cut in two, is planted. During the growth the earth is drawn up once or twice round the root, and the grass hoed from them; they are dug in before the heavy frosts commence, and put away in cellars, covered with earth and straw, or pine leaves." A more extensive account of their cultivation was given by William Logan in the May 1834 issue of the *Southern Agriculturist*. He notes that it was brought to Carolina by enslaved Africans via Jamaica. He noted that "The Tannier should be always pealed before boiling, and the large roots cut into two or

three parts, and three hours boiling will be sufficient."

The boiling was a necessary caution. Poisonous calcium oxalate crystals pervade the leaves, stems, and roots of both forms of the tanya. Eating the corms raw would trigger a burning sensation in the throat, then swelling. Gastrointestinal disruptions then follow. Cooking breaks down the oxalate crystals, permitting one to eat boiled, baked, roasted or grilled tanya with no ill effect. A correspondent of the *Rural Carolinian* provided a summary of cooking instructions in 1875:

Cooking Tanyah

Rural Carolinian (1875)

The Tanyah (*Colocasia antiquorum, var. esculentum*)—never mind the Latin—is one of the best of our peculiar Southern vegetables, and we are glad to know that the recommendations of the Rural Carolinian have led to a considerable extension of its culture beyond the coast region, to which it was formerly almost entirely confined. It should be grown wherever the climate will permit, and we think its northern limit, as a garden vegetable, would be found not far south of the Potomac. It is grown much further north, as an ornamental plant Some of our up-country friends, having found it easy to grow a crop of Tanyah—it asks little but rich moist ground—are somewhat at a loss what to do with it—how to prepare it for the table. The simplest and most common mode of cooking the Tanyah root is by boiling; and it is served, like other vegetables, with the inevitable bacon. Pare the root, as you would a turnip, and, if large, cut it into several pieces; put it into a saucepan with cold water and bring to a boil; pour the water off, to get rid of the acridity which pertains to this plant . . . ; add more water and a little salt, and cook till tender. It may be eaten with butter, like the sweet potato. After boiling, it is sometimes cut into slices and fried. Boiled, finely mashed, and with eggs, milk, and a little flour added, it makes batter cakes, which, once tasted, will be in demand forever afterwards. But the most delicious part of the Tanyah is not the root, but the large, succulent leaf-stalk. The blanched parts of the inner ones are to be used, and the plant may be earthed up, like celery, when the whole, so far as covered, become edible. Cut these blanched stems into short pieces, and boil in the same way as directed for the roots. Serve with butter, like asparagus. We low country people like Tanyah very much, but strangers do not, generally, take to it very kindly, at first; so we shall not be surprised if some of our new growers of the crop shall vote it "not fit to eat." Better try it again— you will soon learn to like it.

Why did the root cease to be cultivated in the wet parts of the South that loved it in the 1870s? Our suspicion is that in the 1910s American health officials made such a fuss about poisons in plants that the entire taro family, which was being promoted by the USDA (see the Dasheen entries in seed catalogs of 1914–1915), got quashed by consumers.

Tomato Gravy

First, we must make a distinction—there is a community of Italian Americans in New Orleans, Atlanta, and other parts of the urban South that call tomato sauce (whole tomatoes cooked down with oil and seasoning) "tomato gravy"—this communal name is not what we are talking about here, and what most non-Italian southerners mean when they speak of tomato gravy.

Tomato gravy begins with a roux—with flour browned in fat or oil. Benne oil, lard, and olive oil all do well. Often pan drippings from a roast or a ham slice served as the lipid in which to brown the flour. And then you moisten the roux with tomato juice, or machine processed tomatoes with the machine set to liquefy. A good shake of salt improves the gravy. This gravy tastes better the longer it cooks—but you must watch your temperature control so as to not let it scorch, or go too dry, or clump. As the sugars in the gravy caramelize, it takes on a greater depth of flavor.

Tomato gravy usually accompanied meatloaf, but in the South, it adorned slices of friend guinea squash, or biscuits for breakfast. It flavored rice for much of the twentieth century. Some serve tomato gravy over freshly baked biscuits or alongside a little fried okra.

The basic formulation was elaborated in a number of ways. In the upper South, heavy cream might be introduced into the gravy, smoothing it out. The seasoning of tomato gravy saw a range of adjustments. Mace was the classic spice added to the mixture in the Lowcountry. Some add a dash of cayenne. Others thought that a teaspoon of Worcestershire gave it greater complexity. Gullah cooks added pigs feet to the gravy and cooked the pot low and slow until the gelatinousness of the foot made the tomato gravy glossy. In no recipe did anyone mention a specific variety of tomato to employ.

Remember: Italian tomato gravy has no roux. Southern tomato gravy has roux.

Tomato Gravy

KEVIN MITCHELL

This recipe does not stray too far from traditional recipes. I love the flavor combination of smoked paprika and tomato, and when the gravy is served with fried okra, it takes me back to my grandmother Doris's kitchen

4 tablespoons butter
    (or pan drippings from
    bacon or lard)
1 cup finely diced onion
1 clove garlic, crushed or grated
1 large bay leaf
1 sprig thyme
1½ teaspoons smoked paprika
¾ teaspoon freshly ground black
    pepper

¼ cup flour
2 cups tomato sauce
    (or a 14.5-ounce can)
1 cup vegetable broth
    (chicken if you like)
2 cups diced tomatoes
    (or a 14.5-ounce can)
2 tablespoons chopped parsley
Salt to taste

Melt the butter or drippings in a deep skillet or Dutch oven over medium heat. Add the onions, garlic, bay leaf, thyme, smoked paprika, and black pepper. Sauté until the onions begin to soften, 2 to 3 minutes. Mix in the flour and continue to cook the roux, stirring constantly, until both the onions and the flour turn light golden brown, about 3 or 4 minutes. Don't let the flour or onions get too brown. Add the tomato sauce and broth. Combine with a whisk until the sauce comes to a boil. Turn the heat down until the gravy is at a low simmer. Cook until the mixture is smooth and thick, about 5 minutes. Add the diced tomatoes and their juice and simmer 15 to 20 minutes. Just before serving, remove the bay leaf. Sprinkle with parsley.

Tomato Pie

While southerners were the first North Americans to embrace the tomato as a culinary ingredient—baking it in casseroles, frying it, preserving it in sugar, pureeing it into soups, and rendering it into sauce by 1810—they were not the first to make tomato pies. All of the earliest pie notices date from the 1830s. All come from New England. A widely republished article from the *Springfield MA Republican* in 1838 announced that tomato pie (a sugared version) was the equal of elderberry or gooseberry.

The appearance of the first pies coincided with the sea change of opinion about tomatoes in the broader nation; from indifference and suspicion to a conviction that they were a medical boon. Andrew F. Smith chronicled the tomato craze of the 1830s in his entertaining book, *The Tomato in America* (1994).

All of the early pies were double crust, but there were decided schools of approach: green tomato pies with sugar, spice, and sometimes vinegar; ripe tomato pies (featuring yellow or light colored tomatoes) that could either be sugared or salted, buttered, and spiced; and there was a now-lost tradition of tomato custard pies. Often these mixed eggs with the tomato syrup used in making preserved "tomato figs."

In the 1870s, the single crust flipped pie came into being. Here we see a step toward the type of open-faced pie that now predominates in the South. The pie is baked with sliced, sugared, ripe tomatoes in a dish and a crust on top; once baked the pie is flipped to expose the tomato filling, glazed with egg and popped into the oven for finishing.

How does this open-faced pie differ from those now popular in the South? I (David) have sampled numbers of the prevailing sort—that of the Tomato Shed outside of Charleston exemplifies the twenty-first-century pie. It has red tomatoes rather than the old yellow. It is salted rather than sugared. The baked tomato face is covered with a mixture of cheddar cheese and Duke's Mayonnaise. The spicing (cinnamon, mace) has been dialed back and salt and pepper and herbs pushed to the fore.

Sugared green tomato pies still exist—I've tasted excellent ones in Kentucky and western Virginia. But I haven't encountered a double crust savory tomato pie in some years, so welcome notices of places that serve such a thing.

I've cooked the earliest baked tomato dishes—Martha Randolph's scalloped tomatoes and Sarah Rutledge's shrimp and tomato bake. I thought the former needed a dash of Worcestershire sauce or something. The latter saw the shrimps shrink and toughen in the baking. So, I think I'll take a wedge of pie.

Tomato Pie prepared by Kevin Mitchell. Rhonda L. Wilson.

TOMATO PIE

Waffles

There is something jolly about waffles. Is it their crispiness? Their crenellations? Their willingness to be slathered in syrup and butter? In southern cities there are never-closing shrines devoted to them—the Waffle Houses. Many a penitent carouser has sought remedy in the late hours of night for a toxic gut and a fogged head with black coffee and waffles.

In 1911, General Electric introduced the electric waffle iron, a countertop dimpled metal device equipped with a plug-in heating element. The design mimicked the stove-top waffle iron patented by Cornelius Swarthout in 1869. In the South, the older design of the waffle iron prevailed until the 1930s. Every household of means had a waffle iron in its kitchen—two plates (round or rectangular) of cast iron, sometimes embossed with a design, sometimes simply indented, at the end of long handles with a hinge allowing one to open and close the plates. They were used for hearthside cooking over embers or the heat source of a cook stove. One greased the plates liberally with bacon grease, heated the plates, poured on a batter, closed the plates, and extended them over the coals. You flipped the iron once. After a modest period of time you removed the irons from the heat, popped them open, and anointed the crispy waffles with butter, cane syrup, sorghum, or your favorite preserves. In the mid-nineteenth century, such waffles were a *sine qua non* of breakfast at a boarding house or hospitable home—served with biscuits and corn bread in a kind of trinity. Certain cooks became famous for their waffles—Mrs. Schwarz, who ran a boarding house in Aiken, prepared waffles and bread so sumptuous they

became the stuff of wonder in Charleston newspapers in 1830.

The formula for waffle batter varied depending upon one's locale. In the Lowcountry, until 1880 or so, the waffle had to have rice, either boiled or in the form of rice flour as a component. The most refined had a crème de riz base, into which one added milk, rice flour, some water, and salt. Others combined boiled rice and rice flour with milk and eggs. Sarah Rutledge, in *The Carolina Housewife*, offered a recipe that used day-old hominy grits as a base into which one added some wheat and a larger measure of rice flour, making a paste which one poured onto the iron.

In the 1880s, the Charleston hotels stopped offering waffles in the bread baskets and on breakfast plates. A generation of public diners went without until Jack Bischoff, an ambitious young restaurateur from a family that ran saloons, revived them. Bischoff championed a Lowcountry version of German food. He opened two restaurants simultaneously in the autumn of 1912—The Hanover at 233 Meeting Street and The German Restaurant at 67 Hasell. His lunchroom, the Rialto, opened across from the Argyle Hotel in 1913. The German Restaurant was surely the most unusual German restaurant in the country, offering roasted raccoon and sweet potatoes, deviled crabs, shad roe, and shrimp salad a la creole along with wiener schnitzel, liver sausages, and real rye bread. It deserves recall in Charleston for being the first place in the city to offer "Hamburger Steak." But its greatest claim to fame was being the restaurant that renovated the reputation of the waffle. Long a fixture of the Lowcountry breakfast, the waffle in Bischoff's hands was slathered in butter and maple syrup and brought back to starring status on a restaurant bill of fare. One of his advertising tags was, "Are you a Waffle Eater?" He would thrive until the anti-German hysteria of World War I drove him out of business. The waffles he repopularized remained a menu staple thereafter, albeit using wheat flour rather than rice. The rice waffle would not enjoy a renaissance until Zingermann's Road House introduced its Carolina Gold Rice Waffle, made from rice flour, to its menu.

Rice Waffles

Stoney Recipes Book, South Carolina Historical Society (1850s)

A small coffee cup of Rice flour to one half pint of rice boiled very soft, to be mixed with one half pint of milk, the boiled rice to be mashed in a mortar, previously to its being mixed with the flour; the iron to be greased with hog's lard or bacon skin previous to the mixture being placed in it. A pot of boiling water may be kept in readiness, should the iron need it, and the iron to be greased each time, before the mixture is placed in it.

Sweet Potato Waffle

Sarah Rutledge,
The Carolina Housewife (1847)

Two tablespoonful of mashed sweet potato, one of butter, one of sugar, one pint of milk, four tablespoonful of what flour. Mix these ingredients well together and bake in a waffle iron.

The watermelon saved the South. In the chaotic year after the Confederacy's defeat in the Civil War, seed for most staple crops (cotton, corn, peanuts, rice) was not available for planting. The liberated African American population had little inclination to reengage in field labor, particularly to benefit white planters or farmers. There was only one plant in Georgia and South Carolina that could be easily grown, that did not require great labor to grow, and that commanded a ready market—watermelon. Boxcars of Rattlesnake and Bradford watermelons sped north from Augusta, Georgia, on the intact rail line in July, August, and September of 1866. They met a rapturous reception. No northern melon tasted as good and the demand in New York was limitless. Indeed, its success kick-started the southern economy, directing it toward truck farming and away from cultivation of staples.

Why did the Georgia Rattlesnake melon and the Bradford melon inspire such ferocious demand? Each had a stable shape and ample size. Consistency mattered because watermelons cross so promiscuously that most varieties cultivated north of Carolina morphed with every season. In 1838, a Philadelphian complained, "I know of none which have not very much degenerated." Both southern melons had been created with rigorous breeding discipline. The Rattlesnake—created in 1850s Augusta—was an oblong picnic melon with wavy stripes (the snakes) crawling the length of the sides. The Bradford—created in the 1850s by Nathaniel Napoleon Bradford of Sumter—was also an oblong picnic melon, with dark green skin and sutures running the length; it looked like a giant cucumber. Both ranged from 20 to 40 pounds—ample food for large families. Both were sweet, and their good flavor derived from a common ancestor—the Lawson melon of Georgia. The former derived from a cross between the Lawson and the Mountain Sweet Watermelon, the latter from a cross between the Lawson and the Carolina Long/Mountain Sprout Watermelon.

Because the Rattlesnake and the Bradford did not survive rough handling in railcars well, they would be supplanted by transport melons bred for shipping. These market melons, such as Kolb's Gem and the Black Diamond, did not taste as good as the Rattlesnake and Bradford, resulting in an odd growing pattern. Truck farmers grew field melons of mediocre flavor for sale in the northern cities. Home gardeners grew the flavorful melons—Rattlesnake, Bradford, Florida Favorite, and Kleckley's Sweet. Unfortunately, the greed of the market growers would spoil the pleasure of the home gardeners. They covered entire counties in Kolb's Gem watermelons, and whenever you monocrop on that scale, sooner or later the pest or pathogen that loves that melon more than anything else will show up and find paradise. In 1893, Fusarium wilt broke out in southern Georgia and spread over the South, killing field melons and garden melons without discrimination. Breeders would then seek to make a shipping melon with resistance to Fusarium and anthracnose. One had to have extraordinary faith to plant the old tasty melons with disease rampant and resistant watermelons

Bradford watermelon. David S. Shields.

available—and much of the watermelon breeding until 1960 was driven by the need to create a productive, disease-resistant melon.

In 1954, breeder C. F. Andrus released the greatest American watermelon produced in the mid-twentieth century, the Charleston Gray. So called for its ashy, gray-green skin, the Charleston Gray is a black-seeded picnic style melon of 23 to 35 pounds in weight. It has four great virtues: it produces multitudes of melons; it resists anthracnose; it keeps the same shape; and it is tough enough to withstand rough handling in shipping. From the late 1950s through the 1980s, it was the most widely cultivated watermelon in the world. The scientists at the USDA Vegetable Lab in Charleston decided to create a new crop melon shortly after World War II. Andrus determined that the flavor should be derived from the Pedigree Seed Company's Garrison melon, an improved form of the striped Georgia Rattlesnake. The anthracnose resistance derived from the Congo Watermelon (the first great anthracnose-resistant watermelon, also bred by Andrus). The configuration derived from the old southern gray watermelons. The watermelon breeding after 1970 was directed at creating the convenience melon—seedless, small, with thin rind. Sweetness rather than nuanced flavor was the hallmark of these refrigerator melons.

In 2009, the Carolina Gold Rice Foundation began looking for the old Carolina melons—the Bradford, the Ravenscroft, and the Odell's White—to provide an alternative to the

Odell's White Watermelon grown by Rodger Winn, Little Mountain, SC. David S. Shields.

insipid convenience melons in our groceries. In 2013, Nat Bradford came forward to announce that his family's famous melon still survived. Nat Bradford was the eighth generation descendent of the creator of the variety. The return of the Bradford watermelon became the heirloom recovery story of 2013. The superlative flavor and thick rind made the Bradford the ideal vehicle to restore a range of watermelon foodways—the distilling of watermelon brandy, the rendering of watermelon meat to molasses, and finally the pickling of the watermelon rind. Watermelon juice also had a wealth of uses in cooking and brewing. Nat organized the Bradford Watermelon Company to oversee the future of his family's horticultural legacy. He made seed available through Sow True Seed in Ashville, North Carolina, to home growers who can make it a resource for home growers.

Once the Bradford had been recovered, southern seed savers sought out the other classic melons. Dr. James Kibler realized that the Stoney Mountain Watermelon preserved through the Metze family in the Dutch Fork and grown by heirloom breeder Rodger Winn was the Odell's White watermelon, a large (up to 60 pounds), round, light-skinned, pink-fleshed melon, originally bred by the Black foreman of Col. A. G. Summer's plantation, and promoted by Milton Odell of Mulhollan. A robust, productive melon, it became the favorite market melon in 1870s California, when Lodi grew truck crops rather than citrus. Its seed is also available from Sow True Seed and has been board on Slow Food's global Ark of Taste. Dr. Kibler believes that the Ravenscroft Watermelon also may survive in the seed collection maintained by Carrold Wicker.

Wildlife officials now call it the Southern Kingfish (*Menticirrhus americanus*), but to fishermen and gastronomes in South Carolina it had another name, a name so savory when pronounced it made a fish lover's gastric juices percolate: Whiting. And the deep water, fully adult version, the most cherished of coastal-caught fishes, is the bullhead whiting. You know it by the one short stubby barbel dangling beneath its chin.

In 1886, a commentator on Charleston's fish market observed, "The whiting is an aristocratic kind of fish with fastidious tastes, and the bull-head variety is the crème de la crème of the whiting family, piscatorial Poo-Bahs, in fact, which are born sneering, and despise such common bait as clams or difflers. 'No swimp, no whitin' is an old proverb in fishing circles." Until the shrimp began to run in

coastal waters—in May—there was no securing whiting in the market.

John Edwards Holbrook, Charleston's resident ichthyologist in the nineteenth century, was a great admirer of the whiting. He indicated that it appeared in the surf in April and stayed on the coast through August but was rarely landed in any numbers in July and August. There were two sorts of whiting: the surf whiting and the deep-water whiting. The former could be caught "where the bottom is hard and sandy, often forming, when the tide is out, an extensive beach" (1855). The front beach of Sullivan's Island was a prime location for this. Many were caught with a seine net and sold in market. The deep-water whiting, or bullhead, was a larger, better flavored fish, darker in color, solitary in habit (surf whiting will school). During spawning season, it would

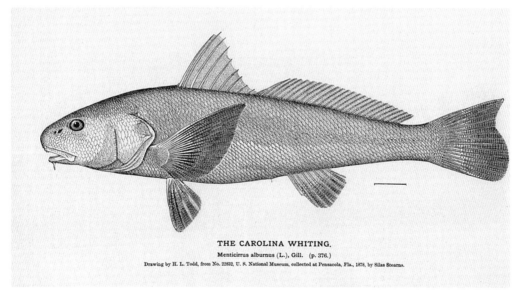

THE CAROLINA WHITING.
Menticirrus alburnus (L.), Gill. (p. 376.)
Drawing by H. L. Todd, from No. 22932, U. S. National Museum, collected at Pensacola, Fla., 1878, by Silas Stearns.

H. L. Todd, engraving of the Whiting from vol. 2 [illustrations] of George Brown Goode, The Fishes and Fishery Industries of the United States *(Washington, DC: GPO, 1887).*

head into deep brackish water and deep fresh rivers to cast eggs. Notices would begin to appear in newspapers in mid-September that the bullhead whiting were running in the rivers.

Fried whiting was standard breakfast fare, often paired with shrimp and grits in hotels and restaurants. Deep fried whiting in the Calabash style became, in the last half of the twentieth century, a standard offering at family restaurants. The recipe was simple—heat cooking oil to 375°F, wash 10 filets of whiting leaving them damp, dust them in seasoned wheat flour, pop them in the bubbling fat, and wait until they brown. Whiting sautéed in butter also had its adherents. Among the other traditional preparations, whiting pilau ranks high. The prolific DIY cookbook author Oscar Vick has a particularly useful version of a preparation of this traditional stew. Needless to say, Carolina Gold rice was the preferred variety to employ in this dish:

Whiting and Rice Pilau

Oscar Vick, *Gullah Cooking: Fish Cooking* (1991)

1 pound diced, skinless whiting fillets
1 cup smoked bacon, diced and fried
1 cup diced celery
1 cup diced onions
1 teaspoon red pepper
6 cups water
1 diced green bell pepper
1 cup beef broth
½ cup diced parsley
3 ounces tomato paste
1 tablespoon garlic
1 tablespoon parsley diced
1 crushed bay leaf
1 tablespoon Tabasco
1 teaspoon vinegar
3½ cup raw rice

Salt and pepper the fish. Bring the water to a boil and then add all of the ingredients except the rice. Boil for 4 to 5 minutes. Stir in 3 ½ cups of rice. Reduce to simmer for 40 to 60 minutes. You should never stir a pilau after the rice has been added. Serve with slaw and dill pickles.

Aside from having a fishing license, you have no restrictions or requirements when harvesting whiting/southern kingfish in South Carolina waters.

The port of Charleston formed a node in a global web of trade during the colonial era, and much of the first-world trading system exchanged drugs of various sorts— tobacco, alcohol, coffee, chocolate, capsicum, sugar, and spice. The coffee shops, taverns, confectioners, smoking parlors, and tea shops that made up the Lowcountry cityscapes in Savannah and Charleston gave eloquent testimony to the people's investment in these physical stimuli. Strangely, many were unaware that the Lowcountry hosted its own Native drug plants: Dahoon Holly *Ilex cassine* and Yaupon Holly *Ilex vomitoria*—thornless members of the holly family whose foliage was saturated with theobromine, the same elation-causing chemical found in chocolate, and also caffeine.

The Native peoples of the southeast knew it of course. Yaupon was their famous "black drink"—a strong beverage used to cleanse the body. In Virginia they sold the tea to settlers and some developed a taste—but its consumption was always limited to the most rural, least cosmopolitan settlers. The same was true in South Carolina. Natives made Yaupon Tea, and a small contingent of the settler population as well, prepping the leaves in the same way. "They are gathered in the fall and laid in a trough chopped up somewhat fine, and then put into an iron pot which is carefully heated, to wilt the leaves; then the whole is packed away in earthen jars, or dried, and is made by infusion in the ordinary way" (1850).

Of the two plants, *Ilex cassine* was deemed the more mild in its effects; *Ilex vomiteria,* as its name suggests, would purge you when ingested in high concentrations. Black Drink was a dense brew by all reports. John Lawson,

Yaupon (dahoon holly) grows in two forms: Ilex cassine *pictured here and* Ilex vomitoria. *It is the one native plant in South Carolina that contains caffeine. It also contains theobromine, the active chemical in chocolate. David S. Shields, photograph of a hedge on Cassina Road in Columbia, SC.*

in his *Voyage to Carolina* from 1703, reported a Native legend in which a chronically ill elder dreamt that he would be cured if he drank a decoction made of the tree against which he rested his head; it was a Yaupon. So began the reputation of the tree as a drug.

Publication of E. M. Hale's treatise, *Ilex Cassine, the Aboriginal American Tea* in 1891, set imaginative horticulturists thinking in South Carolina. Alfred Jouannet made his fortune as a farmer and seedsman long before he had his inspiration to serve Americans' inexhaustible craving for chemical stimulants. He had come to South Carolina in 1882, at the age of twenty-one, bearing packages of asparagus seed and in the sandy fields of the Lowcountry planted the largest farm in North America—acre after acre of Argenteuil spears. With each decade he expanded his offerings: Bermuda onions, Charleston Wakefield Cabbages, Seashore Rye. Yet in the 1910s, Jouannet became enamored of a wild plant growing along the Carolina coast: *Ilex cassine*. The Cassina Tree, Christmasberry, or Dahoon Holly made up windbreak hedges along some of his farms. He read Hale's book. A curious man, he cured some leaves, tried it, and realized that it supplied the same lift, the same elation, as tea.

Banking on the conviction that nothing would hinder Americans' pursuit of a cheap high, Jouannet in 1922 began stockpiling and curing Cassina on a commercial scale at a purpose-built plant in Mt. Pleasant. Agricultural reporter M. L. Willet declared, "I do not believe that I have ever gone on a more important mission than this one to Mt. Pleasant." On the 20th of November, 1922 Jouannet had 3 tons prepped for sale. He could process 200 pounds a day at the cost of 5 cents a pound.

Newspaper articles appeared repeatedly in the early 1920s about the cassina beverage revolution that was supposed to occur. "Japanese producers and exporters of green and black tea which will come in competition with green cassina and black cassina are worried over the prospective new American industry" (1926). A syrup was made from the leaves for use in soda fountains. But Jouannet's Cassina drink revolution died stillborn. Despite assurances that it tasted as invigorating and splendid as tea, the public simply chose to add another teaspoon of sugar to their iced tea, sip their South American coffee, and pay the additional charge for familiar pleasures. Jouannet was the rare individual who bet on Americans' love of drugs . . . and lost.

Periodically over the twentieth century, agronomists and plant scientists would refloat the idea of a yaupon industry. Test plots would be planted. But it was not until the 2010s that a well-funded and thoughtfully designed revival of cassina came about—in Savannah Georgia with the ASI Yaupon Tea Company, in Florida with the Yaupon Brothers American Tea Co., Yaupon Teas in Texas and in Cat Spring, Texas with the Cat Spring Black Tea Company. While all of the companies offer a straight form of the fermented leaf, ASI has noted the odd American fascination for flavored herbal teas or tisanes and determined to offer a range of flavor possibilities. This may prove intelligent in that the black drink by itself does not have the complexity of a good fermented black tea. At any rate, today one can drink Yaupon and have a choice of what company and what flavor one would prefer.

SOURCES

Asparagus

Peter Henderson, *Everything for the Garden* (New York, 1886), 8. Robert. F. M. Hexamer, *Asparagus: Its Culture for Home Use and for Market* (New York: Orange Judd Co., 1903). *Washington Asparagus C. T. & F. C. D. C.* Bulletin 7 (Washington, DC: Government Printing Office, 1919). W. S. Flory, *Genetic and Cytological Investigations on Asparagus Officinais, Genetics* 17, 4 (1931), 432–76. J. Dufault, *History of Asparagus in South Carolina: A Look at Its Potential and How to Grow It* (Clemson University Technical Report, 2013).

Barbecue

Charleston City Gazette (September 17, 1802), 2. "Barbecue," *South Carolina State Gazette* (July 4, 1828), 1. "Fourth of July Celebrations, At Bachelor's Retreat, Pickens District," *Miller's Weekly Messenger* (July 18, 1832), 1. "From Our Correspondent. Fourth of July at Camden No. VIII," *Charleston Southern Patriot* (July 15, 1845), 2. "Hon. Preston S. Brooks at Home," *Charleston Courier* (October 7, 1856), 1. "The Barbecue of Mssrs. Hunter and Birge," *Newberry Herald* (August 1, 1866), 3. [Maybin Griffin], *Edgefield Advertiser* (August 1, 1872), 4. "Grand Barbecue of the Season," *Newberry Herald* (July 21, 1875), 4. "Alcazar," *Augusta Chronicle* (August 26, 1906), 18.

Benne

James Meese, *Archives of Useful Knowledge* (1811). "Bene," *American Farmer* 2, 17 (July 21, 1820), 135. "Raleigh, June 27, 1821," *American Farmer* 3 (August 3, 1821), 150. Robert Goodwin, "Bene," *American Farmer* 6 (1824), 6. Francis Porcher, *Medical Botany of South Carolina* (Charleston, SC: Evans & Cogswell, 1849), 493. "Benne Brittle," *South Carolina: A Guide to the Palmetto State* (Federal Writers Projects, 1938), 156. Sarah Rutledge [1847], "Groundnut Soup" and "Bennie Soup," *The Carolina Housewife* (Columbia: University of South Carolina Press, 1979), 45–46.

Biscuits

Thomas Walter Peyre Plantation Journal (1831–1851) South Carolina Historical Society ms collections, 59. "Buttermilk Biscuit," *Abbeville Press and Banner* (November 7, 1888), 8. "Southern Biscuit. How to Make Them," *Telegram-Herald* (September 30, 1889), 8; this was a widely syndicated story and appeared in at least sixteen newspapers over September and October 1889, albeit with textual alterations. "Ideal Cheese Biscuit," *Abbeville Press and Banner* (October 7, 1896), 4. "Test of Cook's Skill," *Edgefield Advertiser* (September 3, 1913), 2. Toni Patrick, *101 Things to do With Canned Biscuits* (Salt Lake City, UT: Gibbs-Smith, 2008). Nathalie Dupree and Cynthia Graubert, *Southern Biscuits* (Gibbs-Smith, 2011). Carrie Morey, *Callie's Biscuits and Southern Traditions: Heirloom Recipes* (New York: Simon & Schuster, Atria Books, 2013), 121–8. Linda Civitello, *Baking Powder Wars: The Cutthroat Food Fight that Revolutionized Cooking* (Champaign: University of Illinois Press, 2017).

Blackberry

"Blackberry Syrup," *Southern Patriot* (August 12, 1847), 2. "Blackberry Brandy," *Charleston Courier* (August 10, 1858), 1; reprinted from the *Edgefield Advertiser*. "Blackberries In," *Edgefield Advertiser* (June 6, 1894), 1. "Blackberry Jam" and "Southern Blackberry Cobbler," *The State* (June 28, 1908), 18. "Blackberry Culture," *Laurens Advertiser* (October 13, 1909), 9. "Wild Blackberry Dumplings," *Baltimore American* (July 20, 1911), 3. "Find good money in Blackberries," *The State* (February 16, 1915), 9. "Blackberry Time," *Pageland Journal* (June 23, 1915), 2. "Blackberry Wine cause for Action," *The State* (November 28, 1921), 5. "Blackberry time in York claims Center of Stage," *The State* (July 13, 1923), 9.

Blackfish

"How to Make a Chowder," Sentinel of Freedom 60, 1 (July 6, 1858), 3. "Fishing Excursion," *Charleston Courier* 67, 21371 (July 27, 1869), 1. "Black-fish à l'Americaine," Felix Déliée, *Franco-American Cookery* (New York, 1884), 290–91. G. Brown Gordon, *The Fisheries and Fishing Industries of the United States* (Washington, DC: GPO, 1887), "About Clams," *Charleston News and Courier* (July 14, 1888), 8. "Clam Chowder at Riddock House," *Charleston News and Courier* (June 17, 1894), "Business Card—R. R. Whiteley," *Charleston News and Courier* (August 12, 1899), 5. "Blackfish a la Orly," Charles Ranhofer, *The Epicurean* (New York, 1920, 2nd edition), 431. Wilma D. Martin, "Baked Black Sea Bass," *Captain*

Murrell's Savory Seafood Recipes (Murrells Inlet, SC: Rum Gully Press, 1990), 77. "Okra Blackfish Chowder," Oscar Vick, *Gullah Cooking: Fish Cooking* (Charleston, SC: By the Author, 1991), 32. David S. Shields, "Fish Master," *Southern Provisions: The Creation and Revival of a Cuisine* (Chicago: University of Chicago Press, 2015), 184–87.

Boiled Peanuts

Mrs. Washington [pseud.], *The Unrivalled Cook Book* (New York: Harper & Brothers, 1885), 3–4. Andrew F. Smith, "Boiled Peanuts," *Peanuts: The Illustrious History of the Goober Pea* (Champaign: University of Illinois Press, 2002). *Charleston News and Courier* (July 31, 1966), 41. "Boiled Peanuts History and Recipe," whatscookingamerica.com (2006). "Boiled Peanuts Questions and Answers," *The Lee Bros. Boiled Peanuts Catalog*, http://www.boiledpeanuts.com/index2.html. *The Lee Bros. Charleston Kitchen* (Clarkson Potter, 2013). http://www.tonythepeanutman.com/.

Butterbeans and Sieva Beans

"The Culture of the Butter Bean," *Southern Planter and Farmer* (October 1868), 615. Theresa C. Brown, *Modern Domestic Cookery* (1871), 81. "Something to take the place of Cotton," *Progressive Farmer and Southern Farm Gazette* (November 4, 1911), 3. W. F. Fechner, "How to Grow," *Miami District Daily News* (March 10, 1920), 4. "Friendly Indians," *The Columbia Record* (October 13, 1969), 57.

Cabbage

"Sea Island Truck Farming," *Southern Cultivator* 50, 5 (May 1892), 238–40. William C. Geraty, *Catalogue of Cabbage, Sweet Potato, and Strawberry Plants* (Yonge's Island, SC, 1907), 2–4. *Handbook of South Carolina, Resources, Institutions and Industries of the State* (Columbia:

The State Department of Agriculture, 1908), 297. "Smothered Cabbage" [White Gravy Version] *Manning Times* (October 24, 1917), 3. "The Plaza Café," *Columbia Record* (January 21, 1918), 10. "Cabbage King," *Charleston News and Courier,* June 24, 1931, 13. "Smothered Cabbage," [Vinegared Gravy], *Rock Hill Herald* (May 31, 1938), 12. 10. Menu, Sgt. White's Diner, Beaufort, SC, February 5, 2017.

Calabash Fried Fish and Shrimp

Steven V. Roberts, "In Calabash N.C. It's Seafood Aplenty," *New York Times* (August 28, 1983), 10:6. Jason Frye, "Calabash seafood tradition still cooking as diners flock in," StarNews Online (June 12, 2012). Sheri Castle, "Calabash Shrimp," *Our State* (May 30, 2018). Beck's Restaurant http://www.becksrestaurant.com/about-us.

Carolina Gold Rice

"How to Boil Rice," "From the Charleston Courier," *Providence Patriot & Columbian Phoenix* (September 2, 1829), 1. "Pilau of Green Peppers," *Charleston News and Courier* (September 7, 1905), 6. "Eggplant Pilau," *The State* (August 9, 1908), 14. David S. Shields, "Carolina Gold Rice," *The Golden Seed; Writings on the History and Culture of Carolina Gold Rice* (Charleston, SC: The Carolina Gold Rice Foundation, 2010), 5–36. David S. Shields, "Carolina Gold Rice," *Southern Provisions: The Creation & Revival of a Cuisine* (Chicago: University of Chicago Press, 2015), 229–52.

Catfish

Henry William Herbert, *Frank Forester's Fish and Fishing of the United States, and British Provinces of North America* (London: Richard Bentley, 1849), 193. A Cat Fish Stew," *Laurens Advertiser* (July 28, 1909), 4. [Wateree Catfish] *The State* (November 23, 1930), 13. Harry Hampton, "Catfish Stew-Woods & Waters," *The State* (April 16, 1931),

2. David M. Newell, *The Fishing and Hunting Answer Book* (Garden City, NY: Doubleday and Company, Inc., 1948), 33. "Cush Stew," *The State* (April 9, 1950), 64. Vlad Evanoff, *The Freshwater Fisherman's Bible* (New York: Doubleday, 1964), 170. Laverne M. Prosser, "Catfish Farm is Newest Berkeley County Industry," *Charleston News and Courier* (May 28, 1968), 6. "Columbia Catfish Stew, Loved and Lost," *Charleston News and Courier* (November 5, 1974), 8. "Catfish Farmers on the Hook," *The State* (October 28, 1991), 48.

Chestnuts

Mary Lincoln, "Deviled Chestnuts," *Philadelphia Inquirer* (December 30, 1899), 11. "Nut Dainties-Chestnut Soufflé," *Augusta Chronicle* (September 27, 1903), 3. "The Luxurious Chestnut-Chestnut Custard," *Bay City Times* (November 20, 1903), 10. "Thanksgiving Dinner—Chestnut Dressing," *Abbeville Press and Banner* (December 2, 1904), 8. "Damage to Southern Trees," *Keowee Courier* (August 7, 1912), 4. "Edible Fruits of Forest Trees," *Watchman and Southron* (November 17, 1917), 8. Pete Gilpin, "Radiation being employed to Fight Chestnut Blight," *Charleston News and Courier* (December 29, 1958), 6. Susan Freinkel, *American Chestnut: the Life, Death, and Rebirth of a Perfect Tree* (Berkley Los Angeles: The University of California Press, 2007).

Chicken Bog

"Chicken Bog," *Dillon Herald* (May 20, 1920). Kay Rentschler, "Chicken Bog" (Anson Mills, n.d.).

Chinquapins

"Chinquapins on Sale," *Trenton Evening Times* November 26, 1898), 5. "The Immoral Chinquapin," *The State* (September 13, 1912), 4. "Chinquapins," *Baltimore Sun* (September 29, 1920), "Do you Remember," *Charleston News and Courier* (June 29, 1952), 4. "Make the children

happy," *Columbia Record* (October 31, 1956), 4.
"Don Whitehead reports on Chinquapins and Paw
Paws," *Knoxville-News-Sentinel* (October 19, 1971),
63. Susanna Lyle, *Fruit and Nuts: A Comprehensive
Guide to the Cultivation, Uses and Health Benefits
of Over 300 Food-producing Plants* (Ann Arbor:
University of Michigan Press, 2006), 122–23.

Collards

"Greeks and Romans Grew Kale and Collards,"
Columbia [SC] Record (December 31, 1955), 8. F.
R. Irvine, "The Edible Cultivated and Semi-
Cultivated Leaves of West Africa," *Materiae
Vegetabiles* 2 (1956), 35–42. Edna Lewis, "Cooked
Greens" (1988), courtesy Ruth Lewis Smith.
John T. Edge, ed., "Collard Greens," *The New
Encyclopedia of Southern Culture* v.7: Foodways
(Chapel Hill: University of North Carolina
Press, 2007), 172–73. Todd Coleman, "Cabbage
and Collards," *SAVEUR* (April 15, 2011). Judith
Ann Carney and Richard Nicholas Rosomoff, *In
the Shadow of Slavery: Africa's Botanical Legacy
in the Atlantic World* (Berkeley: University of
California Press, 2011). Birney Imes, "Birney
Imes: Amazing Collards," *The Dispatch* (July 12,
2012). Shaylyn Esposito, "How to Make Feijoada,
Brazil's National Dish, Including a Recipe from
Emeril Lagasse," *Smithsonian* (June 13, 2014).
Edward H. Davis and John Morgan, *Collards: A
Southern Tradition from Seed to Table* (Tuscaloosa:
The University of Alabama Press, 2015). David
S. Shields, *Southern Provisions: The Creation and
Revival of a Cuisine* (Chicago: University of
Chicago Press, 2015).

Conch

"President Spends Weekend Relaxing in Fla.,
Bahamas," *Charleston Evening Post* (March 15,
1971), 22. "Conch—Recipes Loved and Lost,"
Charleston News and Courier (April 9, 1978), 85.

"Colony House Conch Fritters," Dawn O'Brien
and Karen Mulford, *South Carolina's Historic
Restaurants and their Recipes* (Winston-Salem,
NC: John F. Blair, 1984), 67. "Short Season Hits
Conch Processors," *The State* (April 6, 1997), 7.
Terri Kirby Hathaway, "What's in a Name—
Conch versus Whelk," *Cross Currents* N.C. Sea
Grants (March 2, 2015), https://ncseagrant.ncsu
.edu/currents/2015/03/whats-in-a-name
-conch-vs-whelk/. http://dnr.sc.gov/swap
/supplemental/marine/whelksguild2015.pdf.

Cooter Soup

"City Affairs," *Charleston Courier* (August 6,
1869), 1. Julia York, "Cooter Soup," *The State*
(July 31, 1949), 65. Bob Talbert, "South Carolina
Outdoors," *The State* (August 28, 1960), 22.
Damon Fowler, ed., *Mrs. Hill's Southern Practical
Cookery and Receipt Book* (Columbia: University
of South Carolina Press, 1995), 27. Joseph
Dabney, *Food, Folklore, and Art of Lowcountry
Cooking* (Naperville, IL: Cumberland House,
2010), 170.

Corn Bread

Philo-Rumford, "On the Use of Maize,"
The Monthly Magazine and American Review
(August 1799), 345–47. Charles A. Wickliffe,
"Letters from the South No. 3," *Charleston
Courier* (December 21, 1840), 2. "Rebel Corn
Bread," *Union News and Herald* (February 22,
1883) 5. Christian Mugel, "Pavilion Hotel Corn
Bread," *The Weekly Union Times* (July 17, 1883),
2. "Corn Bread at its very Best," *Charlotte
Observer* (December 10, 1899), 5. Bessie R.
Murphy, "Spider Corn Bread," *Charleston
Evening Post* (July 31, 1923), 12; reprinted by
permission of *Charleston Post and Courier*. "It's
Birdsey's Flour The Best," *The State* (May 16,
1930), 16.

Cracklin' Bread

W. A. Clark, "Craklin' Bread," *Augusta Chronicle* (December 20, 1904), 6. "Cracklin' Bread," *Columbus GA Daily Inquirer* (January 7, 1911), 4. "Crackling Bread," *Charleston News and Courier* (December 2, 1928), 9. Emma Speed Sampson, "De Way to a Man's Heart," *Richmond Times-Dispatch* (February 11, 1930), 8. "Lillie Rose Tells How She Learned Down in S. Carolina as a Child to Cook Crackling Bread and Hopping John," *Knoxville News-Sentinel* (February 4, 1938), 16.

Duck

Theresa C. Brown, "To Roast a Wild Duck," "To Roast an English Duck," *Modern Domestic Cookery* (Charleston, SC: Edward Perry, 1871), 61–62. A Southern Lady, "To Roast Duck," *Centennial Cook Book* (Charleston, 1876), 29. "My Mother's Cook Book," *Lancaster News* (October 24, 1919), 8. "How to Cook Christmas Poultry and Game," *Columbia Record* (December 16, 1927), 7. Eddie Meier, "Species of Duck Not to Stuff," *The State* (December 26, 1956), 5-B. "Magnificent Duck is Perfect Entrée," *Columbia Record* (November 18, 1968), 23. Harriott Fauette, "Hunter Plays Fare Game," *Columbia Record* (February 6, 1978), 31. Julius M. Reynolds, *Sunrise on the Santee: A Memoir of Waterfowling in South Carolina* (Columbia: University of South Carolina Press, 2002).

Duke's Mayonnaise

Katie McElveen, "3 great make-it-yourself mayonnaise recipes: Cooking Creole," *NOLA.com* (2005). Rebecca Orchant, "Duke's Mayo Is the South's Favorite and Maybe the Best," *Huffington Post* (September 30, 2013). Emily Wallace, "Duke's Mayonnaise: The Southern Spread with a Cult Following," *Washington Post* (November 5, 2013). Kim Severson, "There's No Mayonnaise Like My Mayonnaise," *New York Times* (April 14, 2015). Emily Wallace, "Duke's Mayo: An Obsession," *Southern Living* (2016).

Dumplings

"On indigestion," *Charleston Courier* (August 11, 1824), Damon Lee Fowler, *Mrs Hill's Southern Practical Cookery and Receipt Book* (Columbia: University of South Carolina Press, 1995, rpt. 1872 ed.), 269–72. "A Monster Dumpling," *Elkhart Daily Review* (December 19, 1904), 5. "Here are the Favorite Dishes—How to Cook them," *Augusta Chronicle* (March 29, 1908), 29. "All Worth Sampling," *Edgefield Advertiser* (February 2, 1916), 4. "Recipes from a Dutch Housewife," *Augusta Chronicle* (July 29, 1926), 11. W. Kerrigan, "Hard Cider and the Election of 1840," *American Orchard* (March 11, 2015), https://americanorchard.wordpress.com/tag/william-henry-harrison/.

Field Peas

John MacLean, *American Farmer* 2, no 24. (1822). Sarah Rutledge [1847], *The Carolina Housewife* (Columbia: University of South Carolina Press, 1979), 44. C. A. Fatokun, S. A. Tarawali, B. B. Singh, P. M. Kormawa, and M. Tamò, *Challenges and Opportunities for Enhancing Sustainable Cowpea Production* (Lagos, Nigeria: International Institute of Tropical Agriculture, 2002), 62–80. Richard Fery, Jeffrey Ehlers, Phillip Roberts, "Cowpea Breeding in the USA, New Varieties and Improved Germ Plasm," USDA Vegetable Research, Charleston, SC #255132 (July 21, 2010), https://www.ars.usda.gov/research/publications/publication/?seqNo115=255132. "Peas in Our Time," Red Dirt Productions (September 9, 2015). Kim Severson, "Field Peas, a Southern Good Luck Charm," *The New York Times* (December 29, 2015). David S. Shields, *Southern Provisions:*

The Creation and Revival of a Cuisine (Chicago: University of Chicago Press, 2015).

Figs

John Bachman, "On the Cultivation of the Fig Tree in Carolina," *Southern Cabinet of Agriculture, Horticulture, Rural and Domestic Economy* (October 1840), 603. "Crowing Figs at the South," *American Agriculturist* (February 1848), 45. D. Redmond, "The Pomological Resources of the South," *Southern Cultivator* (November 1850), 339–40. D. Redmond, "The Pomological Resources of the South," *Proceedings of the Seventh Session of the American Pomological Society* (Brooklyn, NY: George C. Bennett, 1858), 210. "Fig Candy," *Charleston Women's Exchange Cook Book* (Charleston, 1901), 87. Gustav Eisen, *The Fig: Its History, Culture, and Curing* (Washington, DC: Government Printing Office, 1901), 61–62. Ira J. Condit, "Fig History in the New World," *Agricultural History* 31, 2 (April 1957), 19–20.

Fritters

New York Commercial Advertiser (March 17, 1830), 1. Sarah Rutledge, *The Carolina Housewife, or House and Home: by a Lady of Charleston* (Charleston, SC: W. R. Babcock & Co., 1847), 119. "Corn Fritters," *Abbeville Press and Banner* (November 11, 1891). "Potato Fritters," *Abbeville Messenger* (December 14, 1887), 7. "Strawberry Fritters," *Abbeville Press and Banner* (March 21, 1888), 8. "Tomato Fritters," *Weekly Union Times* (August 25, 1893), 5. "Orange Fritters," *Anderson Intelligencer* (May 22, 1901), 11. "Salsify Fritters," *Abbeville Press and Banner* (February 1, 1905), 8. "Sweet Potato Fritters," *Abbeville Press and Banner* (May 30, 1906), 7. "Rice Fritters," *Edgefield Advertiser* (July 5, 1911), 3. "Fig Fritters," *Edgefield Advertiser* (May 2, 1917), 4. "Leftovers make Palatable Timbales and Fritters," *Charleston News*

and Courier* (March 12, 1927), 7. Betsy Murphy," Doughnuts, Croquettes and other Recipes," *Charleston Evening Post* (January 20, 1928), 14. Sister Mary, "Fritters," *Charleston Evening Post* (June 6, 1933), 10. "Rice Fritters are Welcome at Any Meal," *Charleston Evening Post* (March 5, 1937), 25. "Temperature Must be Right When All Fritters Are Being Prepared," *Baton Rouge Advocate* (May 29, 1936), 16.

Frogmore Stew

"Frogmore Stew," *The State* (Oct 19, 1983), 6. "Frogmore Stew," *Post and Courier* (December 10, 1992), 102. Joseph Dabney, *The Food, Folklore and Art of Lowcountry Cooking* (Cumberland House, 2010), 73–75, 132–133. Nancie McDermott, *Southern Soups and Stews* (Chronicle Books, 2015), 53. Hannah Raskin, "Expert boils Frogmore Stew Down to Basics," *Charleston Post Courier* (September 20, 2016). John Martin Taylor, "Frogmore Stew," www.hoppinjohns.net (March 12, 2008).

Ginger and Ginger Ale

"Ginger Beer," *Camden Gazette* (April 24, 1817), 3. "prepared and sold by J. Dalton," *Charleston Times* (September 23, 1818), 2. "Ginger Beer," *Charleston Courier* (May 9, 1829), 2. "Freymuth's," *Charleston Courier* (June 27, 1837), 3. William J. Rivers, "Instructions," *A Sketch of the History of South Carolina* (Charleston, SC: McCarter & Co., 1856), 343. "Holloway's Concentrated Essence of Jamaica Ginger," *Charleston Courier* (May 19, 1868), 3. "The Duty of the Hour," *Charleston Evening Post* (November 18, 1896), 5. "Harris Lithia Springs Hotel," *The State* (August 20, 1899), 5. Eppie Richbourg, "Bottling Works Still Brews Ginger Ale," *Charleston News and Courier* (April 20, 1975), 3. Bill McDonald, "Why Fuss Over Ginger Ale, *The State* (March 8, 1982), 23. David Mould,

"Bottler's new-found publicity has ginger ale business bubbling," *Columbia Record* (August 1, 1983), 30. Fred Monk, "New Owner puts zest in Blenheim," *The State* (December 1, 1983), 9. Bethany Aram, "Caribbean ginger and Atlantic trade, 1570–1648," *Journal of Global History,* 10, 3 (2015), 410–430.

Gravy

[Pierre Blot] "More Hints to American Housekeepers," *San Francisco Bulletin* (March 15, 1859), 1. Theresa C. Brown, *Modern Domestic Cookery: Being a Collection of Receipts Suitable for All Classes of Housewives, Together with Many Valuable Household Hints* (Charleston, SC: Edward Perry, 1871), 3. Cornelia C. Bedford, "Fish and Meat Sauces," *The State* (September 13, 1908), 19. "A dissertation on rice—an Gravy," *The State* (October 6, 1909), 4.

Groundnut Cakes

Sarah Rutledge, "Groundnut Cakes," *The Carolina Housewife, or House and Home: by a Lady of Charleston* (Charleston, SC: W. R. Babcock & Co., 1847). "Groundnut Cake and Groundnut Candy," *Centennial Receipt Book* (1876), 25. Janet Grant Gilmore Howard & Florence Brobeck, *Fifty Years in a Maryland Kitchen* (Philadelphia: Lippincott, 1881), 294. "With her Face to the East," *Charleston News and Courier* (January 20, 1895), 12. "The Bread You Eat!" *Charleston Evening Post* (May 24, 1895), 3. "Impressions of Charleston," *Charleston Evening Post* (May 17, 1899), 7. "Fod de Wah," *Charleston Evening Post* (February 5, 1901), 8. "At the Exposition," *Winston-Salem Journal* (February 9, 1902), 3. "Charleston Revisited," *Charleston Evening Post* (March 16, 1905), 2. "Charleston Biscuit Works," *Charleston News and Courier* (July 20, 1906), 6. "Peanut Candy," *Portland Oregonian* (August 22, 1909), 5–6.

"Groundnut Cakes," *Charleston News and Courier* (February 28, 1911), 8. [Local Foods] *Augusta Chronicle* (December 16, 1915), 6.

Guinea Squash

Bernard M'Mahon, *The American Gardener's Calendar* (Philadelphia: B. Graves, 1806), 319–20. Mrs. Mary Randolph, *The Virginia House-Wife: or, Methodical Cook* (Baltimore: Plaskitt, Fite & Co., 1838), 108. "Egg Plant," *The Farmer & Gardener, and Live-Stock Breeder and Manager* 6, 1 (May 1, 1839), 7. Sarah Rutledge, *The Carolina Housewife, or House and Home: by a Lady of Charleston* (Charleston, SC: W. R. Babcock & Co., 1847), 100–101. William N. White, *Gardening for the South; or the Kitchen and Fruit Garden* (New York: C. M. Saxton & Co., 1857), 267–68. Pierre Blot, *What to Eat, and How to Cook It* (New York: D. Appleton & Co., 1863). 182. Mrs. R. L. O. Marion Cabell Tyree, "Egg-Plant Pudding," *Housekeeping in Old Virginia* (Louisville, KY: John P. Morton, 1879), 249. "Dishes of Eggplant," *Edgefield Advertiser* (March 12, 1913), 8. Peter Henry Rolfs, *Subtropical Vegetable Farming* (New York: Macmillan & Co., 1916), 193–203.

Hominy Grits

J. and F. Turner, "Flint Hominy Corn," *The American and Commercial Daily Advertiser* (February 14, 1840), 3. Eliza Leslie, "Hominy," *Lady's New Receipt Book* (Philadelphia: A Hart, 1850), 491–92. "Charlestown Grits," *Alexandria Gazette* (December 28, 1853), 3. William Gilmore Simms, "Maize-in-Milk," *Marie de Berniere* (Philadelphia, 1853), 354–55. Theresa S. Brown, "Lye Hominy," *Modern Domestic Cookery* (Charleston, SC: Perry, 1871), 90–91. Joseph Goldberger, *The Cause and Prevention of Pellagra*, Public Health Reports 29 (Washington, DC: GPO,

1914), 2354. "Pellagra," *The Sage Encyclopedia of Food Issues*, ed. Ken Albala (Los Angeles, Sage Reference, 2015), 1123–24. David S. Shields, *Southern Provisions: On the Creation and Revival of a Cuisine* (Chicago: University of Chicago Press, 2015), 339–51. Erin Byers Murray, *Grits: A Cultural and Culinary Journey Through the South* (New York: St. Martin's Press, 2016), 1–56.

Hoppin' John
Sarah Rutledge, "Hopping John," *The Carolina Housewife, or House and Home: by a Lady of Charleston* (Charleston, SC: W. R. Babcock & Co., 1847), 83. Theresa C. Brown, "Hopping John," *Modern Domestic Cookery* (Charleston, SC: Edward Perry, 1871), 91. "Recipes Loved and Lost," *Charleston News and Courier* (December 31, 1972), 34. "Recipes Loved and Lost," *Charleston News and Courier* (December 27, 1973), 8. Jessica B. Harris, "Prosperity Starts with a Pea," *New York Times* (December 30, 2010), https://www.nytimes.com/2010/12/30/opinion/30harris.html.

Iced and Sweet Tea
"Iced Tea is becoming very popular," *New York Tribune* (July 27, 1868), 8. ["A Trip to the Springs"], *New Orleans Times Picayune* (August 27, 1871), 5. "Tube Drinking," *Dallas Daily Herald*, (August 11, 1874), 2. Christine Arpe Gang, "Iced Tea gains popularity nationwide as a summer drink," *Marietta Journal* (June 30, 1988), 51. Lisa Boalt Richardson, *Modern Tea* (San Francisco: Chronicle Books, 2014), 67–68.

Jerusalem Artichoke
"The Jerusalem Artichoke," *Savannah Morning News* (August 14, 1899). N. L. Willet, "Artichokes," *Augusta Chronicle* (January 7, 1912), 6. "Artichoke Pickles," *Manning Times* (1919). "Meeting of the Women's Council," *Watchman and Southron* ("Jerusalem Artichokes Grown

for Sale Experimentally about Fayetteville," *The State* (July 31, 1934), 5. Cordelia Rhodes, "Cookery Gems—Artichoke Relish, *Augusta Chronicle* (August 8, 1941), 11. Mrs. I Greer Reeves, "Jerusalem Artichoke Pickle," *Charleston News and Courier* (November 7, 1971), 45. "Artichoke has one thing going for it—versatility," *The State* (January 2, 1991), 28. Verna Dugger, "Artichoke Relish," *Charleston Post and Courier* (March 22, 1992), 74. Joseph Anthony Amato, *The Great Jerusalem Artichoke Circus, the Buying and Selling of the Rural American Dream* (Minneapolis: University of Minnesota Press, 1993).

Lady Baltimore Cake
[Florence Ottolengui] *Charleston Evening Post* (July 11, 1906), 6. Camilla S. Pinckney, "Lady Baltimore Cake," *Charleston Evening Post* (July 23, 1906), 4. "Delicious Lady Baltimore Cake and How it Should be Made," *Charleston Evening Post* (November 15, 1906), 6. Cecily Brownstone, "Lady Baltimore Cake Originated in Charleston," *Charleston News and Courier* (August 9, 1953), 30. Anne Bryn, *American Cake, From Colonial Gingerbread to Classic Layer* (New York: Rodale Books, 2016), 110–12.

Liver Pudding
[Mr. Brill], *Columbia Daily Phoenix* (October 3, 1867), 3. [Mrs. Stoudemeyer], *Newberry Herald* (December 21, 1882), 4. J. A. Darwin, "Liver Pudding," *Charleston Evening Post* (December 10, 1897), 5. "Charges Not Sustained," *Charleston Evening Post* (April 23, 1898), 7. Mrs. Willard A. Silcox, "Yonges Island Liver Pudding," *Charleston News and Courier* (February 16, 1971), 5. Joe Waldon, "Liver Pudding [sausage style]," *Charleston News and Courier* (February 1, 1972), 3. Mrs. M. E. Crain, "Old Southern Liver Pudding—Recipes Loved and Lost," *Charleston News and Courier* (May 30, 1974).

Loquat

"Rare Fruit," *New York Evening Post* (May 11, 1848), 2; reprint of a *Charleston Courier* article. "Fruit and Ornamental Trees," *Charleston Courier* (November 18, 1862), 3. "The Loquat Japonica," *Riverside Daily Press* (April 12, 1887), 2. "The Loquat," *The American Garden* 9 (May 1888), 183. C. P. Taft, *Loquats and Other Exotics* (Orange, CA, 1903). "Loquats" *Daily Herald* (May 22, 1910), 57. "Loquats, Loved and Lost," *Charleston News and Courier* (January 26, 1971), 5.

Macaroni and Cheese

"Angelo Santi," *Charleston City Gazette* (August 16, 1794), 3. "Rafle," *Charleston City Gazette* (September 16, 1794), 4. "To Lovers of Music," *Charleston City Gazette* (May 23, 1795), 4. "Angelo Santi Confectioner No. 81, King-street," *Charleston Oracle* (January 5, 1807), 4. "The Subscriber," *Charleston Strength of the People* (January 13, 1810). South Carolina Marriage Index, 1600–1820. "Extract from the tour of Holman, the Blind Man," *Charleston Mercury* (July 31, 1822), 1. John B. Sartori, "Vermicelli & Macaroni," *Federal Gazette* (January 24, 1803), 3. "Stewed Macaroni," *The Port Royal Standard and Commercial* (July 13, 1876), 5. Adrian Miller, *Soul Food: The Surprising Story of an American Cuisine, One Plate at a Time* (Chapel Hill: University of North Carolina Press, 2013), 130–40.

Mullet and Mullet Roe

"Islanders Hanker for Fish; Mullet Soon to Simmer," *Charleston Evening Post* (February 28, 1944), 11. Chalmers S. Murray, "Edisto Islanders have Sea Food Dishes of their Own," *Charleston News and Courier* (January 28, 1953), 8. Jack Leland, "Mullet Run Time, Once Favorite of Rich and Poor," *Charleston News and Courier* (November 23, 1974), 7.

Mustard Greens

"Hints to Home Gardeners," *Columbia Record* (April 9, 1917), 6. "Here's your blood tonic," *The State* (May 10, 1922), 4. "Greens and hog jowl," *Columbia Record* (May 1, 1930), 4. "Pepper Pot," *Columbia Record* (August 30, 1925), 18. "Requests for Favorite Recipes Answered [Pepper Pot]," *Charleston News and Courier* (December 1, 1933), 12. *Columbia Record* (February 4, 1936), 4. J. M. Kemble, ed., *Southeastern U. S. Vegetable Handbook 2018* (Auburn, AL: Southeastern Vegetable Extension Workers Group, 2018): https://www.clemson.edu/cafls/research/coastal/documents/2018_SEVG.pdf.

Okra

"Communications, Charleston, July 25, 1831," *Genesee Farmer and Gardener's Journal* 1, 33 (August 20, 1831), 260. "Clemson Spineless New Okra Developed," *Rock Hill Herald* (March 12, 1937), 6. "Okra Without Spines," *The State* (March 14, 1939), 6. "Clemson Spineless Okra Wins Distinction," *Report of the President of Clemson University* (Clemson, SC, 1939). W. R. Beattie, *Culture and Uses of Okra*, Farmer's Bulletin 232 (Washington, DC: USDA, GPO 1940), 11. "'Mother Walker' to observe birthday today," *The State* (November 18, 1949), 3-c. Jessica B. Harris, *Beyond Gumbo: Creole Fusion Food from the Atlantic Rim* (New York: Simon & Schuster, 2003). Michael Twitty, "The Secret History of Okra," ToriAvey.com (August 27, 2013): https://toriavey.com/history-kitchen/history-okra-soup-recipe/). Chris Smith, *The Whole Okra: A Seed to Stem Celebration* (New York: Orange Rudd, 2019).

Orange

"Fruit Trees," *Charleston City Gazette* (January 10, 1795), 3. "Fresh Orange Juice," *Charleston Courier* 11, 1665 (June 3, 1808), 1. "Orange Marmalade,"

The Carolina Receipt Book (1832), 50. "Shade Trees," Charleston City Gazette 55 (May 18, 1832), 201. 2. "Orange Pie," Abbeville Press and Banner (May 11, 1905). "Household Notes," Wilmington Evening Journal (July 14, 1913), 4. "Orange Fritters," Charleston Evening Post (February 20, 1925), 5. David S. Shields, "Orange," Old Southern Orchards, http://www.digitalussouth .org/oldsouthernorchards/subindex .php?fruitName=Orange.

Oysters

A Lady of Charleston, "To Pickle Oysters," The Carolina Receipt Book (1832), 28. "The Oyster," The Charleston Daily News (April 3, 1869). 1. "Carolina Masons," The State (December 15, 1897), 1. Robert C. Gracey, Willis J. Keith, Survey of the South Carolina Oyster Fishery, Technical Report Number 3 (Charleston, SC: South Carolina Wildlife and Marine Resources Department, 1972). Andre Joseph Gallant, A High Low Tide, The Revival of Southern Oysters (Athens: University of Georgia Press. 2018), 4–5.

Palmetto Pickle

"Palmetto a Marvelous Tree," Charleston News and Courier (July 29, 1911), 6. "Palmetto Pickle has big future," Charleston Evening Post (November 27, 1915), 12. "Palmetto Pickle," Charleston News and Courier (April 3, 1916), 8. "At the Quality Shop," Charleston Evening Post (April 2, 1917), 5. George Horry Townsend, "Palmetto Pickle—claimed New Industry Does Not Threat Extinction of Trees," Charleston News and Courier (May 11, 1917), 4. "An Exhibit of Palmetto Pickle," Charleston Evening Post (May 11, 1916), 9. "Keen Market for Palmetto Pickle," Charleston Evening Post (May 3, 1917), 2. "The Close of the Fair," Columbia Daily Phoenix (November 13, 1869), 2. Southern Cultivator 50, 11 (November 1892), 557.

Peaches

"Spiced Peaches" and "To Pickle Peaches," Sarah Rutledge, The Carolina Housewife (Charleston, SC: W.R. Babcock & Co., 1847), 180. A Lady of Charleston, "Peaches in Brandy," The Carolina Receipt Book (1832), 49–50. Sarah Rutledge, "Forcible Entry of a Citizen's Premises," Southern Patriot of Charleston (May 30, 1842), 2. "To Pickle Peaches," The Carolina Housewife, or House and Home: by a Lady of Charleston (Charleston, SC: W. R. Babcock & Co., 1847), 180–81. J William N. White, Gardening for the South, or How to Grow Vegetables and Fruits (New York: Orange Judd and Co., 1868), 387. James Fitz, The Southern Apple and Peach Culturist (Richmond, VA: Fergusson & Rady, 1872), 230. John Rock, "Pasadena Cling," Semi-Tropic California, and the California Horticulturist, 11, 4 (November, 1881), 186–87. Peter J. Hatch, The Fruit and Fruit Trees of Monticello (Charlottesville: University of Virginia Press,1998), 88–89. David S. Shields, "Peaches," Old Southern Orchards http://www .digitalussouth.org/oldsouthernorchards /subindex.php?fruitName=Peach.

Peach Leather

[Lady Baltimore Tea Room Advertisement], Charleston News and Courier (November 28, 1924), 8. [The Spinning Wheel Advertisement], Charleston News and Courier (December 14, 1924), 5. "Junior League Christmas Sale," Charleston News and Courier (November 26, 1925), 5. [Anchorage Advertisement], Charleston News and Courier (April 11, 1927), 12. "Gift Shop Operated to Aid in Financing Milk Station," Charleston News and Courier (February 15, 1929), 30. "Miss Wilson's Colonial Belle Goodies," Charleston News and Courier (April 10, 1930), 18. Blanche Rhett, 200 Years of Charleston Cooking (New York: Jonathan Cape and Harrison Smith, 1930), 30. "The Colonial Belle Kitchen,"

Charleston News and Courier (February 25, 1931), 30. "Uses Unique Recipes," *Charleston News and Courier* (October 8, 1932), 2. Bessie Murphy, "Peach Leather—The Weekly Cooking School," *Charleston Evening Post* (March 15, 1935), 22. "Slave Market Museum," *Charleston News and Courier* (April 9, 1939), 38. "Slave Recipes Inc.," *Charleston News and Courier* (May 18, 1949), 9. Sterling Bodie, "Ever Tasted Peach Leather," *Charleston News and Courier* (December 4, 1950), 13.

Pecan

[Pecan Trade], *Charleston Courier* (January 29, 1853), 2. Sarah A. Elliott, *Mrs. Elliott's Housewife* (New York: Hurd & Holt, 1870), 318. "Pecan Pie," *Texas Siftings* (February 6, 1886), 3. "World's Biggest Pecan Grove," *Charleston Evening Post* (December 6, 1902), 5. "South Atlantic Pecan Company," *Charleston Evening Post* (November 8, 1912), 14. "Boone Hall had largest Grove," *Charleston News and Courier* (October 22, 1933), 15. "Classic Pecan Pie," *Karo* (n.d.), https://www .karosyrup.com/recipe/classic_pecan_pie.

Persimmons

"The Persimmon and its Uses," *The Rural Carolinian* 3 (Charleston, SC, 1872), 54. R. L. Watts, *Persimmons*, Bulletin University of Tennessee Agricultural Station 11, 1 (April 1899). "Our Persimmon Trees: Factory to be started in Sumter to make Golf Sticks of them," *The State* (January 15, 1900), 8. Francis D. Winston, "Persimmon Beer," *Raleigh Farmer & Mechanic* (December 5, 1911), 7. "Persimmon Crop Fails; Fall Brew is Missed," *The State* (November 22, 1922), 6. Pete Ivey, "Tart but Smart," *Greensboro Daily News* (November 28, 1971), 30. Carson Brewer, "Persimmon Beer High in Indian Lore," *Knoxville News-Sentinel* (October 15, 1981), 43.

Pickles

Sources: William Kitchiner, *The Cooke's Oracle* (London, 1817), 520. Sarah Rutledge, "To Pickle Peaches," *The Carolina Housewife, or House and Home: by a Lady of Charleston* (Charleston, SC: W. R. Babcock & Co., 1847), 180–81. "Premiums Awarded at the Fourth Annual Fair of the Anderson Farmers Association," *Anderson Intelligencer* (November 16, 1871), 3. Mrs. Annabella Hill, "Green Tomato Pickle," *Mrs. Hill's Southern Practical Cookery and Receipt Book* (New York: Carleton Madison Square, 1872), 346. Mrs. Washington, "Pickled Purple Cabbage," *The Unrivalled Cook-book and Housekeeper's Guide* (New York: Harper & Brothers, Franklin Square., 1886), 441. "Pickles Sweet and Pickles Sour," *Camden Journal* (October 9, 1890), 2. "The Vinegar Business," *The State* (Jan 7, 1900), 5. "Pickled Okra," Dee Hryharrow and Isabel M. Hoogenboom, *The Beaufort Cook Book* (Beaufort, SC: Beaufort Book Shop, 1965). Richard L. Lower: http://cuke.hort.ncsu.edu/cgc/conferences /cuc98/Lower1.html. Richard J. Hooker, *A Colonial Plantation Cookbook: The Receipt Book of Harriott Pinckney Horry*, 1770 (Columbia: University of South Carolina Press, 1984), 86–87.

Pilau

Southern Agriculturist (August 1834), 400. Sarah Rutledge, "Carolina Pilau," *House and Home; or, The Carolina Housewife* (Charleston, SC: John Russell, 1855), 73. J. W. Ellis, "Pilau of Rabbit," *What Shall We Eat* (New York: G. P. Putnam & Son, 1868), 97. Annabella Hill, "Rice Pillau," *Mrs. Hill's New Cook Book* (New York: Carleton, 1872), 77–78. "Shrimp Pilau," MS Cookbook, Parker Family Papers, South Carolina Historical Society 28-604-13. "Crab Pilau," *Ladies Home Journal* (November 1892), 32. Deshler Welch, *The Bachelor and the Chafing Dish* (New York & Chicago: F. Tennyson Neely 1895), 131. "Kedgeree," *Union*

Times (April 19, 1895), 17. "Egg Plant Pilau,"
The State (August 9, 1908), 14. "Pilau," *Harper's
Bazaar* (February 1909). "Pilau," *The State*
(July 4, 1912), 11. "Tomato Pilau," *Evening Star*
(March 20, 1913), 18. "Plain Pilau," *Manning
Times* (October 5, 1921). "Fish Pilau," *Tampa
Tribune* (May 14, 1927), 3. "Sally Washington's
Okra Pilau," in Blanche Rhett, *200 Hundred Years
of Charleston Cooking* (New York: J. Cape and
H. Smith, 1930). "Rice and Fowl Pilaf," *Macon
Telegraph* (April 13, 1932), 6. Susan Myrick, "Egg
Pilau," *Macon Telegraph* (October 24, 1934), 3.
"Oyster Pilau," *The State* (October 16, 1936), 1.
"Pilau of Birds," *Charleston News and Courier*
(July 11, 1937), 19; reprinted by permission of
Charleston Post and Courier. Harry Hampton,
"Merganser Pillau," *The State* (January 9, 1940),
11. [Francis Marion Hotel], *Charleston News
and Courier* (March 13, 1949). Mrs. J. G. Giaffis,
"Shrimp Pilau," *The State* (January 2, 1955), 74.
"Tomato Okra Pilau," *Charleston News and Courier*
(March 31, 1965). "Mushroom Pilaf Parisienne,"
Charleston News and Courier (March 30, 1972),
27. "Yellow Squash-Rice Pilau," *Charleston News
and Courier* (June 6, 1974), 38; reprinted by
permission of *Charleston Post and Courier*.

Pine Bark Stew

"Darlington T.P.A.'s Entertain," *Charleston News
and Courier* (September 23, 1907), 2. "The Pee-
Dee Pine Bark Fish Stew," *Charleston News and
Courier* (November 9, 1909), 1–2. "New Method
of Ginning Cotton," *Charleston News and Courier*
(April 25, 1910), 8. "Pine Bark Fish Stew Proves
Popular Canned," *Manning Times* (July 6, 1921), 2.
Clementine Paddleford, "Secret Dishes from Old
Charleston," *New Orleans Times Picayune* (May 20,
1951), 143. F. W. Bradley, "Dr. Pitts on Pine Bark
Stew," *Charleston News and Courier* (April 20, 1952),
4. Katherine W. Eads, "How to Mix a Fish Stew,"
Columbia Record (May 16, 1967), 29.

Porgy

"Piscatory," *Charleston Daily News* (April 18,
1867), 4. "Something About Paint," *Port Royal
Standard and Commercial* (April 6, 1876), 5. "The
Porgy Fishery," *Yorkville Enquirer* (November 8,
1877), 1. Felix Déliée, "Fried Porgies, Tartar
Sauce," *Franco-American Cookery* (1884), 194.
Adolphe Meyer, "Stuffed Porgy, Corsican Style,"
Post Graduate Cookery Book (1903), 94. "The Poor
Man's Fish," *Lexington Intelligencer* (August 20,
1904), 7. Hal Dubose, "Glimpse into the Life of
the Fisher Folk," *Charleston Sunday News* (July 16,
1911), 8.

Pot Likker

"Concerning Pot Liquor," *Augusta Chronicle*
(August 22, 1906), Huey Pierce Long, Jr., *Every
Man a King: The Autobiography of Huey P. Long*
(New Orleans: National Book Club, Inc., 1933),
200–201. "Pot Liquor or Potlikker?" *New York
Times* (23 February 1982). Herbert C. Covey and
Dwight Eisnach, *What the Slaves Ate: Recollections
of African American Foods and Foodways from the
Slave Narratives* (Santa Barbara: Greenwood
Press, 2009), 78. John T. Edge, *The PotLikker
Papers: A Food History of the Modern South* (New
York: Penguin Books, 2017).

Pumpkin

Mrs. T. W. Boone, Stoney Manuscript, South
Carolina Historical Society Collection, College
of Charleston, circa 1855. "Some Pumpkins,"
Newberry Herald (May 19, 1869), 3. "New
Berry at the State Fair," *The Newberry Herald*
(November 27, 1878), 4. "Various and All
About," *Newberry Herald and News* (December
11, 1914), 9. "Some Vines and Pumpkins,"
Newberry Herald (October 3, 1816), 6. "Pumpkin
Bread" and "Southern Pumpkin Pie," *Southern
Gardener & Receipt Book* (1860), 170 and 226.
"Pumpkin Pudding," *Port Royal Standard &*

Commercial (May 16, 1876), 5. "Pumpkin Soup," *Abbeville Press and Banner* (December 16, 1885), 8. "Pumpkins Chips," *Kingstree County Record* (October 4, 1917), 8. Sow True Seed of Ashville, NC: https://sowtrueseed.com/products /pumpkin-dutch-fork.

Punch

"Chupien's," *City Gazette* (May 4, 1824), 3. "Town Talk" [Poem on Punch], *New Orleans Times* (June 20, 1866), page supplement 2. "The Holiday Season," *Charleston Daily News* (December 18, 1872), 1. "Charleston Light Dragoons Punch," Jacqueline Harrison Smith, *Famous Old Receipts* (1908), 189. "St. Cecilia's Punch," Junior League of Charleston, *Charleston Receipts* (1950). *The Winyah Indigo Society of Georgetown, S.C., 1755-1998* (Georgetown: By the Society, 1998). Robert F. Moss, *Southern Spirits; Four Hundred Years of Drinking in the South, with Recipes* (Berkeley, CA: Ten Speed Press, 2016), 190–99.

Red Chicken Stew

"Yank Blandings's Red Chicken Stew," Lady's Aid Society of New Wappetaw Presbyterian Church, *McClellanville, S. C. Favorite Recipes*, Compiled by the Ladies Aid Society of New Wappetaw Presbyterian Church (Kansas City, MO: Bev-Ron Publishing Co., 1956), 16. Keith Deamke, *The Sumter Item* (March 25, 2015).

Red Horse Bread

"Indian Meal Fritters," Christian Isobel Johnston, *Treatise on Domestic Brewing* (1847), 497. "Corn Meal Fritters, without Eggs" Mrs. T. J. Crown, *American Lady's System of Cookery* (1860), 235. Nettie O. Speaks, "Fish Fry at 'Romey's,'" *Bamberg Herald* (June 27, 1907), 2. "Red Horse Bread," *Winter Cover Crop Experiments at the Pee Dee Experiment Station* (1933), 71. Reba Thorne Polattie, "Family Favorites: Red Horse

Bread, Shrimp Are on the Deep-South Menu," *Knoxville News-Sentinel* (August 11, 1955), 29. "Red Horse Bread the perfect complement to any Santee fish fry," *The Sumter Item* (January 20, 2008), 4. Robert Moss, "The Real History of Hush Puppies," *Serious Eats* (June 15, 2015), https://www.seriouseats.com/2015/06/real-history-myths-hushpuppies.html. Liz Biro, "Hush Puppies have Strayed far from Coast," *The Coastal Review On Line* (July 26, 2018), https://www.coastalreview.org/2018/07 /hush-puppies-have-strayed-far-from-coast/.

Rice Bird

"Rice Birds," *Maine Farmer* (December 29, 1853), 1. "The Rice Bird-the Bobolink," *Spirit of the Age* (October 15, 1859), 29. "Rice Birds are Ripe," *Portland Oregonian* (October 26, 1894), 6. "Potting Rice Birds in Carolina," *Springfield Republican* (November 3, 1896), 10. "The Fate of Our Bobolinks," *Springfield Republican* (October 21, 1901), 10. "Fifty Years Ago," *Georgetown Times* (October 2, 1952), 2.

Rice Bread

"Rice Bread," *Charleston Courier* (January 7, 1812), 3. A Lady, "Rice Family Bread," *Southern Agriculturist* (February 1836), 110. Eliza Leslie, "Rice-Flour Bread," *Lady's Receipt-Book* (Philadelphia: Carey & Hart, 1847), 190. "Superior Rice Bread," *Mrs. Goodfellow's Cookery as it Should Be* (Philadelphia: T. B. Peterson & Brothers, 1865), 180. Karen Hess, *The Carolina Rice Kitchen* (Columbia: University of South Carolina Press, 1998), 114–121. John Martin Taylor, "Rice Bread," *Hoppin' John's Lowcountry Cooking* (Chapel Hill: University of North Carolina Press, 2012), 214–15. David S. Shields, *Southern Provisions* (Chicago: University of Chicago Press, 2015), 245–48.

Rye

James Wilson, "Fruit Trees, Fresh Garden," *Charleston Courier* (November 8, 1831), 3. Sarah Rutledge, *The Carolina Housewife, or House and Home: By a Lady of Charleston* (Charleston, SC: W. R. Babcock & Co., 1847), 28. "Rye Pancakes," *Abbeville Press and Banner* (January 18, 1888), 7. Alfred Jouannet, "For Sale," *Charleston Evening Post* (August 25, 1910), 2. William H. Mixson, "South Carolina Seashore," *Garden, Field and Farm Seeds* (Charleston, 1914), 17. David S. Coker, *Coker's Pedigreed Abruzzi Rye and Red Oats* (Hartsville, SC: Pedigreed Seed Company, 1916), [8]. "Our Daily Plant Hint," *Augusta Chronicle* (June 28, 1915), 4. "Our Daily Plant Hints," *Augusta Chronicle* (September 17, 1917), 4. Stanley Ginsburg, "Heirloom Dixie Rye," *The Rye Baker Blog* (August 23, 2016), http://theryebaker.com/dixie-rye-bread-united-states/.

Scuppernong Grape

Proceedings of the American Pomological Society 1871 (Cleveland, OH: Fairbanks, 1872), 54. J. Van Buren, *The Scuppernong Grape, Its History and Mode of Cultivation* (Memphis, 1877), 8. "Subvarieties of Scuppernong," *Bushberg Catalogue, a Grape Manual* (Bushburg, MO, 1895), 178. "Whole carload of Scuppernongs," *Charleston Evening Post* (July 23, 1905), 2. U.S. "The Sweet Smell of Scuppernongs," *The State* (September 20, 2000), 38. Department of Agriculture Pomological Watercolor Collection. Rare and Special Collections, National Agricultural Library, Beltsville, MD 20705, Amanda Newton, 1905.

Shad

A Lady of Philadelphia, "Fried Shad," *The National Cook Book* (1856), 24. E. R. Mordecai, *Food of the Shad of the Atlantic Coast of the United States* (Philadelphia: King & Baird, 1860). Sarah Elliott, *Mrs. Elliott's Housewife* (1870), 27. Dick Swiveller, "Angling in South Carolina," *Field and Stream* (May 4, 1882), 270–71. "Shad Season is Here," *New York Herald* (March 8, 1887), 3. Felix Déliée, "Baked Shad with Roes," *Franco-American Cookery* (1884), 153. "Save the Shad," *The State* (April 4, 1909), 4. "Will Hatch Shad near Orangeburg," *The State* (November 26, 1913), 14. "How to Cook Toothsome Shade," *Augusta Chronicle* (May 14, 1916), 1. William K. Fenn, "The Origin of Planked Shad," *Forest and Stream* (May 1918), 300. "Shad Catch," *Columbia Record* (October 28, 1978), 5. John McPhee, *The Founding Fish* (New York: Farrar, Straus, & Giroux, 2003).

She-Crab Soup

"She-Crab Soup," *Charleston News and Courier* (October 11, 1930), 12. Isabella G. Leland, "Charleston Flavored She-Crab Soup," *Charleston News and Courier* (July 27, 1958), 29. "Recipes Loved and Lost," *Charleston News and Courier* (March 28, 1976), 12. E. John Burbage, "A Brief history of William Deas's Soup," *Charleston Post and Courier* (March 23, 1992), 9. Nancie McDermott, *Southern Soups and Stews: More than 75 recipes from Burgoo and Gumbo to Etouffee and Fricassee* (Chronicle Books, 2015), 62–63. "She-Crab Soup Recipe and History," *What's Cooking America*. Retrieved November 1, 2015, https://www.thespruceeats.com/what-is-a-she-crab-1807055.

Sheepshead

Felix Déliée, "Sheep's-Head a la Caroline," *Franco-American Cookery* (1884). "Make Big Catch," *Charleston Evening Post* (November 9, 1915), 9. "Bait Trained to Hook Sheepshead," *Charleston Evening Post* (October 12, 1916), 5. "Woods and Waters-Carolina Fishes #5 The Sheepshead," *Charleston News and Courier* (February 5, 1930), 9, Jack Leland, "Bait Stealing

Sheepshead is a Prince of Sea Foods," *Charleston Evening Post* (May 30, 1972), 30. Tommy Braswell, "To Catch a Thief, bait with Shrimp," *Charleston Post and Courier* (February 12, 1995), 44. Brian Perry, *The Honest Guide To Successful Pier and Coastal Fishing* (Bloomington, IN: WestBow Press, 2012), 17–18.

Shrimp and Grits

"At the Old Stand," *Charleston News and Courier* (September 9, 1886), 1. "Rather Give up the Shrimp," *Charleston News and Courier* (April 8, 1888), 2. "An Easter Offering," *Charleston News and Courier* (April 7, 1890), 8. "Bulling the Market," *Charleston News and Courier* (August 11, 1892), 8. Craig Claiborne, "For A Carolina Chef, Helpings of History," *New York Times* (July 10, 1985), C-1. Nathalie Dupree and Marion Sullivan, *Shrimp and Grits* (Gibbs and Smith, 2014, revised edition.) David S. Shields, "Song of the Shrimp Fiend," *Charleston Magazine* (June 2016), https://charlestonmag .com/features/song_of_the_shrimp_fiend. Matt and Ted Lee, Robert Stehling, "Iconic Southern Plates: Lowcountry Shrimp and Grits," *Southern Living* (December 13, 2016), https://www.southernliving.com/grains/grits /low-country-shrimp-and-grits.

Shrimp Paste

Sarah Rutledge, *The Carolina Housewife, or House and Home: by a Lady of Charleston* (Charleston, SC: W. R. Babcock & Co., 1847), 216. "S. H. Oppenheim and Company," *Charleston Courier* (February 7, 1855), 3. "Shrimp Paste," Minnie Pringle, *Charleston News and Courier* (February 15, 1929), 17; reprinted by permission of *Charleston Post and Courier*. Mrs. C. Norwood Hastie, "Shrimp Paste," in Blanche C. Rhett, *Rhett's 200 Years of Charleston Cooking* (New York, 1930). S. A. Cothren, "Lowcountry Flavors Captured in Jars,"

Charleston News and Courier (December 19, 1948), 51. "Southern Treat: Potted Shrimps" *Charleston News and Courier* (March 5, 1961), 9-B.

Shrimp Pie

Sarah Rutledge, "Shrimp Pie," *House and Home; or, The Carolina Housewife* (Charleston, SC: John Russell, 1855), 48. Nat Fuller, "Turtle Soup and Wild Turkey," *Charleston Mercury* (September 21, 1864), 2. [Torck's notice], *The Charleston Daily News* (September 10, 1869), 3. Mrs. A. P. Hill, "Shrimp Pie," *Mrs. Hill's Practical Cookery and Receipt Book* (New York: G. W. Carleton, 1872), 44. Ella B. Washington, "Cooking Shrimps," *Frank Leslie's Popular Monthly* IV, 1 (July 1877), 99. "An Earnest Protest Against the 'Raw Shrimp' Fiend," *Charleston News and Courier* (August 24, 1884), 4. "At the Old Stand," *Charleston News and Courier* (September 9, 1886), 1. "Rather Give up the Shrimp," *Charleston News and Courier* (April 8, 1888), 2. "A Paean of Victory," *Charleston News and Courier* (August 16, 1888), 8. "An Easter Offering," *Charleston News and Courier* (April 7, 1890), 8. [Mass Meeting to repress shrimp fiend], *Charleston News and Courier* (July 21, 1892), 8. "Bulling the Market," *Charleston News and Courier* (August 11, 1892), 8. "Song of Raw Swimps," *Charleston New and Courier* (July 22, 1894), 8. "The Editors of the State," *Charleston News and Courier* (August 15, 1894), 8. [Joe Cole's Calls], "Raw, Raw Shrimps," *Charleston News and Courier* (January 2, 1900), 5. "Shrimp Salad," *Charleston News and Courier* (March 16, 1911), 6. "Fishermen have Sport in Plenty," *Charleston Evening Post* (August 6, 1912), 10. "Miss Maizie Jones," *Charleston Evening Post* (August 23, 1916), 5. [eighteenth-century Rhett Family Recipe], *Cleveland Plain Dealer* (July 23, 1939), 86. "Loved and Lost," *Charleston News and Courier* (April 6, 1969), 42.

Soft-Shelled Crab

"Soft Shelled Crabs," *Southern Patriot* (July 19, 1844), 2. "Soft Shell Crabs," *Edgefield Advertiser* (September 30, 1896), 2. "Fried Soft Shell Crabs," *Charleston Evening Post* (January 25, 1929), 16. "Soft-Shell Crab Industry Grows," *Charleston News and Courier* (April 25, 1933), 12. "Soft Shells are bustin' out all over," *Charleston News and Courier* (June 17, 1979), 66. David S. Shields, *Southern Provisions* (Chicago: University of Chicago Press, 2015), 194–98.

Sorghum Syrup

H. W. Wiley, "The Growth of Sorghum Cane and the Manufacture of Sugar and Syrup Therefrom," *Annual Report of the Indiana State Board of Agriculture* 23 (Indianapolis: State Board of Agriculture, 1882), 494. David Dodge, "Domestic Economy in the Confederacy," *The Atlantic Monthly* 58 (1886), 235. "Sorghum Cake," *Edgefield Advertiser* (January 29, 1896), 5. Herbert Myrick, *Sugar: A New and Profitable Industry in the United States* (New York & Chicago: Orange Judd, 1897), 14. David S. Shields, *Southern Provision: the Creation and Revival of a Cuisine* (Chicago: University of Chicago Press, 2015), 271–85.

Spoonbread

Sarah Rutledge, *The Carolina Housewife, or House and Home: by a Lady of Charleston* (Charleston, SC: W. R. Babcock & Co., 1847), 21. "Owendaw Corn Bread," *Dorchester Women's Club Cook Book* (Knight & Company, 1897), 60. "Owendaw," Jane Eddington, "Spring Corn Breads," *Seattle Daily Times* (April 21, 1923), 5. "Sally's Spoonbread," *Columbia Record* (December 27, 1935), 9. "Owendaw Bread," *Charleston News and Courier* (June 24, 1938), 16. "Stop It, Man! You're Killing Us!" *Richmond Times Dispatch* (March 14, 1947), 20. Dorothy Robertson, "The Best Food in Virginia is Spoonbread," *Richmond Times Dispatch* (November 1, 1947), 8. Lia Grabowski, "The South's Soufflé," *The Local Palate* (April 17, 2018).

Strawberry Shortcake

"Strawberry Shortcake, *New York Times* (May 20, 1885), 4. "Strawberry Shortcake, A Delicacy That is Seldom Made Well," *Charleston Evening Post* (May 2, 1900), 2. "Strawberry Shortcake," *Evening Post* (July 10, 1905), 3. Barbara E. Shapleigh, "Strawberry Shortcake," *Charleston Evening Post* (April 6, 1923). "Strawberry Shortcake," *Charleston News and Courier* (April 25, 1957), 22. Alice Ross, "July and Strawberry Shortcake" *Journal of Antiques and Collectibles*, (July 2000). "Sweet Treats around the World," *An Encyclopedia of Food and Culture* (New York: Charles Scribner's, 2004), 365. Anne Byrn, *American Cake* (New York: Rodale Books, 2016), 61–63.

Summer Squash

Gardening for the South, (New York: Saxton & Company, 1857), 213. Mrs. R. L. O. Marion Cabell Tyree, "Cymling Fritters" and "Cymling Pudding," *Housekeeping in Old Virginia* (Louisville: John P. Morton, 1879), 241. "Fried Squash," *Raleigh Progressive Farmer* (July 17, 1894), 6. "Plant to Aid Farmers," *Goldsboro Weekly Argus* (January 24, 1901), 3. "The Yellow Crookneck," *The State* (October 27, 1907), 5. Dr. Frank McCoy, "Questions and Answers," *Macon Telegraph* (May 16, 1928), 13. Frank McCoy, "Summer Squash," *Macon Telegraph* (June 9, 1937), 2. Jessie Marie DeBoth, "Many Varieties Offer Tasty Squash Dishes," *Charlotte Observer* (September 27, 1938), 18. "Crook-Neck Squash Baked in Cream," *Rock Hill Herald* (September 21, 1940), 5.

Sweet Corn

"Evaporating Corn for Market," *Abbeville Press and Banner* (October 9, 1895), 4. "Dried Sweet Corn," *Abbeville Press and Banner* (April 6, 1910), 8. "Sweet Corn Promising Crop," *The State* (August 14, 1923), 7. "Sweet Corn Dishes," *Charleston News and Courier* (August 18, 1929), 11.

Sweet Potato Pie

Rev. Paul T. Gervais, "On the Culture of the Sweet Potato," *Southern Agriculturist and Register of Rural Affairs* 4 (Charleston, SC, July 1831), 622. Annabella Hill, "Sliced Potato Pie," *Mrs. Hill's Southern Practical Cookery* (1867). Comrade, "Sweet Potato Pie, Charleston News and Courier (April 19, 1896). "Southern Lunch Counter Slang," *The State* (April 25, 1896), 5. "Reprinted from the Richmond Times Dispatch," *Baltimore American* (January 17, 1904), 28. C. A. Magoon, *A Study of Sweet-Potato Varieties, with Special Reference to their Canning*, USDA Bulletin #1041 (Washington, DC: Government Printing Office, January 11, 1922), 13. Damon Lee Fowler, ed. *Mrs. Hill's Southern Practical Cookery and Receipt Book* (Columbia: University of South Carolina Press, 1995 reprint of 1872 edition), 255.

Tanya Root

Mark Catesby, *A Natural History of Carolina, Florida and the Bahama Islands* Vol 2 (London, 1743), 45. "Tanya," *American Farmer* (September 9, 1825), 197. William Logan, "The Tannier," *Southern Agriculturist* (May 1834), 231. "Cooking Tanyah," *Rural Carolinian* 6 (1875), 109–10.

Tomato Gravy

Mrs. J. Wily Waters, "Tomato Gravy," *Baltimore Sun* (March 5, 1911), 7. "Italian Mama always called it Tomato Gravy," *Dallas Morning News* (April 10, 1980), 115. Louise Durham, "In the Gravy," *Knoxville News Sentinel* (April 2, 1986), 18.

Waffles

Sarah Rutledge, "Sweet Potato Waffle," *The Carolina Housewife, or House and Home: by a Lady of Charleston* (Charleston, SC: W. R. Babcock & Co., 1847). "Rice Waffles," Stoney family, recipe book, n.d. (34/619), South Carolina Historical Society. Mrs. Washington, *The Unrivalled Cook-book* (New York: Harper's, 1886), 288. Jessup Whitehead, *The American Pastry Book* (Chicago: Whitehead Publishing, 1895), "Waffle Iron history," https://blog.library.si.edu/blog/2010/08/24/waffle-iron-patented/#.XDDP6Px7nKo. "Are you a Waffle Eater," *Charleston Evening Post* (January 4, 1913), 9. "The Rialto," *Charleston Evening Post* (September 20, 1913), 8.

Watermelon

H. "A Hint to our New Jersey Friends," *The Farmers' Cabinet* 3 (1838), 128. William Kenrick, "Long Carolina Watermelon," *The New American Orchardist* Vol. 2 (New York, 1838), 316–17. "Mammoth Melon," *Southern Cultivator* (Augusta, GA, October 1853), 306. W. D. Brinckle, "Watermelons," *The Magazine of Horticulture, Botany, and all Useful Discoveries* 23 (1857), 117. William N. White, *Gardening for the South* (1857), 211. W. C. Hampton [Hardin County Ohio], *The Ohio Cultivator* 14 (January 1858), 11. "Melons" Editor's Portfolio, *Horticulturist and Journal of Rural Art and Rural Taste* (April 1870), 122. "Lawson Watermelon," *Macon Telegraph*, June 6, 1883. "Improve Your Melons," *Watchman & Southron* (January 29, 1884). Col. Rueben Jones, "On Watermelons," *Southern Cultivator* 48, 1 (January 1890), 19.

W. F. Massey, "Newer Vegetables of Promise," *American Agriculturist* 52 (January 1893), 20.

Whiting

John Edwards Holbrook, *Ichthyology of South Carolina* (Charleston, SC: John Russell, 1855), 142. George Brown Goode, "The Whitings," *The Fisheries and Fishing Industries of the United States* (Washington, DC: Government Printing Office, 1884), 1; 376–78. "A Corner in Whiting," *Charleston News and Courier* (May 29, 1886), 8. "Whiting," *Columbia Record* (April 19, 1929), 18. "Deep-Fried Whiting," Columbia Record (December 23, 1987), 19. Oscar Vick, "Whiting and Rice Pilau," *Gullah Cooking: Fish Cooking* (1991).

Yaupon Tea

"Yaupon Tea," *Sumter Banner* (July 24, 1850), 7. C. L. Hunter, "Matte, or Paraguay Tea, supposed to exist in North Carolina," *New Orleans Price Current* (May 31, 1856), 3. E. M. Hale, *Ilex Cassine, the Aboriginal American Tea* USDA Bulletin No. 14 (Washington, DC: Government Printing Office, 1891). M. L. Willet, "Common Sense Comment," *Augusta Chronicle*, Nov. 13, 1922, 4. "Tastes Like Tea and Has 'Kick,'" *San Diego Union* (September 12, 1926), 67.

GENERAL INDEX

Boone Hall Plantation
(Mt. Pleasant), 117–18
Boppe, Charles, 93
Botagra, 99
bouillon cube, 126
Boulware, Ross, 32
Bradford, Nat, 39, 140, 144,
197–98
Bradford Watermelon, 144
brandy, 67, 75, 86, 113–14,
122, 142–43, 185, 195;
blackberry, 15; peaches in,
114; watermelon, 198
bread, 26, 28, 150–52; batter,
176; corn, 47–49;
cracklin', 50; flour, 150;
mix, 48; pumpkin, 141;
rice, 26, 28, 150–52; rice
flour, 152; spoonbread,
175–76
breakfast, 10, 50, 61, 73, 80–81,
93–94, 98,137, 169, 176,
190, 194
Broad River, 61
Brock, Sean, 53
Brookgreen Plantation, 26
Brooks, Preston, 3
Brown, Theresa C., 21, 73;
Modern Domestic Cookery,
21, 73, 81
Bryan, Letitia, 58; *Kentucky
Housewife*, 58
Bull's Bay, SC, 21; Oyster
Company, 109
butcher, 93
butter, 11–12
butterbeans, 21–22, 126
buttermilk, 11, 49, 64, 66, 120,
145–46, 171, 175; biscuit,
11

cabbage, 23–24, 41, 89, 125,
138, 140; Charleston
Wakefield, 23–24, 99, 202;
pickles, 123; smothered, 24
cake, 62, 90–92, 113; batter,
44, 47; chocolate,
53–54; crab, 171; fig,
62; ginger, 173; griddle,
33, 153; groundnut,
75–76; hoe, 50; Lady
Baltimore, 90–92;
persimmon, 119; rye
pancake, 153; shortcake,
178; sorghum, 174–75
Callabash NC, 25; fried fish,
25, 200
callaloo, 100
Camden, SC, 3, 9, 70; *Gazette*,
70; *Journal*, 81, 124
candy, 61, 115–16; benne, 9;
fig, 61; groundnut cake,
75–76; monkey meat, 76;
pecan 118
canning, 2, 89, 123, 182, 184;
clubs, 111, 135; corn, 182;
peach, 113; sweet potato,
185
canola oil, 63
cantaloupe, 122
Captain Benjamin's Calabash
Seafood (Myrtle Beach),
25
carbonation, 71, 142
Carolina Gold Rice Foundation,
152, 197–98
Carolina Housewife, The
(Rutledge), 8, 48, 58, 67,
75, 79, 88, 114, 153, 167,
169, 175, 193, 194–95
Carolina Receipt Book (Lady of
Charleston), 110, 114

Carolina Recipes Inc.
(Charleston), 168
Catesby, Mark, 188; *Natural
History of Carolina,
Florida, and the Bahama
Islands*, 188
catfish, 29–33, 134, 145; Catfish
Galley Restaurant
(Charleston), 29;
farming, 29–30;
fried, 29–30; stew, xi, 5,
30–32
cauliflower, 124
Cayce, SC, 6; Farmer's Market,
22, 155
cayenne, 5, 24, 31, 46, 89, 101,
122, 132, 135, 159–60, 163,
167, 170, 190
Centennial Receipt Book (A
Southern Lady), 51, 76
champagne, 142–43
Charleston, SC, 6, 21, 24, 27, 29,
46, 61, 93, 94–95, 111, 149,
163; boarding houses, 169;
Courier, 27, 151; *Evening
Post*, 49, 178; fish market,
171; Junior League, 115;
News and Courier, 129, 130,
133, 134–35, 165–66, 167;
Oyster Company, 109;
Wakefield Cabbage, 23–
24; Women's Exchange,
90
Charleston Receipts, 46, 135, 143,
170, 176
*Charleston Women's Exchange
Cookbook*, 61
Charlon, Francis Joseph, 113
cheese, 12, 96–97, 170, 175;
cheddar, 193; cream,
54; grits, 165; head, 5;

GENERAL INDEX

Harold's Cabin (Charleston), 89, 116
Harris Lithia Carbonated Water, 71
Hastie, Mrs. C. Norwood, 168
Henderson, Peter, 1–2, 22–23
Heyward, Dubose, 136
High Wire Distillery (Charleston), 113
Hill, Annabella, 45–46, 55, 89, 124, 185
Holloway, Thomas Watson, 140
hominy, 9; corn, 80–81; grits, 80–82, 165–66; shrimp and, 165–66
Hoppin' John, 26, 83–85, 129
Horlbeck, John, 117
Horlbeck, John S., 117–18
Horry, Harriott Pinckney, 125
Housekeeping in Old Virginia (Tyree), 79, 180
hucksters, 19, 75–76, 78, 118, 136–37, 165
Huguenots, 51–53, 169–70
hully gully, 39
hunting, 51–52, 148
hush puppies, 145–46

Ilex Cassine, the Aboriginal American Tea (Hale), 201
In Pursuit of Flavor (Lewis), 41
Italy, 96–97, 153, 181

jam, 15, 113, 155
Jamaica, 70–71, 143, 188
James, Joe, 39
James Beard Award, 53
James's Restaurant (Darlington), 135
Japan, 94–95, 98, 120
Jefferson, Thomas, 9, 120

jelly, 56, 107; apple, 56, 126; loquat, 95; muscadine, 155–57; plum, 119
Jerusalem artichoke, 88–89, 122; relish, 89
Jetty House, 18
Johnsman, Greg, 154
Johnston, Christian Isobel, 145
Jouannet, Alfred, 154, 201–02

Kalanty, Michael, 150
Keith, Cornelius, 139
Kentucky, 10, 58, 193
Kentucky Housewife (Bryan), 58
Kibler, James, 2, 21, 198
Kinard, Solomon P., 5
Kingstree, 140; *County Record,* 140
Kitchiner, William, 122
Kuralt, Charles, 71

Lady Baltimore Cake, 90–92
Lady Baltimore Tea Room (Charleston), 115
Lancaster, SC, 52, 104; *News,* 51–52
lard, 7, 11, 25, 29, 44, 55, 63, 145, 152, 153, 163; cracklins, 50
Laurens, SC, 32; *Advertiser,* 32
Laurens, Eleanor, 61
Lee Brothers (Matt and Ted), 19–20
Leland, Jack, 99
lemon, 75, 122, 124, 141, 143; juice, 9, 51, 65, 70, 91, 118, 131, 140, 157, 162, 170; meringue pie, 106–07, 185; rind, 35, 76
Leslie, Charles C., 17, 137, 171
Leslie, Eliza, 152
Lewis, Edna, 41

Lewis, Eliza, 80; *Ladies' New Recipe Book,* 80
limping Susan, 129
Loomis, Henry, 120
loquat, 94–95
Louisiana, 24–25, 50, 58, 61, 73, 78, 101, 164; sugar, 173
Lowcountry, ix, 1–2, 6, 7–8, 18, 23, 25, 43, 46, 57–58, 65, 74, 75–76, 83, 93, 98, 105, 107, 111, 126–27, 133, 134, 147–48, 150, 158, 161, 165, 167, 169, 187; boil, 68–70
lye, 61, 80–81

McClellanville, S. C. Favorite Recipes, 99
McClung, Anna, 26, 28
McGinty, Rupert, 104
macaroni, 96–97
mace, 45–46, 69, 74, 89, 93, 110, 114, 122–24, 131, 141, 161, 167, 169–70, 190
Macon Telegraph, 128
Madeira, 45–46, 74, 161, 168
Magnolias Restaurant (Charleston), 165
Magwood, William H., 171
Marsh Hen Mill, 82, 154
Martin, Wilma, 18; *Captain Murrell's Savory Seafood Recipes,* 18
martynia, 122
May, Charles R., 71
Mayham, Hezekiah, 26
mayonnaise, 53–54, 111, 169, 193; cake, 54
medicinal plants, 7, 14–15, 70–71, 100, 138, 201–02
Megget, SC, 24
Meier, Franz, 44

Meyer, Adolphe, 137; *Post Graduate Cookery Book,* 137
Middleton Place, 41
Miles, Dolester, 53
Miller, Adrian, 96
Miller, Zell, 138
Milling, Chapman J., 134
mills, 81
Miss Leslie's New Receipts, 152
Mixson, Wiliam H., 154
Modern Domestic Cookery (Brown), 21, 73, 81
Moise, Ben, 68
molasses, 9, 75–76
Monck's Corner, SC, 29, 32
Monetta Asparagus Farm, 2
Moore, James, 14
mosquito fleet, 171
Mount Pleasant, SC, 1, 117–18, 171, 202
Mrs. Elliott's Housewife (Elliott), 118, 159
Mrs. Goodfellow's Cookery as it Should Be, 151
Mrs. Hill's New Cook Book (Hill), 45, 124, 170, 185
Mugal, Christian, 49
mulberry, 15, 105, 119
Murphy, Bessie R., 49
muscadine grape, 155–57
mushroom pilau, 130; stock, 100
mustard, 6, 124; barbecue sauce, 6; greens, 100–01; varieties, 101
Myrtle Beach, 25

Native Americans, 21–22, 33, 43, 47, 61, 109, 115, 155, 158, 160; Cherokee, 33, 139, 179; Catawba, 33; Corn Bread, 47; Eno Shakore,

33; Guale, 112; oysters, 109; Sewee (Siouan), 21; Sugaree, 33; sweet corn, 182–83; Wateree, 33; Yaupon Tea, 201–02
Natural History of Carolina, Florida, and the Bahama Islands (Catesby), 188
Neal, Bill, 82, 165
New Orleans, 117, 190
New York Tribune, 86
Newberry, SC, 4, 139; *Herald,* 140
Ninety Six, SC, 29
nitrogen, 57, 60
Nixon, Richard, 43
nixtamalization, 80

oil, 7–8, 44, 63, 190; benne, 7–9; cotton seed, 12; fish, 137; okra seed, 103; pecan, 49; peanut, 145
okra, 66, 102–03, 122–23; Clemson Spineless, 104; flour, 103; fritter, 66; limping susan, 129; Perkins Long Pod, 104; pilau, 130; seed coffee, 173; seed oil, 103; soup, 102–04
Old Bay, 69
Old Slave Market Museum, 76, 115–16
olive, 7, 137; oil, 31, 59, 67, 103–04, 111, 133, 190
Oliver Farms Artisan Oils, 7, 103
onion, 5, 12, 18, 31–32, 36–37, 42, 44, 45–46, 51, 52, 66, 74, 79, 84, 89, 98; 104; 123–24, 128, 134, 144, 145–46; 161–62, 191, 200

Onslow's Confectionery, 9, 116
orange, 67, 105–07; juice, 107; marmalade, 105; pie, 106; varieties, 106–07
Orangeburg, SC, 6, 24, 55, 153
Otranto Club, 135
Ottolengui, Florence, 90
Our House Restaurant (Charleston), 46
oyster, 7–8, 18, 25, 108–10, 164, 169; fritter, 63; gravy, 73–74; pickled, 110, 123; pilau, 126, 130; poached, 164; roast, 108

Paddleford, Clementine, 116
Palmer Plameto Pickle, 111
Palmetto Farm Brand, 93
palmetto pickle, 111
Panorama Restaurant (Ninety Six), 29
Passmore, Deborah G, 94
pâté, 167–68
Pavilion Hotel (Charleston), 49, 164
paw paw, 119
Pawley's Island, 16
pea pliau, 128
Peach, 65, 112–14; Belle of Georgia, 113; Blood, 112; Elberta, 113; Lemon Cling, 113; Shanghai Honey Nectar, 113; leather, 115–16; Pickled, 114, 123–24; Spiced, 114
peanut, 19–20, 75–76; boiled, 19–20, 69; Carolina African Runner, 19, 75; groundnut cake, 75–76; oil, 63
pecan, 117–18; oil, 49; spiced, 118

GENERAL INDEX

GENERAL INDEX

GENERAL INDEX

RECIPE INDEX

Artichoke:
    relish, 89
Biscuits:
    beaten, 11
    biscuits, 10
    buttermilk, 11
Blackberry:
    cobbler 16
    dumpling, 16
    jam, 16
    syrup, 15
Beans:
    butter (Sewee), 21
Beer, ginger, 70
Bread:
    rice, 151
    rice-flour bread, 152
    Superior rice, 151
Candy:
    fig, 62
    groundnut, 76
Cake:
    Duke's Mayonnaise
      Chocolate, 53
    groundnut, 76
    Lady Baltimore, 91–92
    strawberry shortcake, 178
Catfish:
    stew, 31
Chestnut:
    custard, 34
    deviled, 35
    dressing, 34

    souffle, 35
Chicken:
    bog, 36–37
Collards:
    cooked greens, 41
    spicy, 42
Cornbread:
    Pavilion Hotel, 49
    spider, 49
Duck:
    roasted 51
    with turnips, 52
Eggplant; *see* Guinea Squash:
    baked, 79
    boiled, 78
    fried, 78
    pudding, 79
Fritters:
    apple, 67
    basic, 63
    conch, 44
    corn, 64
    cornmeal, 64
    cymling; *see* summer
      squash, 180
    fig, 67
    fritter; *see* Hoppin John,
      84–85
    okra, 66
    orange, 67
    potato, 64
    rice, 64
    salsify, 65

    sweet potato, 65
    strawberry, 67
    tomato, 65
Frogmore:
    seafood boil, 69
    stew, 69
Gravy:
    Tomato, 190
Hominy, Lye, 81
Hoppin John, 83
Jelly:
    Loquat, 95
Macaroni, 97
Orange:
    marmalade, 105
    pie, 107
Oysters:
    pickled, 110
Peaches:
    in brandy, 114
    pickled, 114
    spiced, 114
Peanuts:
    boiled, 20
Peas, black-eyed, 59
Persimmon:
    beer, 121
    pudding, 120
Pickles:
    cabbage, 123
    chow chow, 124–125
    cucumber, 123
    green tomato, 124